THE WORLD
HAS CHANGED

THE WORLD HAS CHANGED

Conversations with Alice Walker

Edited by Rudolph P. Byrd

THE NEW PRESS

NEW YORK
LONDON

The front cover photograph of Alice Walker is by Dr. Doris A. Derby, Georgia State University (photo.derby1@gmail.com).

Requests for permission to reproduce selections from this book should be mailed to: Permissions Department, The New Press, 38 Greene Street, New York, NY 10013.

Published in the United States by The New Press, New York, 2010
Distributed by Perseus Distribution

LIBRARY OF CONGRESS CATALOGING-IN-PUBLICATION DATA

The world has changed : conversations with Alice Walker / edited by Rudolph P. Byrd.
   p. cm.
  Includes bibliographical references and index.
  ISBN 978-1-59558-496-0 (hc. : alk. paper) 1. Walker, Alice, 1944—Interviews.
2. Authors, American—20th century—Interviews. I. Byrd, Rudolph P.
II. Walker, Alice, 1944–
  PS3573.A425Z96 2010
  813'.54—dc22
  2009052950

The New Press was established in 1990 as a not-for-profit alternative to the large, commercial publishing houses currently dominating the book publishing industry. The New Press operates in the public interest rather than for private gain, and is committed to publishing, in innovative ways, works of educational, cultural, and community value that are often deemed insufficiently profitable.

www.thenewpress.com

Composition by dix!
This book was set in Sabon

Printed in the United States of America

10 9 8 7 6 5 4 3 2

CONTENTS

ACKNOWLEDGMENTS

I would like to express my gratitude to Alice Walker for the great privilege and pleasure of collaborating with her in bringing *The World Has Changed: Conversations with Alice Walker* to publication. From conception to publication, Ms. Walker was generous with her time and open to suggestions, such as they were, from this editor.

Emory University is privileged to serve as the custodian of the Alice Walker archive, which opened to the public in 2009. At Emory, we happily bear the privileges and responsibilities of custodianship of this national treasure. These privileges and responsibilities are shared by many across Emory University, in particular James W. Wagner, President; Earl Lewis, Provost and Vice President for Academic Affairs; and Rick Luce, Vice Provost for University Libraries.

The World Has Changed is the first of many books that will emerge from the Walker archive. In preparing this book for publication, I wish to thank my colleagues in the Manuscript, Archive, and Rare Book Library (MARBL) of the Robert W. Woodruff Library, in particular Randall Burkett, Teresa Burke, Naomi L. Nelson, Elizabeth Russey, and Julie Delliquanti, Director of the Schatten Gallery.

I would be remiss if I did not acknowledge the contributions of Michael Hall, doctoral student in the Graduate Institute in the Liberal Arts at Emory University, who served as my research assistant in the editing of this volume.

I wish to acknowledge the contributions and colleagueship of Beverly Guy Sheftall, Howard Zinn, Wendy Weil, Priyanka Jacob, and the very able Sarah Fan and Marc Favreau of The New Press.

I also wish to record grateful acknowledgment to those who have given permission to reprint the following conversations and interviews. Every effort has been made to contact all rights holders of reprinted material in *The World Has Changed*. If notified, the publisher of the book will be pleased to rectify an omission in future editions.

Chapter 1 is excerpted from *Interviews with Black Writers*, edited by John O'Brien (New York: Liveright, 1973).

Chapter 2, excerpted from *Black Women Writers at Work* by Claudia Tate (1983), is reprinted with the permission of the Continuum International Publishing Group.

Chapter 3 is reprinted with the permission of the Animals and Society Institute (www.animalsandsociety.org), successor organization to *The Animals' Agenda* magazine and its publisher, The Animal Rights Network, Inc., and also with the permission of Ellen Bring, activist, attorney, and educator.

Chapter 4 is reprinted with the permission of Claudia Dreifus, whose forthcoming book is *Higher Education?*, co-authored with Andrew Hacker.

Chapter 5 is reprinted with the permission of Paula Giddings, whose most recent book is *Ida: A Sword Among Lions* and who is the Elizabeth A. Woodson Professor of Afro-American Studies at Smith College.

Chapter 6, "Giving Birth, Finding Form: Where Our Books Come From" (1993), from Creative Conversations Series, is reprinted with the permission of Sounds True (www.soundstrue.com).

Chapter 7 is reprinted with the permission of Jody Hoy.

Chapter 8, "My Life as Myself": A Conversation with Tami Simon (1995), is reprinted with the permission of Sounds True (www.soundstrue.com).

Chapter 9 is reprinted with the permission of Howard Zinn.

Chapter 10, © 1996 by New Dimensions Radio/Media. More than 850 programs with other wisdom leaders are offered on the New Dimensions Web site (www.newdimensions.org).

Chapter 11, copyright *Ms.* magazine, 1998.

Chapter 12, "On the Meaning of Suffering and the Mystery of Joy": Alice Walker and Pema Chödrön in Conversation (1998), is reprinted with the permission of Sounds True (www.soundstrue.com).

Chapter 13, from *Southern Cultures*, © 2004 by the Center for the Study of the American South, is reprinted with the permission of University of North Carolina Press.

Chapter 14 is reprinted with the permission of LIVE from the NYPL/Margo Jefferson.

Chapter 15 is an excerpt from a *Democracy Now!* conversation aired February 13, 2006, titled "I Am a Renegade, an Outlaw, a Pagan"—Author, Poet and Activist Alice Walker in Her Own Words.

Chapter 16, from *The Fidel Castro Handbook*, is reprinted with the permission of George Galloway.

The interview in chapter 17 was conducted by Marianne Schnall, a writer and interviewer, and originally appeared at the women's site and nonprofit organization Feminist.com (http://www.feminist.com). It is reprinted with the permission of Marianne Schnall.

Chapter 18 is reprinted with the permission of Shambhala Sun, 2006.

CHRONOLOGY

1944   Walker is born at home on February 9 in Putnam County,
        Georgia, to Willie Lee Walker and Minnie Lou (Tallulah) Grant
        Walker, both sharecroppers. The last child of eight children, she
        is given the name of Alice Malsenior Walker. The Walkers pay
        the midwife three dollars for her services.

1948   At four years of age Walker enters the first grade of East Putnam
        Consolidated, a primary and middle school established in 1948
        through the leadership of Willie Lee Walker, her father.

1952   In a game of cowboys and Indians with her brothers Bobby and
        Curtis, Walker is accidentally shot in her right eye by Curtis
        with a BB gun. She loses the sight in her eye, over which disfig-
        uring scar tissue forms.

1957   Walker enrolls in Butler-Baker High School, the only school
        open to African Americans in Eatonton, the county seat of Put-
        nam County, Georgia.

1958   With the support of her brother Bill, the scar tissue is removed
        from Walker's right eye by Dr. Morriss M. Henry of Boston's
        Massachusetts General Hospital.

1961   Walker graduates from Butler-Baker High School as vale-
        dictorian of her class and enrolls at Spelman College. She de-
        parts from Eatonton on a segregated Greyhound bus with
        "three magic gifts" from her mother, Minnie Lou Grant
        Walker: a typewriter, a sewing machine, and a suitcase. While

at Spelman, Walker becomes involved in the civil rights movement by participating in events sponsored by the Student Nonviolent Coordinating Committee and other civil rights organizations. She becomes a student of the historian Howard Zinn, a member of the faculty at Spelman College.

1962   Walker travels abroad for the first time as a delegate to the World Festival of Youth and Students in Helsinki, Finland. Coretta Scott King is one of her sponsors.

1963   Walker attends the March on Washington for Jobs and Freedom. She withdraws from Spelman College in December.

1964   In January Walker transfers to Sarah Lawrence College with the assistance of Staughton Lynd, a faculty member in the department of history at Spelman College. She continues to be active in the civil rights movement through voter registration campaigns. Walker travels to Kenya under the auspices of the Experiment in International Living. While at Sarah Lawrence, she becomes a student of the philosopher Helen Lynd and the poets Jane Cooper and Muriel Rukeyser.

1965   Walker discovers that she is pregnant and, with the aid of classmates at Sarah Lawrence, has an illegal abortion.

1966   Walker earns her BA degree from Sarah Lawrence College. She writes an honors thesis on Albert Camus entitled "Albert Camus: The Development of His Philosophical Position as Reflected in His Novels and Plays" under the direction of Helen Lynd, her don, or adviser. After graduation she moves to New York City and accepts an appointment as a caseworker at the Department of Welfare. Walker is appointed a Bread Loaf Writers' Conference Scholar and is awarded the Merrill Writing Fellowship. She accepts an appointment with the NAACP Legal Defense and Educational Fund in Jackson, Mississippi, under the supervision of Marian Wright Edelman. Walker meets Melvyn R. Leventhal, a civil rights lawyer with the NAACP Legal Defense and Educational Fund.

1967   Walker marries Melvyn Leventhal in a civil ceremony in New York City. She is awarded a writing residency at the MacDowell Colony. "The Civil Rights Movement: What Good Was It?" is published in the *American Scholar*. The essay wins the journal's first prize of $300. Walker meets the poet Langston Hughes. "To Hell with Dying," her first short story, is published in *The Best Short Stories by Negro Writers*, edited by Hughes.

1968   *Once*, a volume of poems, is published. Walker becomes writer-in-residence at Jackson State University, where she meets the poet Margaret Walker.

1969   Walker and Mel Leventhal become the parents of a daughter, their only child.

1970   *The Third Life of Grange Copeland*, a novel, is published. Walker becomes a guest lecturer at Tougaloo College and discovers the work of Zora Neale Hurston.

1971   Walker is awarded a Radcliffe Institute fellowship from Harvard University.

1972   Walker accepts an appointment as a lecturer in the English Department at Wellesley College and the University of Massachusetts at Boston.

1973   *In Love and Trouble: Stories of Black Women*, a collection of short stories, is published. *Revolutionary Petunias*, a volume of poems, is published. Walker is awarded the Lillian Smith award for *Revolutionary Petunias*. Walker's father, Willie Lee Walker, dies. She places a marker on the grave of Zora Neale Hurston in Fort Pierce, Florida. Walker is a lecturer at Smith College, where she teaches the first course in the nation on black women writers. She delivers a talk, "In Search of Our Mothers' Gardens," at Radcliffe College.

1974   Walker leaves Mississippi and moves to New York City, where she becomes an editor at *Ms*. She publishes *Langston Hughes:*

American Poet. Walker is awarded the National Institute of Arts and Letters award for *In Love and Trouble.* *Revolutionary Petunias* is nominated for a National Book Award along with Audre Lorde's *From a Land Where Other People Live* (1973) and Adrienne Rich's *Diving into the Wreck* (1973). Walker, Lorde, and Rich agree not to compete with one another. The National Book Award is awarded to Rich. Walker, Lorde, and Rich agree to donate the prize money of $1,000 to the Sisterhood of Black Single Mothers, an advocacy organization in New York City. Walker publishes "In Search of Our Mothers' Gardens" in *Ms.*

1976 Walker and Leventhal divorce. *Meridian,* a novel, is published.

1977 Walker is awarded a Guggenheim Fellowship.

1978 Walker leaves New York City and moves to San Francisco, California. She and Robert L. Allen, senior editor of the *Black Scholar,* establish a life together in Boonville, California, where she begins writing *The Color Purple.* Walker makes the first of four visits to Cuba during which she delivers humanitarian aid to the people of Cuba.

1979 *Good Night, Willie Lee, I'll See You in the Morning,* a volume of poems, is published. Walker also publishes *I Love Myself When I Am Laughing . . . and Then Again When I Am Looking Mean and Impressive: A Zora Neale Hurston Reader.*

1981 *You Can't Keep a Good Woman Down,* a collection of short stories, is published.

1982 *The Color Purple,* a novel, is published. Walker is appointed distinguished writer in Afro-American studies at the University of California at Berkeley. She also accepts an appointment as the Fannie Hurst Professor of Literature at Brandeis University.

1983 Walker is awarded the Pulitzer Prize and the National Book Award for *The Color Purple. In Search of Our Mothers'*

Gardens: Womanist Prose, a collection of essays, is published. Walker visits Nicaragua in order to attend the Managua Book Fair.

1984   Walker establishes Wild Trees Press. *Horses Make a Landscape Look More Beautiful*, a volume of poems, is published.

1985   Steven Spielberg's film adaptation of *The Color Purple* is released. With music by Quincy Jones, and starring Whoopi Goldberg, Danny Glover, and Oprah Winfrey, the film will be nominated for eleven Academy Awards in the following year.

1986   Walker attends the premiere of *The Color Purple* in Eatonton, Georgia, with family members including her mother, Minnie Lou (Tallulah) Grant Walker, and Ruth Walker, a sister, who establishes the Color Purple Scholarship Fund and the Color Purple Trail in Eatonton. Awarded O. Henry Prize for her short story "Kindred Spirits."

1988   "To Hell with Dying," a short story, is published as a book of children's literature. *Living by the Word: Selected Writings, 1973–1987*, a collection of essays, is published. Walker closes Wild Trees Press.

1989   *The Temple of My Familiar*, a novel, is published.

1991   *Finding the Green Stone*, a book of children's literature, is published. *Her Blue Body Everything We Know: Earthling Poems 1965–1990* is also published.

1992   *Possessing the Secret of Joy*, a novel, is published.

1993   *Warrior Marks: Female Genital Mutilation and the Sexual Binding of Women* is published as a companion volume to the documentary *Warrior Marks*, directed by Pratibha Parmar and produced by Walker. Minnie Lou Grant Walker, her mother, dies.

1994   *Alice Walker: The Complete Stories* is published. Walker
        changes her name to Alice Tallulah-Kate Walker in honor of her
        maternal great-grandmother, Tallulah Calloway, and her pater-
        nal grandmother, Kate Nelson.

1996   *The Same River Twice: Honoring the Difficult,* a collection of
        nonfiction, is published. *Alice Walker Banned,* a collection of
        fiction and nonfiction, is published.

1997   *Anything We Love Can Be Saved: A Writer's Activism,* a
        collection of essays, is published. Walker attends the char-
        tering of the Alice Walker Literary Society, a collaborative
        project between Spelman College and Emory University, and
        is named Humanist of the Year by the American Humanist
        Association.

1998   *By the Light of My Father's Smile,* a novel, is published.

2000   *The Way Forward Is with a Broken Heart,* a collection of short
        stories, is published.

2001   *Sent by Earth: A Message from the Grandmother Spirit After
        the Attacks on the World Trade Center and Pentagon,* an essay,
        is published.

2002   James (Jimmy) Walker, brother, dies.

2003   *Absolute Trust in the Goodness of the Earth* and *A Poem Trav-
        eled Down My Arm,* two volumes of poetry, are published.

2004   *Now Is the Time to Open Your Heart,* a novel, is published.
        Scott Sanders's musical stage adaptation of *The Color Purple*
        premieres at the Alliance Theater in Atlanta, Georgia. Walker
        begins discussions with Emory University regarding the custo-
        dianship of her archive.

2005   The musical *The Color Purple* premieres at the Broadway The-
        atre in New York City.

2006   *We Are the Ones We Have Been Waiting For: Inner Light in a Time of Darkness: Meditations,* a collection of essays and talks, is published. Walker also publishes *There Is a Flower at the Tip of My Nose Smelling Me,* a book for children of all ages. The musical *The Color Purple* wins a Tony Award. Walker is inducted into the California Hall of Fame.

2007   *Why War Is Never a Good Idea,* a children's book, is published. Emory University becomes the custodian of the Alice Walker archive. The twenty-fifth-anniversary edition of *The Color Purple* is published.

2008   Walker delivers a reading at Emory University to commemorate its custodianship of her archive. She endorses the candidacy of Barack H. Obama for president of the United States. Walker launches alicewalkersgarden.com, her official Web site. Ruth Walker Hood, a sister, dies.

2009   Walker travels to the Middle East with CODEPINK to deliver humanitarian aid to the women of Gaza. The opening of "A Keeping of Records: The Art and Life of Alice Walker," an exhibition and symposium, takes place at Emory University. Both events commemorate the opening of the Walker archive to researchers and to the public. Walker attends these events and delivers a talk at Emory's Glenn Memorial Auditorium entitled "Reflections on Turning the Wheel: Living a Life of Freedom and Choice." On this occasion she receives the Phoenix Award from the office of Atlanta mayor Shirley Clarke Franklin. Also on this occasion, the city council of Atlanta and the government of DeKalb County declare April 24, 2009, "Alice Walker Day." Walker publishes *Overcoming Speechlessness: A Poet Encounters 'the Horror' in Rwanda, Eastern Congo, and Palestine/Israel.* Walker is awarded the James Weldon Johnson Medal for Literature by the James Weldon Johnson Institute of Emory University.

2010   Walker publishes *The World Has Changed: Conversations with Alice Walker.*

The World Has Changed

Alice Walker
December 7, 2008

The World Has Changed:
Wake up & smell
The possibility.
The world
Has changed:
It did not
Change
Without
Your prayers
Without
Your faith
Without
Your determination
To
Believe
In liberation
&
Kindness;
Without
Your
Dancing
Through the years
That
Had
No
Beat.

The world has changed:
It did not
Change
Without
Your
Numbers
Your
Fierce
Love
Of self
&
Cosmos
It did not
Change
Without

Your
Strength.

The world has
Changed:
Wake up!
Give yourself
The gift
Of a new
Day.

The world has changed:
This does not mean
You were never
Hurt.
The world
Has changed:
Rise!
Yes
&
Shine!
Resist the siren

Call
Of
Disbelief.
The world has changed:
Don't let
Yourself
Remain
Asleep
To
It.
***

THE WORLD
HAS CHANGED

Introduction

Even when we feel we can't change things, it's important to have awareness of what has happened. If you are unaware of what has happened, it means you're not alive in many respects. And to be unalive in many places within yourself means you are missing a lot of the experience of being on this planet. And this planet is not to be missed.

—Alice Walker

The World Has Changed: Conversations with Alice Walker is the first collection of interviews and conversations with Alice Walker, whose expanding corpus is a permanent part of our national literature. Spanning the years from 1973 to 2009, *The World Has Changed* maps many of the changes that have occurred in Walker's writings and life for more than three decades. These changes have occurred within the complex and dynamic context of national and world events. Within the pages of this volume, Walker emerges as an artist and activist who has generated change in the world and who also has been transformed by change in the world. Ever the alert, probing, engaged, and compassionate figure, she is both inside and outside the change that is the subject of her art and the force behind her activism.

Walker's art and activism have their origins in post-Depression, segregated rural Georgia. It is this particular landscape that provided the self-described "daughter of the rural peasantry" with her first words, her first canvas as it were, and a means of establishing through the medium of art a human connection with what would become a worldwide readership. In the opening lines of "Three Dollars Cash," Walker pays tribute to her origins in Putnam County, Georgia, where she was born on February 9, 1944, to Minnie Lou (Tallulah) Grant Walker and Willie Lee Walker, both sharecroppers: "Three dollars cash / For a pair of catalog shoes / Was what the midwife charged / My mama / For bringing me." [1] In the poem Minnie Lou Walker recalls the family's circumstances at the time of the birth of Walker, the last child of eight: "We wasn't so country then / You being the last one—And we couldn't, like / We done / When she brought your / Brother, / Send her out to the / Pen / And let her pick / Out A pig." [2] When Walker was born her parents could

*Minnie Lou Grant Walker and Willie Lee
Walker*

pay Miss Fannie, the midwife, "three dollars cash" for her services.
This represented progress—"We wasn't so country then"—for a family
whose income in the 1940s was approximately $20 per month.

According to Minnie Lou Walker, Walker began to write well before
she began to walk. She and other family members remember how "Baby
Alice" would crawl underneath the house and with a twig "write" in
the Sears, Roebuck catalog. The family library, such as it was, was composed of cast-off books from whites and gifts from black teachers in
Putnam County. As a child, Walker was drawn to other expressive art
forms, namely painting and the piano, but without the resources to buy
oils or to pay for music lessons, she continued to write, a practice that
complemented her already solitary nature. Concerned about the welfare
of her child as she picked cotton, and in defiance of the white landlords
who believed that black children should be in the fields rather than sitting at desks, Minnie Lou Walker enrolled "Baby Alice" in East Putnam
Consolidated, an elementary and middle school established through the

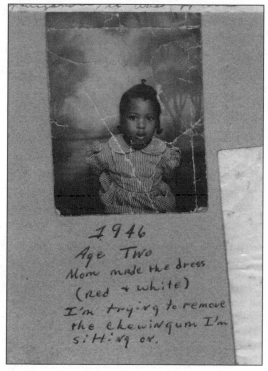

Alice Walker at age two.

leadership of her parents, Willie Lee and Minnie Lou Walker, and other elders in her community. The building of the first school was burned down, presumably by white supremacists. Undeterred, Willie Lee Walker and others rebuilt East Putnam Consolidated, and Walker began her education there at the age of four. Although she would pick cotton along with other family members as a child, Walker flourished in school under the almost parental attention of Miss Reynolds and other black teachers who recognized and nurtured her gifts.[3] As a student, she was curious about everything, mastered her lessons, delivered flawless recitations, and continued to write.

In 1952 the world changed in a dramatic way for Walker. In a game of cowboys and Indians with her brothers Bobby and Curtis, she was accidentally shot in her right eye with a BB gun. In "Beauty: When the Other Dancer Is the Self," Walker reconstructs this pivotal event:

I am eight years old and a tomboy. I have a cowboy hat, cowboy boots, checkered shirt and pants, all red. My playmates are my brothers, two and four years older than I. . . . On Saturday nights we all go to the picture show. . . . Back home, "on the ranch," we pretend we are Tom Mix, Hopalong Cassidy, Lash La Rue . . . we chase each other for hours rustling cattle, being outlaws, delivering damsels from distress. Then my parents decide to buy my brothers guns. These are not "real" guns. They shoot "BBs," copper pellets my brothers say will kill birds. Because I am a girl, I do not get a gun. Instantly I am relegated to the position of the Indian. Now there appears a great distance between us. They shoot and shoot at everything with their new guns. I try to keep up with my bow and arrows.

One day while I am standing on top of our makeshift "garage" . . . holding my bow and arrow and looking outward toward the fields, I feel an incredible blow in my right eye. I look down just in time to see my brother lower his gun.

Both rush to my side. My eye stings, and I cover it with my hand. "If you tell," they say, "we will get a whipping. You don't want that to happen, do you?" I do not. "Here is a piece of wire," says the older brother, picking it up from the roof; "say you stepped on one end of it and the other flew up and hit you." The pain is beginning to start. "Yes," I say. "Yes, I will say that is what happened." If I do not say this is what happened, I know my brothers will find ways to make me wish I had.

Confronted by our parents we stick to the lie agreed upon. . . . There is a tree growing from underneath the porch that climbs past the railing to the roof. It is the last thing my right eye sees. I watch as its trunk, its branches, and then its leaves are blotted out by the rising blood.[4]

The physical result of the accident is that Walker lost the vision in her right eye. The psychological result is that she became alienated and depressed. She also became more observant, detached, and empathetic. Walker delved more deeply into reading and writing. She also turned to nature, which did not look away when she raised her face, now disfigured by the scar tissue covering her right eye, as did many classmates and adults. In the pastoral "O Landscape of My Birth," Walker evokes the loneliness and pain of that dark period and how she was further diminished by the razing of a tree, her "dearest companion": "and

I see again with memory's bright eye / my dearest companion cut down / and can bear to resee myself / so lonely and so small / there in the sunny meadows / and shaded woods / of childhood / where my crushed spirit / and stricken heart / ran in circles / looking for a friend." [5] The loss of vision in her right eye, along with the trauma and isolation that came with it, led to the creation of a strong inner vision that would become the foundation of her art. The scar tissue covering her right eye was eventually removed through the aid of her older brother William when Walker was fourteen. A physician once told her that eyes are sympathetic, and so for many years she lived with the fear of going blind. "The unhappy truth," recalls Walker many years after the event, "is that I was left feeling a great deal of pain and loss and forced to think I had somehow brought it on myself. It was very like a rape. It was the first time I abandoned myself, by lying, and is at the root of my fear of abandonment. It is also the root of my need to tell the truth, always, because I experienced, very early, the pain of telling a lie." [6]

Walker's commitment to truth telling assumed written form in a scrapbook. The first published reference to her scrapbook appears in Gloria Steinem's "Alice" in *Outrageous Acts and Everyday Rebellions* (1983). There Walker observes: "From the time I was eight, I kept a notebook. I found it lately and I was surprised—there were horrible poems, but they were poems. There's even a preface that thanks all of the people who were forced to hear this material—my mother, my teacher, my blind Uncle Frank." [7] As she tells us, Walker began keeping her scrapbook in 1952 at the age of eight years old; the last addition, a photograph taken of her in her room at Packard Hall at Spelman College, was made in March 1962. Like many girls her age, she kept a record of her thoughts, dreams, and experiences, a practice that would prepare her to become a writer. Containing poems, essays, reflections, and photographs of herself, her friends, and her family, the scrapbook is the earliest record we have of Walker's effort to achieve conscious eloquence. One of the most striking features of this record of childhood and adolescence is the dedication: "I, ALICE MALSENIOR WALKER, ON THIS DAY, MY 15TH BIRTHDAY, FEBRUARY 9, 1959, DO DEDICATE THIS COLLECTION OF MY WORKS TO MYSELF, AND TO THOSE WHO HAVE INSPIRED ME MOST: MOTHER, FATHER, RUTH, UNCLE FRANK, MR. ROBERTSON, MR. HORTON, MR. RICE, AND MR. NELSON." [8] The dedication and its bold type reveal many things.

First, there is a sense of the high value Walker attached to her own person and vision, a value that is not grounded in egocentrism but rather in a self-love that is both nurturing and empowering. There is also an awareness, at the age of fifteen, of the contributions she would make as a writer to the world of letters. We would not expect such boldness, self-confidence, and a sense of self-worth from the one-eyed daughter of sharecroppers who came of age in an environment governed by a social order stained by the relentless operations of patriarchy and white supremacy, a social order committed to her subordination, if not annihilation. We are conscious here, as we are in the other parts of her corpus, of the manner in which this "daughter of the rural peasantry" made creative, inspiring use of personal tragedy as well as racism, sexism, class and caste oppression, and any other species of trouble. The bold, self-assured stance Walker assumes in this first of many dedications and throughout the volume prefigures the stance she would assume some years later in the signature poem "On Stripping Bark from Myself": "I find my own / small person / a standing self / against the world / an equality of wills / I finally understand." [9] Following this clear and powerful canto comes the concluding one, in which the speaker delivers a final meditation on her potentiality that is laced with defiance for those intent upon her destruction: "My struggle was always against / an inner darkness: I carry within myself / the only known keys / to my death— to unlock life, or close it shut / forever. A woman who loves wood grains, the color / yellow / and the sun, I am happy to fight / all outside murderers / as I see I must." [10] In addition to prefiguring the self-confidence that would sustain her even during periods when she was suicidal, the dedication also contains, characteristically, an acknowledgment of those who inspired and supported her writerly efforts.

The "small person" who produced the scrapbook, in which she would continue to make entries until 1962, would become the valedictorian of her class at Butler-Baker High School in Eatonton, Georgia, the only high school open to blacks. After her graduation in 1961, Walker would matriculate at Spelman College as a scholarship student. While at Spelman she would meet the scholar and feminist Beverly Guy-Sheftall as well as the scholar and activist Robert Allen, who was enrolled at Morehouse College. She also would become a student of the historians Howard Zinn and Staughton Lynd, and with their support and encouragement become involved in the civil rights movement. Much to her

disappointment, Walker found the culture of Spelman College more oppressive than liberating. She was a student at Spelman during an era
when all students were subjected to the humiliation of pelvic examinations. According to scholar and Spelman alumna Beverly Guy Sheftall,
the pelvic examination was administered during a student's first and
third years. The purpose of the pelvic examination was to determine
if a student was pregnant. Or, put another way, the purpose of these
carefully timed examinations was to police and regulate the sexuality
of Spelman students. Walker herself submitted to such an examination.
Her critique of the culture of Spelman College is on full display in her
second novel, *Meridian* (1976), where the historically black Georgia
women's college emerges as Saxon College, an institution whose mission is to produce virgins and ladies rather than activists and leaders in
the tradition of Harriet Tubman. The scholarship student from Putnam
County had hoped to encounter a guardian at Spelman College, but
instead, as she has observed, she encountered a guard. Walker found
the culture of Spelman intolerable after the dismissal of Zinn by Albert
Manley, then the president, for the historian's involvement in the civil
rights movement and his open support of Walker and other students
involved in the demonstrations organized by the Student Nonviolent
Coordinating Committee (SNCC) and other civil rights organizations
in the Atlanta University Center. After two difficult years at Spelman,
Walker transferred to Sarah Lawrence College with the assistance of
Lynd in December 1963.

Walker began her studies at Sarah Lawrence in January 1964. While
racism was an aspect of the culture of this progressive New York wom-
en's college, she nevertheless flourished in an environment that was
particularly supportive of her aspiration to become a writer. Walker's
teachers at Sarah Lawrence were the poets Jane Cooper and Muriel
Rukeyser, as well as the social philosopher Helen Lynd (the mother of
Staughton Lynd). In "A Talk: Convocation, 1972," she recalled the lessons they modeled as both teachers and women. Through Lynd, Walker
"came to understand that even loneliness has its use, and that sadness is
positively the wellspring of creativity." [11] Through Rukeyser, the daughter of sharecroppers learned the important lesson "that it *is* possible to
live in this world on your own terms." [12] In recalling Cooper's singular
attributes, Walker compares her to a "pine tree. Quiet, listening, true.
Like the tree you adopt as your best friend when you're seven. Only

dearer than that for having come through so many storms, and still willing to offer that listening and that peace." [13] These teachers nurtured and supported Walker's development as both artist and human being. Among them, Rukeyser would play a particularly important role as Walker would confront yet another painful, transforming experience while still a student at Sarah Lawrence.

The world changed again for Walker in the fall of 1965. Returning to Sarah Lawrence after a trip to Kenya and Uganda under the auspices of the Experiment in International Living, she discovered that she was pregnant. The father was David DeMoss, a white student enrolled at Bowdoin College whom Walker had met in 1963 while DeMoss was an exchange student at Morehouse College. At the high point of their relationship, Walker and DeMoss attended together the March on Washington in 1963. While their lives had taken them in different directions, they maintained what both regarded as an important friendship. In 1965, DeMoss was employed by the Peace Corps in Tanzania. He and Walker rendezvoused in Kampala, Uganda, where she conceived. The knowledge of her pregnancy turned Walker's life upside down: it made it impossible for her to concentrate upon her studies at the beginning of a new academic year at Sarah Lawrence after her sojourn in East Africa. She informed DeMoss of the pregnancy by letter and of her decision to seek an abortion. Walker decided that if she could not secure an abortion that she would commit suicide. "It was me or it," remembers the writer, who was twenty-one at the time. "One or the other of us was not going to survive." [14] Pregnant in 1965, eight years before the Supreme Court legalized abortion in *Roe v. Wade* in 1973, Walker was confronted with the terrible choice of an illegal abortion or suicide, for which she prepared with a degree of serenity: "And so, when all my efforts at finding an abortion failed, I planned to kill myself, or—as I thought of it then—to 'give myself a little rest.' " [15] While DeMoss opposed the abortion, he respected Walker's decision to seek one. He contributed all of his savings at the time to a fund Walker's classmates at Sarah Lawrence had established to pay for the abortion, which took place in Manhattan in the fall of 1965.[16]

The abortion behind her, Walker felt as if her life had been returned to her. As with the loss of vision in her right eye, she emerged from the trauma of this event through the cultivation of a strong inner vision. And at this later stage in her life, this inner vision assumed a particular shape and heft through the act of writing. Days after the abortion, Walker began writing a series of poems that she shared with Rukeyser. She wrote the poems from a place of deep silence and relief, one after another, far into the night, and at dawn she would leave them under the door of Rukeyser's office. The poet and teacher circulated the poems to publishers with the assistance of Monica McCall, her literary agent and her companion.[17] This was done without Walker's knowledge. Some years later, these poems would be published in *Once* (1968), Walker's first volume of poetry, which she dedicated to Howard Zinn. Of this debut volume, which arose out of a courageous effort to regain and re-order her life after an unwanted pregnancy and an illegal abortion, Walker has observed: "I had need to write them, but I didn't care if they ever got published. That was irrelevant to me."[18] In her final year at Sarah Lawrence, Walker wrote not only the works that would consti-tute her first volume of poems, but she also wrote such short stories as "To Hell with Dying," "Flowers," and "Suicide of an American Girl." With the encouragement of Rukeyser, the poet Langston Hughes se-lected "To Hell with Dying" for inclusion in his book *The Best Short Stories by Negro Writers* (1967). The story would subsequently be re-printed in *In Love and Trouble: Stories of Black Women* (1973), and then some time later it would have its own special life as a book for juvenile readers in 1988. Written in one of her many spiral notebooks and tucked between lecture notes, "Flowers" would be published in *In Love and Trouble*. "Suicide of an American Girl," a short story that generated much discussion and admiration at Sarah Lawrence, remains unpublished.[19] These early works of poetry and fiction, written while Walker was still an undergraduate, foreshadowed the emergence of an original and powerful voice in American letters.

While writing poetry and fiction, Walker also completed her honors thesis, entitled "Albert Camus: The Development of His Philosophical Position as Reflected in His Novels and Plays" under the direction of her beloved don Helen Lynd.[20] Throughout the twenty-eight-page the-sis Lynd wrote in the margins such questions as this one: "What is the difference between an idea, and a 'philosophical idea'?" Certainly, the objective here was to introduce a greater degree of clarity and precision in the analysis of an exceptional student who came to her through her son. In a very legible longhand, Lynd provides in her summary a bal-anced assessment of Walker's examination of Camus's treatment of the relationship between innocence and evil, between one's present condition and one's potentiality, and between the recognition of the absurd and rebellion, questions that would assume a particular significance in the future writings of her honor student: "I think that you got a great deal from doing this paper and I got a great deal from reading it. You combine very well the pertinent analysis of detail and the major trends in his thought. I like particularly the way you use recognition of the absurd as a basis for human solidarity and a preparation for rebellion. A good paper." [21]

Having fulfilled the last requirement of her studies, which spanned English, French, philosophy, and creative writing, Walker graduated from Sarah Lawrence in 1966. After graduation, she worked as a caseworker at New York City's Department of Welfare. Not long after her appointment, Walker was awarded a Merrill Fellowship and also was named a Bread Loaf Writers' Conference Scholar. [22] Drawn to the possibility of traveling to Senegal and the opportunity to improve her French with funds from the Merrill Fellowship, yet also riveted by the upheavals in her native South born of the civil rights movement, Walker accepted an internship at the National Association for the Advancement of Colored People's Legal Defense and Educational Fund in Jackson, Mississippi. There she was under the very able supervision of Marian Wright Edelman, a graduate of Spelman College and future founder of the Children's Defense Fund. During her tenure at the Legal Defense and Educational Fund in Jackson, Walker would seek to bring about progressive social change in Mississippi through the taking of depositions from blacks in nearby Greenwood who had been evicted from their homes for attempting to register to vote. [23] Soon after her arrival in Jackson the world would change again for Walker, for she met there a "struggling young Jewish law student" who became her husband. [24]

The "struggling young Jewish law student" was Melvyn R. Leventhal, a native of Brooklyn, New York, who was enrolled in the law school of New York University. Walker met Leventhal only hours after her arrival in Mississippi at Steven's Kitchen, "a black owned, soul food restaurant in downtown Jackson where civil rights workers routinely gathered to fill their stomachs and replenish their spirits after battling Jim Crow." [25] At the time of their meeting in June 1966, Leventhal had completed his second year of law school and was an intern at Jackson's Legal Defense and Educational Fund, where he reported to Edelman.

Walker says, "I was introduced to Mel when I arrived at the restaurant and I remember thinking he was cute, [but] at the same time, I was very mistrusting of white people in the Movement. I believed what SNCC had been saying about how whites needed to be in their own communities doing civil rights work. I agreed that they were often a detriment in the struggle because of the way blacks in the South had been conditioned to automatically defer to whites." [26] Walker eventually overcame her mistrust of Leventhal after observing his commitment to social justice through his defiance of white supremacy, often at the risk of his own life. In due course, they moved from being colleagues to friends, and finally to lovers.

At the end of their summer internships in 1966, Walker and Leventhal, now deeply in love, decided to return to New York in order for him to complete his final year of law school at NYU. They established a life together in a one-room apartment in Greenwhich Village above Washington Square Park. Leventhal gave himself over completely to the study of law; Walker turned her attention to writing the earliest drafts of *The Third Life of Grange Copeland*. In the winter of 1967, she accepted a residency at the MacDowell Colony in Peterborough, New Hampshire. Missing Wangari (the leopard clan), the name given to Walker by the Kikuyu during her sojourn in Kenya the year before in the summer of 1965, the Jewish boy who had attended public school and a yeshiva in Brooklyn writes to his future bride with the following salutation in a letter of February 2, 1967: "Dear Alice Wangari Lucky Stiff! Back to Uncle Sam for any communication from you. . . . Nothing in my life has dimension without you present. I miss you and love you—I will play cards tonight at Mike's and win a fortune so that we can spend the rest of our lives in the woods of New Hampshire talking to trees and birds and not shoveling snow. . . . More soon sweetheart. In the meantime—do all of the writing and laughing and observing for both of us. Mel." [27] Leventhal writes again to Wangari on February 3: "Shalom: I LOVE YOU (Run your fingers over the back of the page and tell me: how does love feel?)" [28] Reporting his bad luck at cards the night before, he writes: "Nothing else to say except that we lost at cards last night so I guess we cannot spend the rest of our lives in New Hampshire." Bereft at 33 Washington Square West, in Jesuitical fashion the law student deploys the trees in the neighborhood as both evidence and analogue for his own forlorn state: "The trees outside of our window are asking for you and I don't know what to tell them. They ask: 'aren't we as good as any other trees, that she should travel a long distance?' I must think of something to tell them for if I don't I will not be able to look at them with smiling eyes." Anxious for word from Wangari and ever supportive of her calling to become a writer, he closes his passionate epistle thusly: "Write soon—I suspect that you have already completed a major piece of fiction? a poem? Nothing? Love Mel."[29]

The following month, Walker and Leventhal would marry in a civil ceremony in New York City Family Court on March 17, 1967, three months before the Supreme Court would outlaw state bans on interracial marriage in *Loving v. Virginia*.[30] Not everyone was pleased, including Carole Darden, a friend of Walker who attended the ceremony. Mrs. Miriam Leventhal, the groom's mother, dismissed her daughter-in-law as a *schvartze* and in her racism and rage sat shivah.[31] In love and in trouble but nevertheless undeterred, Leventhal wrote to Edelman in Jackson seeking her guidance when the newlyweds decided to return to Mississippi to continue their lives together as well as their important work at the Legal Defense and Educational Fund. After a cheerful acknowledgment of the groom's happy state—"You still sound blissful! which is lovely"—Edelman turns to the serious matter of advising an idealistic interracial couple who have decided to establish a household in a state that has become a national symbol of white supremacy and where, predictably, interracial marriage is illegal. In offering advice, Edelman was also doubtless drawing upon her own experience as a member of an interracial couple living in the Magnolia State; the first African American woman admitted to the bar in Mississippi delivered her advice in the crisp form of a legal brief:

(1) Whether or not your marriage comes to the attention of the authorities really depends on how you conduct yourself. It is reasonable that they may eventually find out but with discreet conduct, I don't think it will provoke any major reaction. We have had interracial couples in the State for varying degrees of time, but they got along without difficulty and the authorities were either unaware or deliberately ignored it.

(2) I would not volunteer that you are married to strangers who may be dangerous. If the news did get to the Sovereignty

Commission the more likely approach may be a publicity campaign, but I feel with their current cool way of operating they would cool it for publicity would likely have to result in prosecution, and I don't think Mississippi is anxious to test its miscegenation laws as they are sure of losing. . . .

(3) I don't feel housing is a problem. You will, of course, stay in the Negro community.[32]

Before leaving Greenwich Village to establish a household with Leventhal in a three-bedroom bungalow previously owned by Edelman in Jackson's most recently constructed Negro subdivision, i.e., "community,"[33] Walker wrote to Mrs. Leventhal, her mother-in-law, who remained firm in her opposition to the marriage. She carefully set the stage for her last written communication to Mrs. Leventhal. Significantly, the letter opens with the notation "Mother's Day," a subtle, ironic criticism of Mrs. Leventhal's abdication of her role as mother to her daughter-in-law. This opening is followed by the date of May 14, 1967, and these stage directions for a family drama conclude with the formal salutation "Dear Mrs. Leventhal." As part of what Walker terms the "preliminaries" in a carefully composed, three-page, typed, single-spaced letter, she reconstructs for Mrs. Leventhal the contrasting reaction of Minnie Lou Grant and Willie Lee Walker to the decision of their daughter to marry a Jew, or as the men and women of their generation would phrase it, to marry outside of the race:

My own mother is more fearful than unhappy about our marriage. I am sure my father, deep down, is very upset. By "historical" rights, my father should not have allowed your son into our house. And yet, whatever agonizing occurred between my parents was never done in my hearing—not to mention Mel's. And I know that their silence did not mean they loved me less. Considering their rather dubious view of the white man, it could only mean they loved me more. My marrying your son is comparable to a Jewish girl—in Nazi Germany—marrying a German. Somehow one expects the Jewish experience to enlighten the followers of Judaism. It is always disappointing to find a prejudiced Jew. And yet, most of them are, and as Americans and as at last part of the leadership of a racist country, they seem proud of thus assimilating into American mores. This is a fact that will never cease to amaze me.[34]

Walker then challenges Mrs. Leventhal to reflect upon the dangerous world of Jackson, Mississippi, that she and Mel are about to enter with only her anger as a remembrance:

> I want you to consider this too, in three months we will be living in Jackson. Mississippi is dangerous country. Your son who is one of the finest, kindest, bravest, most gentle, men in the world will have to face other people who will also be very angry that he married me. Unfortunately they will, without doubt, be much more violent than you. Will they try to kill us? by beating us to death, shooting us to death, bombing us to death? Or all three? You should realize too that in Mississippi "miscegenation" is against the law. We will have no protection that we do not provide ourselves. If something happens to us—to your son—and you are sitting here on your pride and anger, how will you feel? Will you respond like a southerner with a cheer? Will you say "I told him so, he shouldn't have married her?!" But I hope you will remember, if that is indeed the way you feel now, that nothing will bring a dead man to life. If you are contrite after the fact you will be contrite all by yourself. Your son, whom you "never want to see again," will be out of your sight forever. These are the little maneuvers of life that we must consider before giving in to our rages.[35]

More in the role of a younger woman who was providing an older woman with instruction, Walker introduces at this point in the letter the delicate matter of grandchildren: "There is a lot in the future to think about. You may be scandalized to know that we plan to raise a family. . . . Grandchildren are grandchildren, even if you never see them. If you never want to see them, fine, if they never know you how can they miss you? But is this really what you want? Try to be sure. Life is both long and difficult. It can also be lonely."[36] Recalling another scene in this family drama, Walker addresses Mrs. Leventhal's insistence that certain gifts be returned to her:

As for your insistence that Mel return presents, etc. that you gave him, as you know he will do exactly that. He is actually a finer person than either you or I, he knows his mind and knuckles under for nobody. Neither does he hate. If you carry this further so that you figure we owe you money let us know, we won't rest until it is paid. I have money, you can have it all. We are all probably responding to the situation like children, but I don't suppose we can help the way we are, that is what Mel says all the time anyway. Frankly I always think people can do better than they're doing at the time.[37]

Walker closes her letter to Mrs. Leventhal without sentimentality, keenly aware of the implications of the gulf that has opened up between them:

Since we will never see one another again this is good-bye. I will do my best to make Mel happy and I will never recall in his presence your disrespect of our marriage. Your son will do great things in life because he is a great man. And if that great God of the Jews exists I am sure he will be pleased that at least one of the chosen has not forgotten his teachings in a world where it is so easy to forget. We will take what comes, love and trust each other, love and try to understand our children.[38]

Maintaining a defiant and principled stance throughout the letter, the daughter of Minnie Lou Grant Walker and Willie Lee Walker signed the letter "Sincerely, Alice Walker Leventhal."

Mrs. Leventhal was apparently affected by her daughter-in-law's letter. Some time later, Mrs. Leventhal returns this extraordinary letter to Walker, and on the third and last page writes the following reply in longhand: "If you need money I promise to see you thru this I will do. I am your mother in spite of a broken heart."[39] In her own way, Walker would reply to Mrs. Leventhal's postscript some years later in a fictionalized treatment of her marriage to Leventhal in "To My Young Husband," a story that appears in the collection of short stories *The Way Forward Is with a Broken Heart* (2000).

During the years of her marriage to Leventhal, from 1967 to 1976, Walker published the first of the foundational works in her expanding body of work. In the genre of the essay, she published in 1967 "The Civil

Rights Movement: What Good Was It?" This powerful reflection on the meaning of her involvement in the civil rights movement is Walker's first published essay, and "it won the three-hundred-dollar first prize in the annual *American Scholar* essay contest."[40] Widely reprinted, it would appear in *In Search of Our Mothers' Gardens* (1983), Walker's first collection of essays. Soon after Walker and Leventhal arrived in Jackson, Mississippi, *Once* (1968) was published. This debut collection of poetry was soon succeeded by a second such volume, *Revolutionary Petunias* (1973), which earned Walker the Lillian Smith Award and was nominated for the National Book Award. During this particularly fecund period, she published the fiction that would establish her as a leading figure in the renaissance of African American women's writings of the 1970s. A year after the birth of their daughter, Leventhal and Walker celebrated the publication of *The Third Life of Grange Copeland* (1970), a historical novel of redemption and transformation grounded in the lives of black sharecroppers of Walker's native Georgia. Three years later, while a lecturer at Wellesley College, where she taught the first course on black women writers, she published *In Love and Trouble: Stories of Black Women* (1973). For this debut collection of short stories Walker was awarded the National Institute of Arts and Letters Award. In 1974, she accepted an appointment in New York as editor at *Ms.*, thus leaving Mississippi and beginning a long friendship with the magazine's co-founder Gloria Steinem. In her first year at *Ms.* (the magazine that largely defined the national debate on feminism in the 1970s), Walker wrote her landmark essay "In Search of Our Mothers' Gardens," which would be reprinted almost a decade later in a collection of essays under the same title. In 1974 she also published *Langston Hughes: American Poet*, her tribute to the poet of Harlem and the nation who provided her with support at a critical stage in her artistic development. A year later Walker published in *Ms.* "Looking for Zora," the reconstruction of her now well-known pilgrimage to Fort Pierce, Florida, where she placed a marker on the unmarked grave of an influential literary ancestor: Zora Neale Hurston. The poet Michael S. Harper dramatically evokes this pilgrimage in his splendid poem "Alice": "You stand waist-high in snakes / beating the weeds for the gravebed / a quarter mile from the nearest / relative, an open field in Florida: lost, / looking for Zora."[41] Widely reprinted, "Looking for Zora" also would appear in *In Search of Our Mothers' Gardens*, and Joyce Carol Oates would include it in

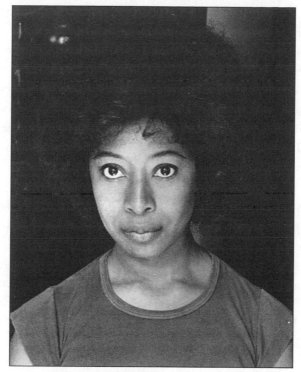

Alice Walker portrait by R. Nathans, 1976

The Best American Essays of the Century (2000). In the final year of her marriage, Walker published *Meridian* (1976), a meditation on the civil rights movement and in particular the role of women in the movement. This is an experimental novel of great depth and power that, in structural and thematic terms, bears the deep imprint of Jean Toomer's *Cane* (1923) and Zora Neale Hurston's *Their Eyes Were Watching God* (1937).

After nine years of marriage, Walker and Leventhal agreed to divorce in 1976. The parting was amicable, though marked by sadness. Reflecting upon the divorce, Walker remarks that a desire for greater states of freedom was the basis for the end of her first and only marriage: "As long as you exist, you are changing. I cared for Mel, but I didn't want to live with him anymore. I needed to be free." [42] Leventhal subsequently married Judith Goldsmith, and not long after the divorce Walker resumed a friendship with scholar Robert Allen, whom she had met in Howard Zinn's Russian history course while at Spelman College. Walker and Allen would remain together until 1990, the break occasioned by many factors, including Allen's infidelity and Walker's full embrace of her bisexuality.[43]

A year after her divorce, Walker was awarded a Guggenheim Fellowship. With this important recognition of her work she acquired a new degree of financial security; thus positioned, she left New York for San Francisco in 1978. With Robert Allen, Walker established a new life in a region of the nation Mark Twain and Ralph Ellison termed "the territory." The search for a place to write and think led to Boonville, California, where she would write the novel that would establish her as a national and international figure in letters.

In characteristic fashion, Walker completed other writing projects even as she prepared to write the novel that would transform her into an iconic figure in American letters and culture. In 1979 she published *Good Night Willie Lee, I'll See You in the Morning*, a third volume of poems, which contains the signature poem "On Stripping Bark from Myself." Walker's 1973 pilgrimage to Fort Pierce, Florida, in search of Zora Neale Hurston culminated in the 1979 publication of *I Love Myself When I Am Laughing . . . and Then Again When I Am Looking Mean and Impressive: A Zora Neale Hurston Reader*, a collaboration with the scholar Mary Helen Washington. This commitment to the reformation of the American canon would lead Walker to establish in 1984 Wild Trees Press.[44] Thriving in the new landscape of Northern California, which bears a striking resemblance to her native Putnam County, Georgia, in 1981 Walker published her second collection of short stories, *You Can't Keep a Good Woman Down*. A celebration of the tradition of resistance, resilience, and grace of black women, the invitation to the book party held at San Francisco's Women's Building invokes the tradition Walker honors in each story: "Your Grandmama Survived / Taft / Your Mama Survived / Hoover / You've Already Survived / Nixon / and / One Hundred and Forty Days / of / Reagan / Why? Because / *YOU CAN'T KEEP A GOOD WOMAN DOWN* / Celebrate / the / Tradition!"[45]

With funds from the Guggenheim Fellowship almost depleted, Walker pieced together an income based upon the advance for *You Can't Keep a Good Woman Down*, a three-hundred-dollar-a-month retainer from *Ms.*, and fees for lectures, which she soon stopped altogether out of respect for the demands of the characters who were taking up residence in her head.[46] "I don't always know where the germ of a story comes from, but with *The Color Purple* I knew right away," recalls Walker:

I was hiking through the woods with my sister, Ruth, talking about a lover's triangle of which we both knew. She said:
"And you know, one day The Wife asked The Other Woman for
a pair of her drawers." Instantly the missing piece of the story I
was mentally writing—about two women who felt married to the
same man—fell into place. And for months—through illnesses,
divorce, several moves, travel abroad, all kinds of heartaches and
revelations—I carried my sister's comment delicately balanced in
the center of the novel's construction I was building in my head.[47]

In her key to the characters of *The Color Purple*, Walker provides
details of the background of characters based on family members and
others beyond her kinship group. "The Wife" was Rachel Walker, the
wife of Henry Clay Walker, or "Pa Pa," the "man" in question, who
reluctantly married Rachel after the murder of his first wife, Kate Nelson, "who was shot by [a] lover in [a] pasture on [her] way home from
church. Died at home after much suffering."[48] The murdered Kate Nelson was the mother of Willie Lee Walker, Walker's father, who witnessed his mother's murder. "The Other Woman" was Estella "Shug"
Perry of Ohio: "Lover of Henry. Mother of two of his children. Elegant
dresser. Honest woman. Kind and frank."[49] This ménage à trois involv-
ing her grandparents was the "germ," or rather the gem, of the story that
became *The Color Purple*. In correspondence many years later, Walker
reveals that the character Celie was based upon her "great-grandmother
[Anne[50]]. Raped by white plantation owner when 11. Had grandpa
Albert when she was 12."[51] Yet another character who emerged from
family history is Nettie: "My mother's mother. Died when I was two.
Mother of twelve. Black. Color struck. Abusive husband. Married to
William Grant, whose name is left out (unconsciously) as statement
of—?"[52] Interestingly, in the key Walker also reveals that the character
Harpo is a "transliteration of Buree [pronounced Bur-yee[53]], my father's
nickname."[54] The character of Sofia has her origins in Hollywood and
the community of Putnam County: "Sophia. Sophia Loren and Miss So-
phie, independent woman I confused with Miss Lillie Orange who had
a house on a hill, raised flowers and was husband and child free."[55]
But, more importantly, Sofia is named for Sophia, the Goddess of Wisdom. And concerning the character of Squeak, or Mary Agness, Walker
records in her key that this character's name is that of a neighbor in

Boonville.[56] Many of the characters in Walker's classic novel are composites of her ancestors as well as women who are relations of a different kind.

During the writing of *The Color Purple*, Walker remembers, there "were days and weeks and even months when nothing happened. Nothing whatsoever." [57] During these fallow periods she turned to quilting. The writer was initiated into the tradition of quilting by her mother, Minnie Lou Grant Walker, and the other women of Putnam County. Walker made her first quilt during the writing of *In Love and Trouble*. Seeking to create art out of family history, she turned again to a traditional art form introduced to her by her family. "I knew that in order for me to have the kind of meditative depth to [*The Color Purple*] that I needed, that I had to work with my hands and I asked my mother to suggest a pattern that would be easy, and she said that there was nothing easier than the Nine-Patch. You know, you just get some fabric and cut up the pieces into nine blocks and you sew them together and that's it. So, I followed her advice. . . . And as I worked on [the quilt], the novel formed." [58] After a long gestation, Walker committed herself to several years of writing the novel: "I had planned to give myself five years to write *The Color Purple* . . . But . . . less than a year after I started writing, I wrote the last page." [59]

Walker wrote *The Color Purple* in her favored spiral notebooks; the first few pages of the novel were written in longhand in green ink, her homage to Langston Hughes, who wrote for much of his life in green ink. As the novel assumed a definite form, Walker continued to write in longhand in the multiplying spiral notebooks, choosing more often to write in black ink. It was out of these simple materials, the unassuming props of the writer, that she elevated to the level of art aspects of a family history possessing universal power and significance.

On April 18, 1983, the world changed again for Walker when she became the first African American woman to be awarded the Pulitzer Prize for Fiction. When members of the press began calling her for interviews she was disbelieving, as she had not been contacted by the fiction jury for the Pulitzer Prize: "I thought it was a joke and a mean-spirited one at that. I was completely stunned." [60] After receiving confirmation of the award, Walker confided the news of this historic achievement in American letters to fellow activist Belvie Rooks, who had dropped by her San Francisco co-op on Galilee Lane for a visit: "Well . . . I just

Alice Walker reading from The Color Purple

won the Pulitzer for *The Color Purple*. The phone's been ringing all day and good news can be just as stressful as bad." [61] Ever the independent daughter of sharecroppers who tolerates no limits on her autonomy and who is generally indifferent to awards from strangers, Walker declined to attend the award ceremony for the Pulitzer Prize. She instead requested that the award money, $1,000, and the citation be mailed to her. "Actually, I think life is the award," observes Walker. "I love being a black Southern woman. All three add incredible enlargements to being a writer." [62] In the weeks to come, *The Color Purple* also would be awarded the National Book Award.

    The Color Purple and the recognition the novel garnered from the American literary establishment dramatically elevated Walker's status as an American writer, or to summon again her own language, as a southern, black woman writer. By extension, the awarding of the Pulitzer Prize to Walker also elevated and legitimized the literary renaissance among African American women writers of which she was a pioneering figure. A deep believer in the importance of creating councils, circles,

Alice Walker and The Sisterhood. Back row, left to right: Vertamae Grosvenor, Alice Walker, Lori Sharpe, Toni Morrison, June Jordan; seated, left to right: Nana Maynard, Ntozake Shange, and Audrey Edwards. The blues singer Bessie Smith, pictured in the photograph, was an example for the Sisterhood of fearlessness and independence.

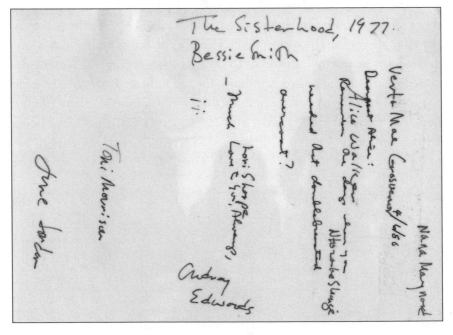

and other methods of support in a society that encourages isolation and competition, Walker had established with her friend and fellow writer June Jordan the Sisterhood in the late 1970s. At Jordan's Brooklyn home, Walker prepared gumbo for the first meeting of the Sisterhood, which included Toni Morrison, Ntozake Shange, Vertamae Grosvenor, and Audrey Edwards. "I remember wanting us black women writers not to be strangers to each other and felt after a couple of gatherings that we weren't," remembers Walker, who at that time had published a significant number of works in both fiction and poetry that heralded a new generation of black women writers. "It was like a council. Being together was the medicine." [63] Among those writers of the Sisterhood, Walker was the first to be awarded a Pulitzer Prize; in 1988 she was succeeded by Toni Morrison, who was awarded the Pulitzer for *Beloved* (1987), and who also would become the first African American and the first American-born woman writer to be awarded the Nobel Prize for Literature in 1993.

After the publication of *The Color Purple*, Walker needed the support of the Sisterhood more than ever. While she had always been attacked by critics, black and white, male and female, for her alleged negative portrayal of African American men, she could not have anticipated the new wave of attacks that came even as the accolades for *The Color Purple* rolled in. Following the release of Steven Spielberg's adaptation of the novel for film in 1985, along with its eleven Academy Award nominations, the naysayers redoubled their efforts. Breaking a long-held silence in the mid-1990s, Walker describes in full detail the impact of the criticism on her:

> The attacks, many of them personal and painful, continued for many years, right alongside the praise, the prizes, the Oscar award nominations. I often felt isolated, deliberately misunderstood and alone. This too is the writer's territory; I accepted it with all the grace and humor I possessed. Still, there is no denying the pain of being not simply challenged publicly, but condemned. It was said that I hated men, black men in particular; that my work was injurious to black male and female relationships; that my ideas of equality and tolerance were harmful, even destructive of the black community. That my success, and that of other black women writers in publishing our work, was at the

expense of black male writers who were not being published sufficiently. I was "accused" of being a lesbian, as if respecting and honoring women automatically discredited anything a woman might say. I was the object of literary stalking: one black male writer attacked me obsessively in lecture, interview and book for over a decade, to the point where I was concerned about his sanity and my safety. In the country north of San Francisco, where I had always sought peace and renewal, I regularly found myself the target of hostile, inflammatory comments by the editor and publisher of the local paper. Because I was the only black woman resident in the community, I was highly visible and felt exposed and vulnerable. This feeling prevented my working at the depth of thought at which I feel most productive. I eventually sought temporary refuge in Mexico, where I was able to work in peace. By then I had grown used to seeing my expressions taken out of context, rearranged, distorted. It was a curious experience that always left me feeling as if I had ingested poison.[64]

While Walker remains for many a polarizing figure, the naysayers are far outnumbered by those who admire and respect her unwavering commitment to "honor [art's] sacred function." Among those admirers is Scott Sanders, the lead producer of the musical adaptation of *The Color Purple*. After a careful courtship, as it were, of Walker, he was granted permission to adapt her novel for the stage. The musical premiered in September 2004 at Atlanta's Tony Award–winning Alliance Theatre, in a collaboration with Susan Booth, the theater's artistic director. After a successful, critically acclaimed run in the capital of Walker's native Georgia, Sanders brought the musical to New York, where it opened at the Broadway Theatre in December 2005. At both venues, the actors performed in theaters filled with diverse and enthusiastic audiences. Nominated for eleven Tony Awards, *The Color Purple* earned a Tony Award for LaChanze as best leading actress for her portrayal of Celie. The return of *The Color Purple* as a musical, a fact that coincided with the twenty-fifth anniversary of the publication of the novel, was not stained by controversy. Through his intelligently and sensitively conceived musical, Sanders introduced Walker's most well-known work to a new generation of readers.

The Color Purple is an important, pivotal work in Walker's corpus because it established her as a canonical figure in American letters and an iconic figure in American culture. This epistolary novel based upon aspects of her family history is also important because it marks a shift in her work. The writings between *Once* and *The Color Purple*, from 1968 to 1983, constitute the first phase of an impressive artistic career. In them Walker explores the impact of a region—the South in general and her native Georgia in particular—with its peculiar history, its race-based, race-privileging structures of dominance, its cultural traditions, its complex, evolving racial and gender formations, and the social justice movement that in large part transformed it. In exploring these questions, Walker also endows with artistic significance the impact of region and social change upon the individual.

And then there is the enormous, complex body of work written after 1983, that is, after *The Color Purple*. The novels of this second rich period include *The Temple of My Familiar* (1989), which rivals *The Color Purple* in popularity, along with *Possessing the Secret of Joy* (1992); *By the Light of My Father's Smile* (1998); and *Now Is the Time to Open Your Heart* (2004). As a poet, Walker produced in this second period *Horses Make a Landscape Look More Beautiful* (1984), *Her Blue Body Everything We Know: Earthling Poems 1965–1990* (1991), *Absolute Trust in the Goodness of the Earth* (2003), and *A Poem Traveled Down My Arm* (2003). In the genre of the essay, Walker's productivity parallels that in other genres: *Living by the Word: Selected Writings, 1973–1987* (1988), *Anything We Love Can Be Saved: A Writer's Activism* (1997), *Sent by Earth: A Message from the Grandmother Spirit After the Attacks on the World Trade Center and Pentagon* (2001), and *We Are the Ones We Have Been Waiting For: Inner Light in a Time of Darkness: Meditations* (2006). And in this second, highly productive period, she continued to write books for the juvenile reader, namely *Finding the Green Stone* (1991), *There Is a Flower at the Tip of My Nose Smelling Me* (2006), and *Why War is Never a Good Idea* (2007). As a writer of short stories, Walker solidified her strong reputation in this genre with the publication of *Alice Walker: The Complete Stories* (1994) and enlarged it with *The Way Forward Is with a Broken Heart* (2000).

The work Walker produced from 1984 up to the present differs from the writing of the first period in a number of important ways. To begin, Walker is interested in exploring questions related to history, but in this second period her interest in history is limited neither to the South nor

Alice Walker being arrested, 1977

the nation but rather encompasses the history of humankind in an effort
to weave a narrative across millennia. This interest in human history is
most evident in *The Temple of My Familiar,* Walker's tribute to Lucy—
the oldest archaeological remains of a human being found to date. Further, as a storyteller Walker has moved beyond her native Georgia to
California and to Hawaii as well as to Mexico, Central America, and
Europe, and once again in *Possessing the Secret of Joy* there is a return
to Africa. The corpus that flows from *The Color Purple* is also more
deeply concerned with questions related to spirituality and the need for
a spiritual practice, and also with human psychology, human sexuality, and human development. Another hallmark of the work of this second period is voice. Throughout this body of work, Walker not only
speaks as witness and rebel but also assumes the voice of the elder and
earthling. This new voice is a function of the achievement of a particular maturity, which is accompanied by an increased awareness of the
interrelatedness of all human existence, and thus also a responsibility
to make her readers aware of this fact, and of the urgency of working

for peace, justice, and reconciliation through art-governed expressions that both instruct and illuminate. The work of this second period is also distinguished by an increased concern for the health and well-being of the planet and other beings, that is, all forms of life in nature, with whom we must learn to coexist. It is through this concern that Walker explores questions related to ecology, the environment, vegetarianism, the culture and history of indigenous peoples, and why war is never a good idea.

While there are, inevitably, some points of convergence between these two organically related bodies of work, they nevertheless have emerged as quite distinct from one another. What they reflect is the manner in which Walker herself has changed and the impact of change upon her own development as a human being and artist. This division is also evidence of an expansive imagination and of a curious, compassionate, and probing intelligence that reflects her openness to new stories, new visions, and new points of view *irregardless* (an ungrammatical, forceful rendering of "in spite of" that appears on Walker's license plate) of the expectation of some critics that her art conform to their demands.

Across this rich division in Walker's writing is the continuity of her belief in activism. The Georgia writer's earliest examples of activism are within her own family. There is the powerful example of May Poole, Walker's great-great-great-great-grandmother who was "enslaved in the North American South" and who walked from Virginia to Georgia with a child on each hip. She died at the age of 125. In the year of her death Willie Lee Walker, Walker's father, "was a boy of eleven." Some have observed that in her own life Walker exhibits the "attitude and courage" of May Poole, qualities that made it possible for this former slave to "attend the funerals of almost everyone who'd owned her." [65] After May Poole, there is, of course, the courageous example of Walker's parents. Willie Lee Walker and Minnie Lou Grant Walker resisted white supremacy in Putnam County in a variety of ways, but in particular through their insistence upon their right to exercise the franchise; through their leadership as members of Ward Chapel, a Methodist church in Putnam County where Walker was baptized; through their leadership in the establishment of East Putnam Consolidated, an elementary and middle school for blacks in segregated Putnam County; and through the high value they placed upon spiritual values and humor as an antidote to the absurdity and brutality of white supremacy. Their defiant stand against injustice, often at the risk of their own lives, is also part of the foundation of Walker's activism.

At Butler-Baker High School, where she graduated as valedictorian of her class, Walker's activism was nurtured by Mr. McGlockton, her "quietly heroic principal," and also through the example of such teachers as Trellie Jeffers, Mrs. Brown, and Mr. Robertson, all of whom had high expectations of their honor student and who did their utmost to prepare her to "encounter the world beyond [her] small community." "Their simple belief in doing their jobs properly, and with concern for my welfare after I left their instruction," remembers Walker, "was activism at its very best." [66]

The earliest record of Walker's resistance to injustice took place while she was employed as a salad girl at Rock Eagle, a 4-H center in Eatonton. Then a student at Butler-Baker High School, Walker and her black classmates were discussing the consequences of segregation in their daily lives as they drove to Rock Eagle to report to work. Captured in Evelyn White's indispensable biography of Walker, this episode is remembered by Porter Sanford III, a classmate of Walker, and his recollection includes Bobby "Tug" Baines, another classmate:

> We were in my parents' car and Alice started talking about how unfair it was that we had to walk to school while the white kids had a bus; about how white people got paid more for doing the same work that we did; about how they constantly had their foot on our necks. I said that we just had to accept it and there was no use complaining.
>
> Alice got so mad at me that she demanded to be let out of the car. She dragged Tug out with her, telling him he should be ashamed to ride with me and they walked the rest of the way to work.[67]

In his adulthood, Sanford would recall in admiration that "Alice was always real serious about her issues." [68]

Walker would express again her contempt for segregation while en route to Spelman College in August 1961. Inspired by the example of Rosa Parks of Montgomery, Alabama, who refused to surrender her seat on a city bus to a white passenger, thereby catalyzing the Montgomery Bus Boycott of 1955, Walker adopted a similarly defiant stance after boarding a segregated Greyhound bus leaving Eatonton for Atlanta. In open defiance of the Jim Crow laws, she sat in the bus's white section until she was forced to move by the driver. Walker recalled the event years later in the following manner: "A white woman (may her fingernails now be dust!) complained to the driver, and he ordered me to move. But even as I moved, in confusion and tears, I knew he had not seen the last of me. In those seconds of moving, everything changed. I was eager to bring an end to the South that permitted my humiliation." [69]

While a student at Spelman, Walker committed herself "to bring[ing] an end to the South that permitted [her] humiliation" through her involvement in the civil rights movement. With the encouragement of Howard Zinn and Staughton Lynd, teachers, activists, and mentors at Spelman at the time, Walker took part in the demonstrations sponsored by student organizations based at the Atlanta University Center who were working in partnership with the Student Nonviolent Coordinating Committee (SNCC). She acquired a global framework for dissent through her selection as a delegate to the World Festival of Youth and Students in Helsinki, Finland, in 1962. As a delegate representing Spelman College, one of Walker's sponsors was Coretta Scott King, whom she would much later interview for an article after King's husband's assassination. This article would appear in *In Search of Our Mothers' Gardens*. Walker's commitment to the civil rights movement was deepened through her attendance of the historic 1963 March on Washington organized by Bayard Rustin, a model for Grange Copeland of *The Third Life of Grange Copeland*. As already mentioned, after graduating from Sarah Lawrence College she accepted an internship at the NAACP Legal Defense and Educational Fund in Jackson, Mississippi, where, with her future husband, Mel Leventhal, she wrote depositions based upon the testimony of black sharecroppers who had been evicted from their homes as a result of their efforts to register to vote.

Walker's participation in the civil rights movement served as the foundation and framework for her participation in other social justice movements. Her deep commitment to the women's movement and the end of violence against women is manifest in her life in a variety of ways, including her attendance at Boston's first Take Back the Night rally in the 1970s. In her role as editor at *Ms.* and through her many groundbreaking essays published during her tenure at the magazine, Walker has been unstinting in her condemnation of sexism and patriarchy, in

Alice Walker hugging Fidel Castro, 1995

documenting the racism in the women's movement as well as the particular forms of oppression experienced by black women and other women
of color. In her highly regarded definition of womanism, Walker has
provided a theoretical model useful to activists and academics in their
efforts to map and theorize about the interlocking oppressions of African American women. Walker's commitment to end violence against
women has led her to resist the practice of clitoridectomy, or what has
been termed female genital mutilation (FGM). In collaboration with the
British filmmaker and activist Pratibha Parmar, she produced the documentary *Warrior Marks* (1993), which she describes as a liberation film.
With the accompanying eponymous volume, Walker and Parmar suc-
cessfully elevated FGM to a global issue, and this has led to a reduction
of this practice in African countries.

As the daughter of sharecroppers in the segregated South, Walker
has been inspired by the revolution in Cuba in 1959 led by Che Guevara
and Fidel Castro. She first visited Cuba in 1978 and has made three
trips since then. Wishing to make sense of the revolution and to stand

in solidarity with the people of Cuba, on these trips Walker has been accompanied by such artists, cultural workers, and revolutionaries as Bernice Johnson Reagon, Angela Davis, Pratibha Parmar, and Margaret Randall. On a visit to Cuba in 1995 she and others in her delegation had an audience with Fidel Castro. The trips to Cuba are an effort on Walker's part to learn as much as possible about the implementation of the goals of the revolution so that she might continue to defend Cuba's sovereignty against critics in the United States. On her several trips to Cuba she has not only delivered medicine but also raised with Cuban citizens, government officials, and with Castro himself difficult questions concerning racism and homophobia in Cuban society, and she continues to track the efforts of the Cuban government to address these and other forms of discrimination.

As an activist and revolutionary, Walker also visited Nicaragua in 1983, on the occasion of the Managua Book Fair, where Daniel Ortega charmed her by "strolling through the stalls and emerging with a copy of *The Color Purple* held aloft, over his head, proclaiming it 'the best book of the festival.' "[70] Walker and her companion at the time, Robert Allen, were guests at the home of Ortega and his wife, Rosario. What struck her during the visit was "how little food there was." "I was vegan," she says, "but there wasn't any rice or beans. We ate very stringy meat which taught me a good lesson: it is a privilege, sometimes a luxury, to be able to decide what you will eat."[71] Away from the residence of the president, Walker remembers there were "constant Contra attacks [as she and Allen] traveled roads lined with soldiers, for miles and miles." "It was amazing," she says. "I felt no fear. Only the joy of being able to show my support."[72]

Walker's unwavering commitment to justice, peace, and an end to all forms of suffering has encompassed other revolutionary struggles, including the abolition of apartheid in South Africa; the Native American movement; the lesbian, gay, bisexual, and transgendered movement; the human rights movement; and the animal rights movement. For many years she has been an opponent of nuclear war and capital punishment. Coming of age during the movement against the Vietnam War of the 1960s, she has been arrested three times, most recently for her opposition to the U.S. invasion of Iraq. Walker's deep concern about the impact of AIDS upon communities in the U.S. and abroad has manifested itself in a variety of ways, including her support of Marlon Riggs's documentary *Black Is . . . Black Ain't: A Personal Journey Through Black Identity* (1995). In the aftermath of Katrina, she traveled to Houston to deliver aid to the families displaced by a disaster that had its origins in both nature and the failures of the state. As a member of CODEPINK, a U.S. women-initiated grassroots peace and social justice movement working to end wars in Iraq and Afghanistan, Walker traveled to the Middle East in March 2009 to deliver humanitarian aid to the women of Gaza. She also has raised her voice and pen in support of political prisoners, including Assata Shakur, now living in exile in Cuba, and Aung San Suu Kyi of Myanmar, and also those fellow writers and freedom fighters who have been threatened with death or killed for their courage in confronting the backwardness, venality, and brutality of the state. In this regard, Walker has stood in solidarity with Salman Rushdie of India and Ken Saro-Wiwa of Nigeria.

In *Anything We Love Can Be Saved: A Writer's Activism*, Walker reflects upon, in deep and specific ways, the origins, the value, and the foundation of her own activism. "My activism—cultural, political, spiritual—is rooted," she writes, "in my love of nature and my delight in human beings. . . . Everything I would like other people to be for me, I want to be for them." [73] As we are confronted with so much bad news, in Walker's view activism generates "a different kind of 'news.' A 'news' that empowers rather than defeats." [74] According to the great-great-great-great-granddaughter of May Poole, when people stand in solidarity together much is revealed: "Because whatever the consequences, people, standing side by side, have expressed who they really are, and that ultimately they believe in the love of the world and each other enough *to be that*—which is the foundation of activism." [75] Of course, there is the alternative—passivity, indifference, complacency, pessimism—but this is a choice that Walker spurns: "The alternative, however, not to act, and therefore to miss experiencing other people at their best, reaching toward fullness, has never appealed to me."

In the preceding pages, I have attempted to reconstruct, using the broadest of strokes, the various ways in which the world has changed for Walker in her long, productive, unique, and meaningful life. The topics I have examined, her origins in rural Putnam County, Georgia, her education, the events that have shaped her emergence as one of the most gifted and influential writers of our time as well as an activist, are addressed by Walker in the various interviews and conversations that compose this volume. In the following pages, she is in conversation with scholars, activists, religious leaders, psychologists, feminists, and writers concerning the vital issues of our time. Walker's interlocutors include such women and men as John O'Brien, Claudia Tate, Paula Giddings, Jean Shinoda Bolen, Isabel Allende, Jody Hoy, Evelyn White, Pema Chödrön, William R. Ferris, Margo Jefferson, Amy Goodman, Marianne Schnall, and Howard Zinn.

As already noted, this volume is the first collection of conversations and interviews with Alice Walker. *The World Has Changed* spans almost four decades and addresses a worldwide readership that now bridges several generations. In many ways the great value of her interviews and conversations has been overlooked until now; this volume seeks to elevate this genre to a new place of importance within her growing corpus.

In *The World Has Changed*, Walker addresses a number of important subjects that she has treated with varying degrees of specificity in her own nonfiction writings and that scholars have examined in their scholarship. These include commentary on the formal and thematic elements in her work and writing process; the shifting set of interests that has led to changes in the direction of her art; the manner in which she defines herself in relation to other major writers; her stance as a writer, especially her solitary, sometimes suicidal nature, the experience of her illegal abortion, and her position as outcast, rebel, and elder; her belief in human potentiality and the great value she places upon the importance of growth and development, of transformation and the power of the spirit, and the ways in which the act of witnessing and activism are catalysts to these states; and finally the factors that shape our lives as earthlings. In many places in the volume Walker speaks of the great power of sexuality; the role of pain and suffering as teachers; the value and challenge of being oneself; the vital difference between trying and doing; the necessity of forgiveness, of love, and also of her love of the earth and her embrace of the earth as her god; as well as her fears that we may have irreparably damaged the earth—our only home.

In Walker's commentary on these and other subjects, which further enlarges our understanding of the origins and scope of her artistic and activist concerns, we are struck by the power of her voice with its strong sense of immediacy and spontaneity. We also are struck by her engagement with her interlocutors and, by extension, with us. These are elements that are distinctive to the genre of the interview at its best, of course, an important research tool in the humanities and the humanistic social sciences. Whether written or oral, the interview is both accessible and immediate. As readers we occupy a peculiar position in relation to the interviewer and her subject, for we are engaged in the act of reading and listening, and of hearing and interpreting. In instances where rapport intersects with preparation, the outcome is a genuine conversation where both the interviewer and the subject learn something new. These elements account, in part, for the special value of this volume for scholars, biographers, activists, and writers.

In *The World Has Changed* we are keenly aware of the importance of possessing an awareness of what has happened—of change. Through Walker's example and words we are also keenly aware of the dangers, risks, and consequences of remaining ignorant of change. While the world has changed there are some things, happily for us, that have not changed. The first is Walker's unwavering commitment to the highest standards of art, a commitment everywhere in evidence in her luminous corpus. Another constant is Walker's approach to the creation of art. "The way I understand my work," she observes, "is that it is a prayer to and about the world." [76] In the act of prayer or of writing Walker has held us, *held us*, in her cupped hands, and from this position we have been seen, beheld, and loved. Even when we have rejected what she has given to us out of love, her stance toward us, toward the world, has not changed.

We know, now, because of Walker's loving excavation of the life and work of Zora Neale Hurston, that we cannot throw our geniuses away. We do so at great peril to ourselves. And so let us keep faith with Walker, as she has kept faith with us, in this changing world.

As a writer and activist, Walker "continues to change the world, heart by heart." [77]

Rudolph P. Byrd
Emory University

1

Interview with John O'Brien from
Interviews with Black Writers (1973)

JOHN O'BRIEN: Could you describe your early life and what led you to begin writing?

ALICE WALKER: I have always been a solitary person, and since I was eight years old (and the recipient of a disfiguring scar, since corrected, somewhat), I have daydreamed not of fairy tales but of falling on swords, of putting guns to my heart or head, and of slashing my wrists with a razor. For a long time I thought I was very ugly and disfigured. This made me shy and timid, and I often reacted to insults and slights that were not intended. I discovered the cruelty (legendary) of children, and of relatives, and could not recognize it as the curiosity it was.

I believe, though, that it was from this period—from my solitary, lonely position, the position of an outcast—that I began to really see people and things, to really notice relationships and to learn to be patient enough to care about how they turned out. I no longer felt like the little girl I was. I felt old, and because I felt I was unpleasant to look at, filled with shame. I retreated into solitude, and read stories and began to write poems.

But it was not until my last year in college that I realized, nearly, the consequences of my daydreams. That year I made myself acquainted with every philosopher's position on suicide, because by that time it did not seem frightening or even odd—but only inevitable. Nietzsche and Camus made the most sense, and were neither maudlin nor pious. God's displeasure didn't seem to matter much to them, and I had reached the same conclusion. But in addition to finding such dispassionate commentary from them—although both hinted at the cowardice involved, and that bothered me—I had been to Africa during the summer, and returned to school healthy and brown, and loaded down with sculptures and orange fabric—and pregnant.

I felt at the mercy of everything, including my own body, which I had learned to accept as a kind of casing, over what I considered my real self. As long as it functioned properly, I dressed it, pampered it, led it into acceptable arms, and forgot about it. But now it refused to function properly. I was so sick I could not even bear the smell of fresh air. And I had no money, and I was, essentially—as I had been since grade school—alone. I felt there was no way out, and I was not romantic enough to believe in maternal instincts alone as a means of survival; in any case, I did not seem to possess those instincts. But I knew no one who knew about the secret, scary thing abortion was. And so, when all my efforts at finding an abortionist failed, I planned to kill myself, or—as I thought of it then—to "give myself a little rest." I stopped going down the hill to meals because I vomited incessantly, even when nothing came up but yellow, bitter bile. I lay on my bed in a cold sweat, my head spinning.

While I was lying there, I thought of my mother, to whom abortion is a sin; her face appeared framed in the window across from me, her head wreathed in sunflowers and giant elephant ears (my mother's flowers love her; they grow as tall as she wants); I thought of my father, that suspecting, once-fat, slowly shrinking man, who had not helped me at all since I was twelve years old, when he bought me a pair of ugly saddle-oxfords I refused to wear. I thought of my sisters, who had their own problems (when approached with the problem I had, one sister never replied, the other told me—in forty-five minutes of long-distance carefully enunciated language—that I was a slut). I thought of the people at my high-school graduation who had managed to collect seventy-five dollars to send me to college. I thought of my sister's check for a hundred dollars that she gave me for finishing high school at the head of my class: a check I never cashed, because I knew it would bounce.

I think it was at this point that I allowed myself exactly two self-pitying tears; I had wasted so much, how dared I? But I hated myself for crying, so I stopped, comforted by knowing I would not have to cry—or see anyone else cry—again.

I did not eat or sleep for three days. My mind refused, at times, to think about my problem at all—it jumped ahead to the solution. I prayed to—but I don't know Who or What I prayed to, or even if I did. Perhaps I prayed to God awhile, and then to the Great Void awhile. When I thought of my family, and when—on the third day—I began to see their faces around the walls, I realized they would be shocked and hurt to learn of my death, but I felt they would not care deeply at all, when they discovered I was pregnant. Essentially, they would believe I was evil. They would be ashamed of me.

For three days I lay on the bed with a razor blade under my pillow. My secret was known to three friends only—all inexperienced (except verbally), and helpless. They came often to cheer me up, to bring me up-to-date on things as frivolous as classes. I was touched by their kindness, and loved them. But each time they left, I took out my razor blade and pressed it deep into my arm. I practiced a slicing motion. So that when there was no longer any hope, I would be able to cut my wrists quickly, and (I hoped) painlessly.

In those three days, I said good-bye to the world (this seemed a high-flown sentiment, even then, but everything was beginning to be unreal); I realized how much I loved it, and how hard it would be not to see the sunrise every morning, the snow, the sky, the trees, the rocks, the faces of people, all so different (and it was during this period that all things began to flow together; the face of one of my friends revealed itself to be the friendly, gentle face of a lion, and I asked her one day if I could touch her face and stroke her mane. I felt her face and hair, and she really was a lion; I began to feel the possibility of someone as worthless as myself attaining wisdom). But I found, as I had found on the porch of that building in Liberty County, Georgia—when rocks and bottles bounced off me as I sat looking up at the stars—that I was not afraid of death. In a way, I began looking forward to it. I felt tired. Most of the poems on suicide in *Once* come from my feelings during this period of waiting.

On the last day for miracles, one of my friends telephoned to say someone had given her a telephone number. I called from the school, hoping for nothing, and made an appointment. I went to see the doctor and he put me to sleep. When I woke up, my friend was standing over me holding a red rose. She was a blonde, gray-eyed girl, who loved horses and tennis, and she said nothing as she handed me back my life. That moment is engraved on my mind—her smile, sad and pained and frightfully young—as she tried so hard to stand by me and be my friend. She drove me back to the school and tucked me in. My other friend, brown, a wisp of blue and scarlet, with hair like thunder, brought me food.

That week I wrote without stopping (except to eat and go to the toilet) almost all of the poems in *Once*—with the exception of one or two, perhaps, and these I no longer remember.

I wrote them all in a tiny blue notebook that I can no longer find— the African ones first, because the vitality and color and friendships in Africa rushed over me in dreams the first night I slept. I had not thought about Africa (except to talk about it) since I returned. All the sculptures and weavings I had given away, because they seemed to emit an odor that made me more nauseous than the smell of fresh air. Then I wrote the suicide poems, because I felt I understood the part played in suicide by circumstances and fatigue. I also began to understand how alone woman is, because of her body. Then I wrote the love poems (love real and love imagined) and tried to reconcile myself to all things human. "Johann" is the most extreme example of this need to love even the most unfamiliar, the most fearful. For, actually, when I traveled in Germany I was in a constant state of terror, and no amount of flattery from handsome young German men could shake it. Then I wrote the poems of struggle in the South. The picketing, the marching, all the things that had been buried, because when I thought about them the pain was a paralysis of intellectual and moral confusion. The anger and humiliation I had suffered was always in conflict with the elation, the exaltation, the *joy* I felt when I could leave each vicious encounter or confrontation whole, and not—like the people before me—spewing obscenities, or throwing bricks. For, during those encounters, I had begun to comprehend what it meant to be lost.

Each morning, the poems finished during the night were stuffed under Muriel Rukeyser's door—her classroom was an old gardener's cottage in the middle of the campus. Then I would hurry back to my room to write some more. I didn't care what she did with the poems. I only knew I wanted someone to read them as if they were new leaves sprouting from an old tree. The same energy that impelled me to write them carried them to her door.

This was the winter of 1965 and my last three months in college. I was twenty-one years old, although *Once* was not published till three years later, when I was twenty-four (Muriel Rukeyser gave the poems to her agent, who gave them to Hiram Haydn—who is still my editor at Harcourt, Brace—who said right away that he wanted them; so I cannot claim to have had a hard time publishing, yet). By the time *Once* was published, it no longer seemed important—I was surprised when it went, almost immediately, into a second printing—that is, the book it-self did not seem to me important; only the writing of the poems, which clarified for me how very much I love being alive. It was this feeling of gladness that carried over into my first published short story, "To Hell with Dying," about an old man saved from death countless times by the love of his neighbor's children. I was the children, and the old man.

I have gone into this memory because I think it might be important for other women to share. I don't enjoy contemplating it; I wish it had never happened. But if it had not, I firmly believe I would never have survived to be a writer. I know I would not have survived at all.

Since that time, it seems to me that all of my poems—and I write groups of poems rather than singles—are written when I have success-fully pulled myself out of a completely numbing despair and stand again in the sunlight. Writing poems is my way of celebrating with the world that I have not committed suicide the evening before.

Langston Hughes wrote in his autobiography that when he was sad, he wrote his best poems. When he was happy, he didn't write anything. This is true of me, where poems are concerned. When I am happy (or neither happy nor sad), I write essays, short stories, and novels. Poems—even happy ones—emerge from an accumulation of sadness.

J.O.: Can you describe the process of writing a poem? How do you know, for instance, when you have captured what you wanted to?

A.W.: The writing of my poetry is never consciously planned, although I become aware that there are certain emotions I would like to explore. Perhaps my unconscious begins working on poems from these emotions long before I am aware of it. I have learned to wait patiently (sometimes refusing good lines, images, when they come to me, for fear they are not lasting), until a poem is ready to present itself—*all* of itself, if possible. I sometimes feel the urge to write poems way in advance of ever sitting down to write. There is a definite restlessness, a kind of feverish excite-ment that is tinged with dread. The dread is because after writing each batch of poems I am always convinced that I will never write poems again. I become aware that I am controlled by them, not the other way around. I put off writing as long as I can. Then I lock myself in my study, write lines and lines and lines, then put them away, underneath other papers, without looking at them for a long time. I am afraid that if I read them too soon they will turn into trash; or worse, something so topical and transient as to have no meaning—not even to me—after a few weeks. (This is how my later poetry-writing differs from the way I wrote *Once*.) I also attempt, in this way, to guard against the human tendency to try to make poetry carry the weight of half-truths, of cleverness. I realize that while I am writing poetry, I am so high as to feel invisible, and in that condition it is possible to write anything.

J.O.: What determines your interests as a writer? Are there preoccupations you have which you are not conscious of until you begin writing?

A.W.: You ask about "preoccupations." I am preoccupied with the spiritual survival, the survival *whole*, of my people. But beyond that, I am committed to exploring the oppressions, the insanities, the loyalties, and the triumphs of black women. In *The Third Life of Grange Copeland*, ostensibly about a man and his son, it is the women and how they are treated that colors everything. In my new book *In Love and Trouble: Stories of Black Women*, thirteen women—mad, raging, loving, resentful, hateful, strong, ugly, weak, pitiful, and magnificent—try to live with the loyalty to black men that characterizes all of their lives. For me, black women are the most fascinating creations in the world.

Next to them, I place the old people—male and female—who persist in their beauty in spite of everything. How do they do this, knowing what they do? Having lived what they have lived? It is a mystery, and so it lures me into their lives. My grandfather, at eighty-five, never been out of Georgia, looks at me with the glad eyes of a three-year-old. The pressures on his life have been unspeakable. How can he look at me in this way? "Your eyes are widely open flowers / Only their centers are darkly clenched / To conceal / Mysteries / That lure me to a keener blooming / Than I know / And promise a secret / I must have." All of my "love poems" apply to old, young, man, woman, child, and growing things.

J.O.: Your novel, *The Third Life of Grange Copeland*, reaffirms an observation I have made about many novels: there is a pervasive optimism in these novels, an indomitable belief in the future and in man's capacity for survival. I think that this is generally opposed to what one finds in the mainstream of American literature. One can cite Ahab, Gatsby, Jake Barnes, Young Goodman Brown. . . . You seem to be writing out of a vision which conflicts with that of the culture around you. What I may be pointing out is that you do not seem to see the profound evil present in much of American literature.

A.W.: It is possible that white male writers are more conscious of their own evil (which, after all, has been documented for several centuries— in words and in the ruin of the land, the earth) than black male writers, who, along with black and white women, have seen themselves as the recipients of that evil, and therefore on the side of Christ, of the oppressed, of the innocent.

The white women writers that I admire, Chopin, the Brontës, Simone de Beauvoir, and Doris Lessing, are well aware of their own oppression and search incessantly for a kind of salvation. Their characters can always envision a solution, an evolution to higher consciousness on the part of society, even when society itself cannot. Even when society is in the process of killing them for their vision. Generally, too, they are more tolerant of mystery than is Ahab, who wishes to dominate, rather than be on equal terms with the whale.

If there is one thing African Americans have retained of their African heritage, it is probably animism: a belief that makes it possible to view all creation as living, as being inhabited by spirit. This belief encourages knowledge perceived intuitively. It does not surprise me, personally, that scientists now are discovering that trees, plants, flowers, have feelings . . . emotions, that they shrink when yelled at; that they faint when an evil person is about who might hurt them.

One thing I try to have in my life and in my fiction is an awareness of and openness to mystery, which, to me, is deeper than any politics, race, or geographical location. In the poems I read, a sense of mystery, a deepening of it, is what I look for—for that is what I respond to. I have been influenced—especially in the poems in *Once*—by Zen epigrams and by Japanese haiku. I think my respect for short forms comes from this. I was delighted to learn that in three or four lines a poet can express mystery, evoke beauty and pleasure, paint a picture—and not dissect or analyze in any way. The insects, the fish, the birds, and the apple blossoms in haiku are still whole. They have not been turned into something else. They are allowed their own majesty, instead of being used to emphasize the majesty of people, usually the majesty of the poets writing.

J.O.: A part of your vision—which is explored in your novel—is a belief in change, both personal and political. By showing the change in Grange Copeland you suggest the possibility of change in the political and social systems within which he lives.

A.W.: Yes. I believe in change: change personal, and change in society. I have experienced a revolution (unfinished without question, but one whose new order is everywhere on view) in the South. And I grew up—until I refused to go—in the Methodist Church, which taught me that Paul *will* sometimes change on the way to Damascus, and that Moses—that beloved old man—went through so many changes he made God mad. So Grange Copeland was *expected* to change. He was fortunate enough to be touched by love of something beyond himself. Brownfield did not change, because he was not prepared to give his life for anything, or *to* anything. He was the kind of man who could never understand Jesus (or Che or King or Malcolm or Medgar) except as the white man's tool. He could find nothing of value within himself and he did not have the courage to imagine a life without the existence of white people to act as a foil. To become what he hated was his inevitable destiny.

A bit more about the "Southern Revolution." When I left Eatonton, Georgia, to go off to Spelman College in Atlanta (where I stayed, uneasily, for two years), I deliberately sat in the front section of the Greyhound bus. A white woman complained to the driver. He—big and red and ugly—ordered me to move. I moved. But in those seconds of moving, everything changed. I was eager to bring an end to the South that permitted my humiliation. During my sophomore year I stood on the grass in front of Trevor-Arnett Library at Atlanta University and I listened to the young leaders of SNCC. John Lewis was there, and so was Julian Bond—thin, well starched and ironed in light-colored jeans, he looked (with his cropped hair that still tried to curl) like a poet (which he was). Everyone was beautiful, because everyone (and I think now of Ruby Doris Robinson, who since died) was conquering fear by holding the hands of the persons next to them. In those days, in Atlanta, springtime turned the air green. I've never known this to happen in any other place I've been—not even in Uganda, where green, on hills, plants, trees, begins to dominate the imagination. It was as if the air turned into a kind of water—and the short walk from Spelman to Morehouse was like walking through a green sea. Then, of course, the cherry trees—cut down, now, I think—that were always blooming away while we, young and bursting with fear and determination to change our world, thought, beyond our fervid singing, of death. It is not surprising, considering the intertwined thoughts of beauty and death, that the majority of the people in and around SNCC at that time were lovers of Camus.

Random memories of that period: myself, moving like someone headed for the guillotine, with (as my marching mate) a beautiful girl who spoke French and came to Spelman from Tuskegee, Alabama ("Chic Freedom's Reflection" in *Once*), whose sense of style was unfaltering, in the worst of circumstances. She was the only really black-skinned girl at Spelman who would turn up dressed in stark white from head to toe—because she knew, instinctively, that white made an already beautiful black girl look like the answer to everybody's prayer. Myself, marching about in front of a restaurant, seeing—inside—the tables set up with clean napkins and glasses of water. The owner standing in front of us barring the door. A Jewish man who went mad on the spot, and fell to the floor. Myself, dressed in a pink faille dress, with my African roommate, my first real girlfriend, walking up the broad white steps of a broad white church. And men (white) in blue suits and bow ties materializing on the steps above with ax-handles in their hands (see: "The Welcome Table" in *In Love and Trouble*). We turned and left. It was a bright, sunny day. Myself, sitting on a porch in Liberty County, Georgia, at night, after picketing the jailhouse (where a local black schoolteacher was held) and holding in my arms the bleeding head of a little girl—where is she now?—maybe eight or ten years old, but small, who had been cut by a broken bottle held by one of the mob in front of us. In this memory there is a white girl I grew to respect because she never flinched and never closed her eyes, no matter what the mob— where are they now?—threw. Later, in New York, she tried to get me to experiment with LSD with her, and the only reason I never did was because on the night we planned to try it I had a bad cold. I believe the reason she never closed her eyes was because she couldn't believe what she was seeing. We tried to keep in touch—but, because I had never had very much (not even a house that didn't leak), I was always conscious of the need to be secure. Because she came from an eleven-room house in the suburbs of Philadelphia and, I assume, never had worried about material security, our deepest feelings began to miss each other. I identified her as someone who could afford to play poor for a while (her poverty interrupted occasionally by trips abroad), and she probably identified me as one of those inflexible black women black men constantly complain about: the kind who interrupt lighthearted romance by saying, "Yes, well . . . but what are the children going to eat?"

The point is that less than ten years after all these things I walk about Georgia (and Mississippi)—eating, sleeping, loving, singing, burying the dead—the way men and women are supposed to do in a place that is the only "home" they've ever known. There is only one "for coloreds" sign left in Eatonton, and it is on a black man's barbershop. He is merely outdated. Booster, if you read this, *change* your sign!

J.O.: I wonder how clear it was to you what you were going to do in your novel before you started. Did you know, for instance, that Grange Copeland was capable of change?

A.W.: I see the work that I have done already as a foundation. That being so, I suppose I knew when I started *The Third Life of Grange Copeland* that it would have to cover several generations, and nearly a century of growth and upheaval. It begins around 1900 and ends in the sixties. But my first draft (which was never used, not even one line, in the final version) began with Ruth as a civil-rights lawyer in Georgia going to rescue her father, Brownfield Copeland, from a drunken accident, and to have a confrontation with him. In that version she is married—also to a lawyer—and they are both committed to ensuring freedom for black people in the South. In Georgia, specifically. There was lots of lovemaking and courage in that version. But it was too recent, too superficial— everything seemed a product of the immediate present. And I believe nothing ever is.

So, I brought in the grandfather. Because all along I wanted to explore the relationship between parents and children: specifically between daughters and their father (this is most interesting, I've always felt; for example, in "The Child Who Favored Daughter" in *In Love and Trouble*, the father cuts off the breasts of his daughter because she falls in love with a white boy; why this, unless there is sexual jealousy?), and I wanted to learn, myself, how it happens that the hatred a child can have for a parent becomes inflexible. *And* I wanted to explore the relationship between men and women, and why women are always condemned for doing what men do as an expression of their masculinity.

Why are women so easily "tramps" and "traitors" when men are heroes for engaging in the same activity? Why do women stand for this?

My new novel will be about several women who came of age during the sixties and were active (or not active) in the movement in the South. I am exploring their backgrounds, familial and sibling connections, their marriages, affairs, and political persuasions, as they grow toward a fuller realization (and recognition) of themselves.

Since I put together my course on black women writers, which was taught first at Wellesley College and later at the University of Massachusetts, I have felt the need for real critical and biographical work on these writers. As a beginning, I am writing a long personal essay on my own discovery of these writers (designed, primarily, for lectures), and I hope soon to visit the birthplace and home of Zora Neale Hurston, Eatonville, Florida. I am so involved with my own writing that I don't think there will be time for me to attempt the long, scholarly involvement that all these writers require. I am hopeful, however, that as their books are reissued and used in classrooms across the country, someone will do this. If no one does (or if no one does it to my satisfaction), I feel it is my duty (such is the fervor of love) to do it myself.

J.O.: Have women writers, then, influenced your writing more than male? Which writers do you think have had the most direct influence upon you?

A.W.: I read all of the Russian writers I could find, in my sophomore year in college. I read them as if they were a delicious cake. I couldn't get enough: Tolstoy (especially his short stories, and the novels *The Kreutzer Sonata* and *Resurrection*—which taught me the importance of diving through politics and social forecasts to dig into the essential spirit of individual persons, because otherwise, characters, no matter what political or current social issue they stand for, will not live), and Dostoyevsky, who found his truths where everyone else seemed afraid to look, and Turgenev, Gorky, and Gogol—who made me think that Russia must have something floating about in the air that writers breathe from the time they are born. The only thing that began to bother me, many years later, was that I could find almost nothing written by a Russian woman writer.

Unless poetry has mystery, many meanings, and some ambiguities (necessary for mystery) I am not interested in it. Outside of Bashō and Issa and other Japanese haiku poets, I read and was impressed by the poetry of Li Po, the Chinese poet, Emily Dickinson, e.e. cummings (deeply), and Robert Graves—especially his poems in *Man Does, Woman Is*, which is surely a pure male-chauvinist title, but I did not think about that then. I liked Graves because he took it as given that passionate love between man and woman does not last forever. He enjoyed the moment and didn't bother about the future. My poem "The Man in the Yellow Terry" is very much influenced by Graves.

I also loved Ovid and Catullus. During the whole period of discovering haiku and the sensual poems of Ovid, the poems of e.e. cummings and William Carlos Williams, my feet did not touch the ground. I ate, I slept, I studied other things (like European history) without ever doing more than giving it serious thought. It could not change me from one moment to the next, as poetry could.

I wish I had been familiar with the poems of Gwendolyn Brooks when I was in college. I stumbled on them later. If there was ever a *born* poet, I think it is Brooks. Her natural way of looking at anything, of commenting on anything, comes out as a vision, in language that is peculiar to her. It is clear that she is a poet from the way your whole spiritual past begins to float around in your throat when you are reading, just as it is clear from the first line of *Cane* that Jean Toomer is a poet, blessed with a soul that is surprised by nothing. It is not unusual to weep when reading Brooks, just as when reading Toomer's "Song of the Son" it is not unusual to comprehend—in a flash—what a dozen books on black people's history fail to illuminate. I have embarrassed my classes occasionally by standing in front of them in tears as Toomer's poem about "some genius from the South" flew through my body like a swarm of golden butterflies on their way toward a destructive sun. Like Du Bois, Toomer was capable of comprehending the black soul. It is not "soul" that *can* become a cliché, but rather something to be illuminated rather than explained.

The poetry of Arna Bontemps has strange effects on me too. He is a great poet, even if he is not recognized as such until after his death. Or is never acknowledged. The passion and compassion in his poem "A Black Man Talks of Reaping" shook the room I was sitting in the first time I read it. The ceiling began to revolve and a breeze—all the way from Alabama—blew through the room. A tide of spiritual good health tingled the bottom of my toes. I changed. Became someone the same, but different. I understood, at last, what the transference of energy was.

It is impossible to list all of the influences on one's work. How can you even remember the indelible impression upon you of a certain look on your mother's face? But random influences are these: music, which is the art I most envy.

Then there's travel—which really made me love the world, its vastness and variety. How moved I was to know that there is no center of the universe. Entebbe, Uganda, or Bratislava, Czechoslovakia, exist no matter what we are doing here. Some writers—Camara Laye, or the man who wrote *One Hundred Years of Solitude* [Gabriel García Márquez]—have illumined this fact brilliantly in their fiction, which brings me to African writers I *hope* to be influenced by: Okot p'tek has written my favorite modern poem, "Song of Lawino." I am also crazy about *The Concubine* by Elechi Ahmadi (a perfect story, I think), *The Radiance of the King*, by Camara Laye, and *Maru*, by Bessie Head. These writers do not seem afraid of fantasy, of myth and mystery. Their work deepens one's comprehension of life by going beyond the bounds of realism. They are like musicians: at one with their cultures and their historical subconscious.

Flannery O'Connor has also influenced my work. To me, she is the best of the white southern writers, including Faulkner. For one thing, she practiced economy. She also knew that the question of race was really just the first question on a long list. This is hard for just about everybody to accept, we've been trying to answer it for so long.

I did not read *Cane* until 1967, but it has been reverberating in me to an astonishing degree. *I love it passionately*, could not possibly exist without it. *Cane* and *Their Eyes Were Watching God* are probably my favorite books by black American writers. Jean Toomer has a very feminine sensibility (or phrased another way, he is both feminine and masculine in his perceptions), unlike most black male writers. He loved women.

Like Toomer, Zora Neale Hurston was never afraid to let her characters be themselves, funny talk and all. She was incapable of being embarrassed by anything black people did and so was able to write about everything with freedom and fluency. My feeling is that Zora Neale Hurston is probably one of the most misunderstood, least appreciated writers of this century. Which is a pity. She is great. A writer of courage, and incredible humor, with poetry in every line.

When I started teaching my course in black women writers at Wellesley (the first one, I think, ever), I was worried that Zora's use of black English of the twenties would throw some of the students off. It didn't. They loved it. They said it was like reading Thomas Hardy, only better. In that same course I taught Nella Larsen, Frances Watkins Harper (poetry and novel), Dorothy West, Ann Petry, Paule Marshall, etc. Also Kate Chopin and Virginia Woolf—not because they were black, obviously, but because they were women and wrote, as the black women did, on the condition of humankind from the perspective of women. It is interesting to read Woolf's *A Room of One's Own* while reading the poetry of Phillis Wheatley, to read Larsen's *Quicksand* along with *The Awakening*. The deep-throated voice of Sojourner Truth tends to drift across the room while you're reading. If you're not a feminist already, you become one.

J.O.: Why do you think that the black woman writer has been so ignored in America? Does she have even more difficulty than the black male writer, who perhaps has just begun to gain recognition?

A.W.: There are two reasons why the black woman writer is not taken as seriously as the black male writer. One is that she's a woman. Critics seem unusually ill-equipped to intelligently discuss and analyze the works of black women. Generally, they do not even make the attempt; they prefer, rather, to talk about the lives of black women writers, not about what they write. And, since black women writers are not—it would seem—very likable—until recently they were the least willing worshippers of male supremacy—comments about them tend to be cruel.

In Nathan Huggins's very readable book, *Harlem Renaissance*, he hardly refers to Zora Neale Hurston's work, except negatively. He quotes from Wallace Thurman's novel, *Infants of the Spring*, at length, giving us the words of a character, "Sweetie Mae Carr," who is allegedly based on Zora Neale Hurston. "Sweetie Mae" is a writer noted more "for her ribald wit and personal effervescence than for any actual literary work. She was a great favorite among those whites who went in for Negro prodigies." Mr. Huggins goes on for several pages, never quoting Zora Neale Hurston herself, but rather the opinions of others about her character. He does say that she was "a master of dialect," but adds that "Her greatest weakness was carelessness or indifference to her art."

Having taught Zora Neale Hurston, and of course, having read her work myself, I am stunned. Personally, I do not care if Zora Hurston was fond of her white women friends. When she was a child in Florida, working for nickels and dimes, two white women helped her escape. Perhaps this explains it. But even if it doesn't, so what? Her work, far from being done carelessly, is done (especially in *Their Eyes Were Watching God*) almost too perfectly. She took the trouble to capture the beauty of rural black expression. She saw poetry where other writers merely saw failure to cope with English. She was so at ease with her blackness it never occurred to her that she should act one way among blacks and another among whites (as her more sophisticated black critics apparently did).

It seems to me that black writing has suffered, because even black critics have assumed that a book that deals with the relationships between members of a black family—or between a man and a woman—is less important than one that has white people as a primary antagonist. The consequence of this is that many of our books by "major" writers (always male) tell us little about the culture, history, or future, imagination, fantasies, etc. of black people, and a lot about isolated (often improbable) or limited encounters with a nonspecific white world. Where is the book, by an American black person (aside from *Cane*), that equals Elechi Ahmadi's *The Concubine*, for example? A book that exposes the *subconscious* of a people, because the people's dreams, imaginings, rituals, legends, etc. are known to be important, are known to contain the accumulated collective reality of the people themselves. Or, in *The Radiance of the King*, the white person is shown to be the outsider he is, because the culture he enters into in Africa *itself* expels him. Without malice, but as nature expels what does not suit. The white man is mysterious, a force to be reckoned with, but he is not glorified to such an extent that the Africans turn their attention away from themselves and their own imagination and culture. Which is what often happens with "protest literature." The superficial becomes—for a time—the deepest reality, and replaces the still waters of the collective subconscious.

When my own novel was published, a leading black monthly admitted (the editor did) that the book itself was never read; but the magazine ran an item stating that a *white* reviewer had praised the book (which was, in itself, an indication that the book was no good—such went the logic) and then hinted that the reviewer had liked my book because of my lifestyle. When I wrote to the editor to complain, he wrote me a small sermon on the importance of my "image," of what is "good" for others to see. Needless to say, what others "see" of me is the least of my worries, and I assume that "others" are intelligent enough to recover from whatever shocks my presence might cause.

Women writers are supposed to be intimidated by male disapprobation. What they write is not important enough to be read. How they live, however, their "image," they owe to the race. Read the reason Zora Neale Hurston gave for giving up her writing. See what "image" the Negro press gave her, innocent as she was. I no longer read articles or reviews unless they are totally about the work. I trust that someday a generation of men and women will arise who will forgive me for such wrong as I do not agree I do, and will read my work because it is a true account of my feelings, my perception, and my imagination, and because it will reveal something to them of their own selves. They will also be free to toss it—and me—out of a high window. They can do what they like.

J.O.: Have you felt a great deal of coercion to write the kind of fiction and poetry that black writers are "supposed" to write? Does this ever interfere with what you *want* to write?

A.W.: When I take the time to try to figure out what I am doing in my writing, where it is headed, and so on, I almost never can come up with anything. This is because it seems to me that my poetry is quite different from my novels (*The Third Life of Grange Copeland* and the one I am working on now); for example, *Once* is what I think of as a "happy" book, full of the spirit of an optimist who loves the world and all the sensations of caring in it; it doesn't matter that it began in sadness; *The Third Life of Grange Copeland*, though sometimes humorous and celebrative of life, is a grave book in which the characters see the world as almost entirely menacing. The optimism that closes the book makes it different from most of my short stories, and the political and personal content of my essays makes them different—again—from everything else. So I would not, as some critics have done, categorize my work as "gothic." I would not categorize it at all. Eudora Welty, in explaining why she rebels against being labeled "gothic," says that to her "gothic" conjures up the supernatural, and that she feels what she writes has "something to do with real life." I agree with her.

I like those of my short stories that show the plastic, shaping, almost painting quality of words. In "Roselily" and "The Child Who Favored Daughter" the prose is poetry, or prose and poetry run together to add a new dimension to the language. But the most that I would say about where I am trying to go is this: I am trying to arrive at that place where black music already is; to arrive at that unself-conscious sense of collective oneness; that naturalness, that (even when anguished) grace.

The writer—like the musician or painter—must be free to explore, otherwise she or he will never discover what is needed (by everyone) to be known. This means, very often, finding oneself considered "unacceptable" by masses of people who think that the writer's obligation is not to explore or to challenge, but to second the masses' motions, whatever they are. Yet the gift of loneliness is sometimes a radical vision of society or one's people that has not previously been taken into account. Toomer was, I think, a lonely, wandering man, accustomed to being tolerated and misunderstood—a man who made choices many abhorred—and yet, *Cane* is a great reward, though Toomer himself probably never realized it.

The same is true of Zora Neale Hurston. She is probably more honest in her fieldwork and her fiction than she is in her autobiography, because she was hesitant to reveal how different she really was. It is interesting to contemplate what would have been the result and impact on black women—since 1937—if they had read and taken to heart *Their Eyes Were Watching God*. Would they still be as dependent on material things—fine cars, furs, big houses, pots and jars of face creams—as they are today? Or would they, learning from Janie that materialism is the drag-rope of the soul, become a nation of women immune (to the extent that is possible in a blatantly consumerist society like ours) to the accumulation of things, and aware, to their core, that love, fulfillment as women, peace of mind, should logically come before, not after, selling one's soul for a golden stool on which to sit? Sit and be bored.

Hurston's book, though seemingly apolitical, is, in fact, one of the most radical novels (without being a tract) we have.

J.O.: Christianity is implicitly criticized in your work. Is that because it has historically been both racist and antifeminist?

A.W.: Although I am constantly involved, internally, with religious questions—and I seem to have spent all of my life rebelling against the church and other peoples' interpretations of what religion is—the truth is probably that I don't believe there is a God, although I would like to believe it. Certainly I don't believe there is a God beyond nature. The world is God. Man is God. So is a leaf or a snake. . . . So, when Grange Copeland refuses to pray at the end of the book, he is refusing to be a hypocrite. All his life he has hated the church and taken every opportunity to ridicule it. He has taught his granddaughter, Ruth, this same humorous contempt. He does, however, appreciate the humanity of man-womankind as a God worth embracing. To him, the greatest value a person can attain is full humanity, which is a state of oneness with all things, and a willingness to die (or to live) so that the best that has been produced can continue to live in someone else. He "rocked himself in his own arms to a final sleep" because he understood that man is alone—in his life as in his death—without any God but himself (and the world).

Like many, I waver in my convictions about God, from time to time. In my poetry I seem to be for; in my fiction, against.

I am intrigued by the religion of the black Muslims. By what conversion means to black women, specifically, and what the religion itself means in terms of the black American past: our history, our "race memories," our absorption of Christianity, our *changing* of Christianity to fit our needs. What will the new rituals mean? How will this new religion imprint itself on the collective consciousness of the converts? Can women be free in such a religion? Is such a religion, in fact, an anachronism? So far I have dealt with this interest in two stories, "Roselily," about a young woman who marries a young Muslim because he offers her respect and security, and "Everyday Use," a story that shows respect for the "militance" and progressive agricultural programs of the Muslims, but at the same time shows skepticism about a young man who claims attachment to the Muslims because he admires the rhetoric. It allows him to acknowledge his contempt for whites, which is all he believes the group is about.

In other stories, I am interested in Christianity as an imperialist tool used against Africa ("Diary of an African Nun") and in voodoo used as a weapon against oppression ("The Revenge of Hannah Kemhuff"). I see all of these as religious questions.

J.O.: Could you tell me about the genesis of your title poem "Revolutionary Petunias"? Why was "Sammy Lou" chosen as the heroine of the poem?

A.W.: The poem "Revolutionary Petunias" did not have a name when I sat down to write it. I wanted to create a person who engaged in a final struggle with her oppressor, and won, but who, in every other way, was "incorrect." Sammy Lou in the poem is everything she should not be: her name is Sammy Lou, for example; she is a farmer's wife; she works in the fields. She goes to church. The walls of her house contain no signs of her blackness—though that in itself reveals it; anyone walking into that empty house would know Sammy Lou is black. She is so incredibly "incorrect" that she is only amused when the various poets and folksingers rush to immortalize her heroism in verse and song. She did not think of her killing of her oppressor in that way. She thought—and I picture her as tall, lean, black, with short, badly straightened hair and crooked teeth—that killing is never heroic. Her reaction, after killing this cracker-person, would be to look up at the sky and not pray or ask forgiveness but to say—as if talking to an old friend—"Lord, you know my heart. I never wanted to have to kill nobody. But I couldn't hold out to the last, like Job. I had done took more than I could stand."

Sammy Lou is so "incorrect" she names her children after presidents and their wives; she names one of them after the founder of the Methodist church. To her, this does not mean a limitation of her blackness, it means she feels she is so black she can absorb—and change—all things, since everybody knows that a black-skinned Jackie Kennedy still bears resemblance only to her own great aunt, Sadie Mae Johnson.

But the most "incorrect" thing about Sammy Lou is that she loves flowers. Even on her way to the electric chair she reminds her children to water them. This is crucial, for I have heard it said by one of our cultural visionaries that whenever you hear a black person talking about the beauties of nature, that person is not a black person at all, but a Negro. This is meant as a put-down, and it is. It puts down all of the black folks in Georgia, Alabama, Mississippi, Texas, Louisiana—in fact, it covers just about everybody's mama. Sammy Lou, of course, is so "incorrect" she does not even know how ridiculous she is for loving to see flowers blooming around her unbearably ugly gray house. To be "correct" she should consider it her duty to let ugliness reign. Which is what "incorrect" people like Sammy Lou refuse to do.

Actually, the poem was to claim (as Toomer claimed the people he wrote about in *Cane*, who, as you know, were all as "incorrect" as possible) the most incorrect black person I could, and to honor her as my own—on a level with, if not above, the most venerated saints of the black revolution. It seems our fate to be incorrect (look where we live, for example), and in our incorrectness, stand.

Although Sammy Lou is more a rebel than a revolutionary (since you need more than one for a revolution) I named the poem "Revolutionary Petunias" because she is not—when you view her kind of person historically—isolated. She is part of an ongoing revolution. Any black revolution, instead of calling her "incorrect," will have to honor her single act of rebellion.

Another reason I named it "Revolutionary Petunias" is that I like petunias and like to raise them because you just put them in any kind of soil and they bloom their heads off—exactly, it seemed to me, like black people tend to do. (Look at the blues and jazz musicians, the blind singers from places like Turnip, Mississippi, the poets and writers and all-around blooming people you know, who—from all visible evidence—achieved their blooming by eating the air for bread and drinking muddy water for hope.) Then I thought, too, of the petunias my mother gave me when my daughter was born, and of the story (almost a parable) she told me about them. Thirty-seven years ago, my mother and father were coming home from somewhere in their wagon—my mother was pregnant with one of my older brothers at the time—and they passed a deserted house where one lavender petunia was left, just blooming away in the yard (probably to keep itself company)—and my mother said, "Stop! Let me go and get that petunia bush." And my father, grumbling, stopped, and she got it, and they went home, and she set it out in a big stump in the yard. It never wilted, just bloomed and bloomed. Every time the family moved (say twelve times) she took her petunia—and thirty-seven years later she brought me a piece of that same petunia bush. It had never died. Each winter it lay dormant and dead-looking, but each spring it came back, more lively than before.

What underscored the importance of this story for me is this: modern petunias do not live forever. They die each winter and the next spring you have to buy new ones.

In a way, the whole book is a celebration of people who will not cram themselves into any ideological or racial mold. They are all shouting, "Stop! I want to go get that petunia!"

Because of this they are made to suffer. They are told that they do not belong, that they are not wanted, that their art is not needed, that nobody who is "correct" could love what they love. Their answer is resistance, without much commentary, just a steady knowing that they stand at a point where—with one slip of the character—they might be lost, and the bloom they are after wither in the winter of self-contempt. They do not measure themselves against black people or white people; if anything, they learn to walk and talk in the presence of Du Bois, Hurston, Hughes, Toomer, Attaway, Wright, and others—and when they bite into their pillows at night these spirits comfort them. They are aware that the visions that created them were all toward a future where all people—and flowers too—can bloom. They require that in the midst of the bloodiest battles or revolution this thought not be forgotten.

When I married my husband there was a law that said I could not. When we moved to Mississippi three years after the lynching of Chaney, Schwerner, and Goodman, it was a punishable crime for a black person and a white person of opposite sex to inhabit the same house. But I felt then—as I do now—that in order to be able to live at all in America I must be unafraid to live anywhere in it, and I must be able to live in the fashion and with whom I choose. Otherwise, I'd just as soon leave. If society (black or white) says, "Then you must be isolated, an outcast"— then I will be a hermit. Friends and relatives may desert me, but the dead—Douglass, Du Bois, Hansberry, Toomer, and the rest—are a captive audience. . . . These feelings went into two poems, "Be Nobody's Darling" and "While Love Is Unfashionable."

J.O.: There is one poem in *Revolutionary Petunias* which particularly interests me—"For My Sister Molly Who in the Fifties." Can you tell me about what went into the structuring of this rather long poem, and perhaps something about the background of it?

A.W.: "For My Sister Molly Who in the Fifties" is a pretty real poem. It really is about one of my sisters, a brilliant, studious girl who became one of those Negro Wonders—who collected scholarships like trading stamps and wandered all over the world. (Our hometown didn't even have a high school when she came along.) When she came to visit us in Georgia it was—at first—like having Christmas with us all during her vacation. She loved to read and tell stories; she taught me African songs and dances; she cooked fanciful dishes that looked like anything but plain old sharecropper food. I loved her so much it came as a great shock—and a shock I don't expect to recover from—to learn she was ashamed of us. We were so poor, so dusty and sunburnt. We talked wrong. We didn't know how to dress, or use the right eating utensils. And so, she drifted away, and I did not understand it. Only later, I realized that sometimes (perhaps), it becomes too painful to bear: seeing your home and family—shabby and seemingly without hope—through the eyes of your new friends and strangers. She had felt—for her own mental health—that the gap that separated us from the rest of the world was too wide for her to keep trying to bridge. She understood how delicate she was.

I started out writing this poem in great anger; hurt, really. I thought I could write a magnificently vicious poem. Yet, even from the first draft, it did not turn out that way. Which is one of the great things about poetry. What you really feel, underneath everything else, will present itself. Your job is not to twist that feeling. So that although being with her now is too painful with memories for either of us to be comfortable, I still retain (as I hope she does) in memories beyond the bad ones, my picture of a sister I loved, "Who walked among the flowers and brought them inside the house, who smelled as good as they, and looked as bright."

This poem (and my sister received the first draft, which is hers alone, and the way I wish her to relate to the poem) went through fifty drafts (at least) and I worked on it, off and on, for five years. This has never happened before or since. I do not know what to say about the way it is constructed other than to say that as I wrote it the lines and words went, on the paper, to a place comparable to where they lived in my head.

I suppose, actually, that my tremendous response to the poems of W.C. Williams, cummings, and Bashō convinced me that poetry is more like music—in my case, improvisational jazz, where each person blows the note that she hears—than like a cathedral, with every stone in a specific, predetermined place. Whether lines are long or short depends on what the poem itself requires. Like people, some poems are fat and some are thin. Personally, I prefer the short thin ones, which are always like painting the eye in a tiger (as Muriel Rukeyser once explained it). You wait until the energy and vision are just right, then you write the poem. If you try to write it before it is ready to be written you find yourself adding stripes instead of eyes. Too many stripes and the tiger herself disappears. You will paint a photograph (which is what is wrong with "Burial") instead of creating a new way of seeing.

The poems that fail will always haunt you. I am haunted by "Ballad of the Brown Girl" and "Johann" in *Once*, and I expect to be haunted by "Nothing Is Right" in *Revolutionary Petunias*. The first two are dishonest, and the third is trite.

The poem "The Girl Who Died #2" was written after I learned of the suicide of a student at the college I attended. I learned, from the dead girl's rather guilty-sounding "brothers and sisters," that she had been hounded constantly because she was so "incorrect," she thought she could be a black hippie. To top that, they tried to make her feel like a traitor because she refused to limit her interest to black men. Anyway, she was a beautiful girl. I was shown a photograph of her by one of her few black friends. She was a little brown-skinned girl from Texas, away from home for the first time, trying to live a life she could live with. She tried to kill herself two or three times before, but I guess the brothers and sisters didn't think it "correct" to respond with love or attention, since everybody knows it is "incorrect" to even think of suicide if you are a black person. And, of course, black people do not commit suicide. Only colored people and Negroes commit suicide. (See "The Old Warrior Terror": warriors, you know, always die on the battlefield). I said, when I saw the photograph, that I wished I had been there for her to talk to. When the school invited me to join their board of trustees, it was her face that convinced me. I know nothing about boards and never really trusted them; but I can listen to problems pretty well. . . . I believe in listening—to a person, the sea, the wind, the trees, but especially to young black women whose rocky road I am still traveling.

2

Interview with Claudia Tate from
Black Women Writers at Work (1983)

CLAUDIA TATE: Critics have frequently commented about the nonlinear structure of *Meridian*. Did you have a particular form or symbolic structure in mind when you wrote this novel?

ALICE WALKER: All I was thinking of when I wrote *Meridian*, in terms of structure, was that I wanted one that would continue to be interesting to me. The chronological structure in *The Third Life of Grange Copeland* was interesting as a onetime shot, since I had never before written a novel. So when I wrote *Meridian*, I realized that the chronological sequence is not one that permits me the kind of freedom I need in order to create. And I wanted to do something like a crazy quilt, or like *Cane* [by Jean Toomer]—if you want to be literary—something that works on the mind in different patterns. As for the metaphors and symbols, I suppose, like most writers, I didn't really think of them; they just sort of happened.

You know, there's a lot of difference between a crazy quilt and a patchwork quilt. A patchwork quilt is exactly what the name implies—a quilt made of patches. A crazy quilt, on the other hand, only *looks* crazy. It is not "patched"; it is planned. A patchwork quilt would perhaps be a good metaphor for capitalism; a crazy quilt is perhaps a metaphor for socialism. A crazy-quilt story is one that can jump back and forth in time, work on many different levels, and one that can include myth. It is generally much more evocative of metaphor and symbolism than a novel that is chronological in structure, or one devoted, more or less, to rigorous realism, as is *The Third Life of Grange Copeland*.

The Third Life of Grange Copeland is a very realistic novel. I wanted it to be absolutely visual. I wanted the reader to be able to sit down, pick up that book, and see a little of Georgia from the early twenties through the sixties—the trees, the hills, the dirt, the sky—to feel it, to feel the pain and the struggle of the family, and the growth of the little girl Ruth. I wanted all of that to be very real. I didn't want there to be any evasion on the part of the reader. I didn't want the reader to say, "Now, I think she didn't mean this." I wanted him or her to say, "She has to mean this. This is a mean man: she *means* him to be a mean man." I had a lot of criticism, of course, about Brownfield, and my response is that I know many Brownfields, and it's a shame that I know so many.

I will not ignore people like Brownfield. I want you to know I know they exist. I want to tell you about them, and there is no way you are going to avoid them. You are going to have to deal with them. I wish people would do that rather than tell me that this is not the right image. You know, they say this man Brownfield is too mean; nobody's this mean.

c.t.: Brownfield's meanness is balanced against Grange's third life of compassion and understanding. So the statement is not entirely negative.

a.w.: The people who criticize me about Brownfield rarely even talk about Grange. Loyle Hairston is the only black male critic who understood the balance between Grange and Brownfield. Frankly, I think it's because he has read a lot. I'm not convinced that many of the reviewers have read very much literature, and as a result they seem to think you don't put in negative characters, period. But I think Loyle's background in Russian literature, which I like very much—where you get "meanies" and "goodies" and everything—helped him to deal with that book. But it didn't help him at all when it came to *Meridian*. I know because he told me that he just didn't understand it and would have to read it again. And I said, "Sure, go right ahead."

When you asked about critical response to *Meridian*, I must in all honest humility say I don't know of any critics who could do it justice because I can't think of anyone. The reviews I've seen have taken little parts of the book, never treating it in its entirety. For example, there was a wonderful review by Greil Marcus in the *New Yorker*, but he concentrated totally on the influence of Camus on the work. His whole thing was guilt and expiation. Somebody else talked about the strictly social and political issues of the sixties. Someone else talked about the Indians! And somebody else talked about the invention of legend in the first section where the women's tongue is buried under the tree and the tree grows miraculously and all that.

Oh yes, then there are the people, mostly Jewish "girls," who get to the part about Lynn. And every Jewish "girl" I meet under fifty is Lynn or thinks she is. And they claim a) Lynn's a stereotype, or b) she's just like them. And then there's the whole dilemma about black men and what their responsibility is to black women and vice versa. Some Spelman students even called me up and said, "We've been all over the campus looking for the tree. Where is it?" So I said, "Where is there a reviewer who can put it all together?"*

But anyway, the first novel is easy for the critics to deal with. It's real. The realism is there even though people do not want to accept Brownfield as a real character. But with *Meridian*, there's just a lot going on. And when people tell me they just read it once, I do have to smile because I just don't see how you can read it once and understand anything.

So, what I feel about *Meridian* is that I knew while I was writing it, it remained interesting to me, and that is very important because often when you write things, they're no longer interesting to you halfway through. Then the best thing to do is to throw them away because they don't hold up. But *Meridian*'s structure is interesting, and it's really very carefully done. It's like the work of one of my favorite artists, Romare Bearden. In some ways *Meridian* is like a collage.

Another reason I think nobody has been able to deal with *Meridian* as a total work is the whole sublayer of Indian consciousness, which as I get older becomes more and more pronounced in my life. I know this sounds very strange, but I had been working very hard, but not consciously really, to let into myself all of what being in America means, and not to exclude any part of it. That's something I've been working on, on a subconscious level. I've also been trying to rid my consciousness and my unconscious of the notion of God as a white-haired, British man with big feet and a beard. You know, someone who resembles Charlton Heston. As a subjected people that image has almost been imprinted on our minds, even when we think it hasn't. It's there because of the whole concept of God as a person. Because if God is a person, he has to look like someone. But if he's *not* a person, if she's not a person, if *it's* not a person . . . Or, if it is a person, then everybody is it, and that's all

---

* Barbara Christian in her book *Black Women Novelists: The Development of a Tradition, 1892–1976* (Westport, CT: Greenwood Press, 1980) does an incredibly rich and full interpretation of *Meridian*.

right. But what I've been replacing that original oppressive image with is everything there is, so you get the desert, the trees; you get the birds, the dirt; you get everything. And that's all God.

I don't know how to explain this really, but sometimes it's like when you hear voices. Well, I don't really hear voices, you'll be happy to know. But sometimes I have something like visitations and I know they come from what is Indian in me, and I don't necessarily mean Indian blood because I'm not getting back to that; you know my grandmother was such-and-such, although I'm sure the Cherokees were very thick with black folks in Georgia, until they got run out. But anyway, I had this visitation, and it was about smoking grass, which I had been smoking, and he said, "It's okay to smoke grass to help you temporarily forget or ease your problems, but you must go through a time when you engage with your problems without the smoke; otherwise, they will not be worked out, but only become layer on layer, like crisscross webs."

I like that. I like these visitations popping into my mind. I don't know any Indians. When I was in the desert, not long ago, I saw Indians. But I don't know them except on a level of longing. In Georgia there are so many remnants of their presence that there is a real kinship with these people who were forced off the land that was theirs.

c.t.: How did you go about characterizing *Meridian*?

a.w.: I think it started when I became aware that the very brave and amazing people whom I knew in the civil rights movement were often incredibly flawed, and in a way, it was these flaws that both propelled them and "struck" them. I mean they were often stricken because of their flaws which at the same time kept them going. I was fascinated by the way you hardly ever saw their flaws. And yet, they were there, hidden. The image you got on television showed their remarkable control, their sense of wholeness and beauty. In short, they were heroic. It's just that the other side of that control was the cost of their heroism, which I think as black people, as Americans, we don't tend to want to look at because the cost is so painful.

To most people Meridian's illness seems sort of exotic, and they can't quite figure out why she gets ill. But the fact is that when you are under enormous stress, as most of the civil rights people were, the things that the body will do are just incredible. I fully expect that the people who were

very brave and who had endured racial brutality and intimidation . . .
I fully expect that throughout their lives they will have some sort of physical disorder. Because suffering is not all psychological. The body and
the mind really are united and if the central nervous system is crucially
unbalanced by something, then there are also physical repercussions.

Guilt is also stress, and if it is compounded by intense political activity in a dangerous situation and compounded further by the giving away
of your child, the losing of someone you love, then that stress becomes
so intense that physical problems result.

I think Marge Piercy was right in one way in her review of *Meridian*,
although in another way she was very humorous. She said that what the
book needed to end it was a marriage or a funeral. Marriage is absurd.
Meridian is not interested in marriage, but I can see that the expected
end of that kind of struggle is death. It's just that in addition to all of her
other struggles, her struggle is to not die. That's what she means when
she's talking about martyrs not permitting themselves to be martyrs,
but at some point just before martyrdom they should just go away and
do something else.

She talks about Malcolm and King going off to farm or raise Dalma-
tians or doing something else other than permitting martyrdom. This
impulse to flee represents her struggle to break with Christianity, because Christianity really insists on martyrdom. She can see that the life
of Christ is exemplary. It truly is. It's a fine life. But just before the crucifixion, according to Meridian, Jesus should have just left town.

c.t.: Does Truman assume Meridian's struggle at the end of the novel?

a.w.: Oh yes, Meridian's struggle is in this sense symbolic. Her struggle
is the struggle each of us will have to assume in our own way. And Truman will certainly have to assume his because his life has been so full
of ambivalence, hypocrisy, and obliviousness of his actions and their
consequences.

c.t.: Are black women writers more concerned with dramatizing intimate male-female encounters than social confrontations with white
society?

a.w.: I can't think of any twentieth-century black woman writer who is
first and foremost interested in what white folks think. I exempt Phillis

Wheatley and all the nineteenth-century black women writers who *did* have that problem. Twentieth-century black women writers all seem to be much more interested in the black community in intimate relationships, with the white world as a *backdrop*, which is certainly the appropriate perspective, in my view. We black women writers know very clearly that our survival depends on trust. We will not have or cannot have anything until we examine what we do to and with each other. There just has not been enough examination or enough application of findings to real problems in our day-to-day living. Black women continue to talk about intimate relationships so that we can recognize what is happening when we see it, then maybe there will be some change in behavior on the part of men *and* women.

When you see *For Colored Girls Who Have Considered Suicide When the Rainbow Is Enuf,* for example, and you see what the behavior looks like onstage and you recognize it, you are recognizing it as behavior you've seen in the real world and you can judge the consequences of it. This recognition has to become very ordinary for all black people. We must be able to see what is happening, recognize such behavior and *make a judgment.* Judgment is crucial because judgment is lacking in black people these days.

Let's see if I can explain what I mean by that. There was a time when behavior was judged much more strictly than it is now. If you were walking down the street and some black man felt he was perfectly right to accost you and say sneaky, nasty little things to you, there was a time when the community rose up and said, "That's wrong! You can't do that. This is Miss so-and-so's child." There was a time when the community looked at this kind of behavior with the eyes of judgment. But today black people see without judgment. They think that to be nonjudgmental is progress. But in fact, it isn't when your non-judgment means that people suffer. And they do because there is no one saying with the whole authority of the community that what you are doing is hurting us as a community.

c.t.: Do you think that black women are capitalizing on an antagonistic press, as Ishmael Reed said not too long ago?

a.w.: I read somewhere that Reed said he had sold only eight thousand copies of his last book, and he was upset. He felt that if he had been a black lesbian poet he would have sold many more. But I have bought nearly all of Reed's books, and I did not buy them because he is a black lesbian poet. I bought them because he is writing about the black community, presumably from inside it. Since I *am* the black community, I represent his audience. And it is this audience that is ultimately important.

In any case, I think anybody can *only write*. Writing or not writing is not dependent on what the market is—whether your work is going to sell or not. If it were, there is not a black woman who would write. And that includes Phillis Wheatley. Think of *her* antagonistic market! I mean if you really thought about the market, you would probably just take a job canning fish. Even the most successful black women writers don't make a lot of money, compared to what white male and female writers earn just routinely. We live in a society that is racist and white. That is one problem. Another is, we don't have a large black readership; I mean, black people, generally speaking, don't read. That is our *main* problem. Instead of attacking each other, we could try to address that problem by doing whatever we can to see that more black works get out into the world—which, for example, Reed does with his publishing company—and by stimulating an interest in literature among black people. Black women writers seem to be trying to do just that, and that's really commendable.

This brings to mind Ntozake Shange's book *Nappy Edges*, which I just read and liked a lot. It has a wonderful introduction where she refers to a speech she made at Howard. She talked about how black people should try to relate to their writers and permit them the same kind of individuality they permit their jazz musicians. It's beautifully written, and funny, and I'm sure the audience loved what she was saying. Black women instinctively feel a need to connect with their reading audience, to be direct, to build a readership for us all, but more than that, to build *independence*. None of us will survive except in very distorted ways if we have to depend on white publishers and white readers forever. And white critics. If Reed only sold a few thousand copies of his book, he might look at who *controls* publishing first, and then he might look at who is buying his stuff or not buying it, in order to determine whether there is some serious breakdown in communication between him and his potential readers. Although I have all of his early books, it gets harder to lay out money for books that speak of black women as barracudas. As black women become more aware of sexism—when, in fact, they are as sensitive to sexism as they are now to racism, *and they will become so*—then a lot of black male writers are going to be in serious trouble. You notice we do not buy books by William Styron in droves, either.

In any case, to blame black women for one's low sales is just depressing to think about, considering the sad state of our general affairs. Skylab is falling; the nukes are leaking; we're running out of oil and gas; there's a recession. People don't have jobs. Most writers I know, white and black, live with an enormous amount of anxiety over just getting by. That black male writers, no less than black men generally, think that when they don't get something they want, it is because of black women, and not because of the capitalist system that is destroying us all, is almost too much irony to bear. Capitalist society. Racist capitalist society. Racist, sexist, and colorist capitalist society which doesn't give a damn about art except art that can be hoarded or sold for big bucks. It doesn't care about art that is crucial to our community because it doesn't care about our community—which is perhaps its only consistency.

If the black community fails to support its own writers, it will never have the knowledge of itself that will make it great. And for foolish, frivolous, and totally misinformed reasons—going directly back to its profound laziness about the written message as opposed to one that's sung—it will continue to blunder along, throwing away this one and that one, and never hearing or using what is being said. That is basically what happened with Zora Neale Hurston. The time has to come when the majority of black people, not just two or three, will want their own novels and poems, will want their own folktales, will want their own folk songs, will want their own whatever. There is so much that is ours that we've lost, and we don't even know we're missing it: ancient Egypt; ancient Ethiopia; Eatonville, Florida! And yet there's no general sense that the spirit can be amputated, that a part of the soul can be cut off because of ignorance of its past development. But I know one thing: when we really respect ourselves, our own minds, our own thoughts, our own words, when we really love ourselves, we won't have any problem whatsoever selling and buying books or anything else.

Look what happens with Jews and books. Jews make Jewish books bestsellers. Whatever is written by and about them they cherish and keep it going. When we feel *we* are worth money, when we feel that *we* are worth time, when we feel that *we* are worth love, we'll do it. But until we do, we won't. And that's that! This whole number about depending on white people for publicity and for this and that and so forth . . . All I can say is I hope it will soon be over. I am tired of it.

By and large black women writers support themselves, they support each other and support a sense of community much more so than any other group I've ever come in contact with, except for the civil rights era when people tended to be collective. That was true of them, and it is true of us. And I like that.

c.t.: What is your responsibility to your audience?

a.w.: I'm always happy to have an audience. It's very nice because otherwise it would be very lonely and futile if I wrote and had no audience. But on the other hand, although *I'm willing* to think about the audience before I write, usually I don't. I try, first of all, to know what I feel and what I think and then to write that. And if there's an audience, well, fine, but if not, I don't worry about it.

Have I ever written a story with all white characters? Well, of course I have. Years ago I wrote a wonderful story which I must find, if it's not packed in a trunk somewhere back in Brooklyn. It's a good story, and I know I'll publish it one day. But at the time I wrote it, nobody would buy it because it was a very chilling view of white people, of these particular white people. I had written what I saw. I had written what I thought. I had written what I felt, but this was a view that was totally unacceptable to everyone. Nobody wanted this particular view.

So what I do generally is write, and if there's an audience, there is one, but if there isn't one, I just pack it up and wait.

c.t.: Have people asked you whether *Meridian* is autobiographical?

a.w.: Oh yes. I don't think people really understand that a book like *Meridian* is autobiographical only in the sense of projection. Meridian is entirely better than I am, for one thing. She is an exemplary person; she is an exemplary, *flawed* revolutionary because it seems to me that the revolutionary worth following is one who is flawed. When I was talking about the flaw before I didn't mean that it made these people less worthy of following. It made them more worthy of following.

My life has been, since I became an adult, much more middle class than Meridian's. Although what happens often when I write is that I try to make models for myself. I project other ways of seeing. Writing to me is not about audience actually. It's about living. It's about expanding myself as much as I can and seeing myself in as many roles and situations as possible. Let me put it this way. If I could live as a tree, as a river, as the moon, as the sun, as a star, as the earth, as a rock, I would.

Writing permits me to be more than I am. Writing permits me to experience life as any number of strange creations.

c.t.: Are you drawn toward the folk hero/heroine as the focal point of your work?

a.w.: I am drawn to working-class characters as I am to working class people in general. I have a basic antagonism toward the system of capitalism. Since I'm only interested in changing it, I'm not interested in writing about people who already fit into it. And the working class can never fit comfortably into a capitalist society.

I think my whole program as a writer is to deal with history just so I know where I am. It was necessary for me to write a story like *The Third Life of Grange Copeland*, which starts in the twenties and has passages that go back even further, so I could, later on, get to *Meridian*, to *In Love and Trouble*, and then on to *The Color Purple*. I can't move through time in any other way, since I have strong feelings about history and the need to bring it along. One of the scary things is how much of the past, especially our past, gets forgotten.

c.t.: You've often written that some of your stories were also your mother's stories:

> Yet so many of the stories that I write, that we all write, are our mothers' stories. Only recently did I fully realize this: that through years of listening to my mother's stories of her life, I have absorbed not only the stories themselves, but something of the manner in which she spoke, something of the urgency that involves the knowledge that her stories—like her life—must be recorded. . . . She had handed down respect for possibilities— and the will to grasp them. . . . Guided by my heritage of love and beauty and a respect for strength—in search of my mother's garden, I found my own.
> —"In Search of Our Mothers' Gardens," *Ms.*, May 1974, p. 70

a.w.: Yes, some of the stories in *In Love and Trouble* came out of my mother's stories, for instance, "Strong Horse Tea." She often talked about how poor people, "in the olden days," had to make up home remedies for sick people. She used to crack me up with the story about my brother who stuttered and how he was stuttering and stuttering and they couldn't figure out what to do about it. So finally someone told her to hit him in the mouth with a cow's melt. As far as I can figure out, it's something like the spleen. Anyway, it's something raw and wet and bloody, and you get a grip on it and just hit the stutterer in the mouth with it. That would make anyone stop stuttering or stop talking altogether. But anyway, she did that; she hit him in the mouth with the cow's melt and he stopped stuttering.

Anyway, my mother would ramble on and tell about how she would make tea out of the cow's hoof when one of us felt ill. Years later when I was living in Mississippi, when I wrote most of those stories, her world was all around me.

People tend to think that life really does progress for everyone eventually, that people progress, but actually only *some* people progress. The rest of the people don't. There's always somebody using "strong horse tea" in the world; this day, this minute, there's some poor woman making strong horse tea for a child because she's too poor to get a doctor. Now that may not be the case in California; it may not even be in Georgia or Mississippi; it might be in India. But somewhere it is current. This is what I started to understand while I was in Mississippi. So I made up the story about the woman who tried to save her baby because the doctor wouldn't come. You know that the baby died and most of the people around the mother, the white people especially, could not even comprehend that she suffered, that she suffered as any mother would suffer.

"The Revenge of Hannah Kemhuff" in *In Love and Trouble* is also based on one of my mother's stories about a time during the Depression when she went to a local commissary to get food and was refused. I carried the germ for that story of hers with me for years and years, just waiting for an opportunity to use it where it would do the most good.

I wrote "The Child Who Favored Daughter" [from *In Love and Trouble*] in 1966, after my first summer in Mississippi. I wrote it out of trying to understand how a black father would feel about a daughter who fell in love with a white man. Now, this was very apropos because I had just come out of a long engagement with a young man who was white, and my father never accepted him. I did not take his nonacceptance lightly. I knew I needed to understand the depth of his antagonism.

After all, I was twenty or so, and couldn't quite understand his feelings since history is taught in the slapdash fashion that it is taught. I needed to comprehend what was going on with him and what would go on with any black man of his generation brought up in the South, having children in the South, whose child fell in love with someone who is "the enemy."

I had been writing the story for, oh, I guess, almost six months and I took it with me to Mississippi. Ironically, it was over that story, in a sense, that I met the man I did, in fact, marry. We met in the movement in Mississippi, and I was dragging around this notebook, saying, "I'm a writer." Most people think when you say you're a writer, and especially when you're twenty, that you can't be serious. Well, I read the story to him and he was convinced.

"To Hell with Dying" [from *In Love and Trouble*] was the first story I wrote and it was also my first published story. I wrote that story when I was still at Sarah Lawrence. It is my most autobiographical story. But again, the way autobiography works for a writer is different from what you'd think of as being autobiographical. It's autobiographical though, in fact, none of it happened. The *love* happened.

The story is created out of a longing. There was this man I really loved, not in the romantic sense, but I loved, cared about him, and he died while I was away at school. I didn't have any money to go home for the funeral. So the story was my tribute. It was what I could give. Referring to your question about audience, this story really wasn't about having an audience at all. All the audience I gave a damn about was dead. *He* was the audience. I would have been happy if he had known this was what I was thinking about when I couldn't go to his funeral.

3

"Moving Towards Coexistence": An Interview with Ellen Bring from *The Animals' Agenda* (1988)

ELLEN BRING: In your book *In Search of Our Mothers' Gardens*, you wrote about connections, about seeing a larger perspective in a diverse world. What, for you, is the common thread, the unifying theme that connects movements for animal liberation, women's liberation, civil rights, and others?

ALICE WALKER: I think we all suffer oppression. We all suffer from a lack of having others perceive us as being basically the same, in having the same feelings, and the same dreams and desires. I remember when I gave a benefit for Winnie Mandela, I was thinking at the time that there were two things really important to me. One was to raise money for Winnie Mandela and South Africa. The other was to raise money for animal rights because I was just beginning to deal with my own feeling of responsibility towards animals. There were people who were very critical of that because they immediately thought that I was equating human beings with animals in a negative way. I mean I definitely do equate them, but positively. It seemed to me so *right* because the oppression that black people suffer in South Africa—and people of color, women, and children face all over the world—is the same oppression that animals endure every day to a greater degree.

E.B.: In terms of public activism, the animal rights movement is predominantly white and middle-class. Why is that?

A.W.: I think white, middle-class people are the only people who have the time to do the things that have to be done.

At the same time, I feel that, inasmuch as I am a citizen of the planet, my responsibility to other beings is clear. I don't see the responsibility for promulgating an animal rights agenda falling just on white middle-class people. I think that everyone has to nurture an awareness of the ways that we are connected to animals—the essence of what being animal is—and to cherish and literally try to save animals.

I think many people of color feel that they're facing extinction. It's a little difficult, then, to put the energy that you have to fight for your own life into trying to fight for the lives of creatures that you are also exploiting. It's a very heavy bind.

E.B.: Although every day provides us with an opportunity to feel better about ourselves by personally resisting and boycotting violence towards nonhuman animals, many people are hostile and defensive about changing their lifestyles. Why do you think that is?

A.W.: I think that people are defensive about change because people are basically lazy. If they already feel that they are suffering under a horrible government, the world is going crazy, and war is everywhere, then it's a little hard to now have to think about everything they eat and wear.

It would be nice to think that universal enlightenment occurs at once, but it doesn't. I think you can only hope to inspire people—to move them by what you see yourself, by what you feel yourself, and by what you do. It may take them weeks, months, years, but once you reach them, they start to work on the problem, whatever it is. If I didn't have faith that that is what happens, I wouldn't bother to work at all.

When I write a novel about child abuse and sexist violence, I expect that a lot of the wife beaters and a lot of the child abusers are going to be really hostile and resentful. Of course, they don't want to stop this behavior. This is the behavior they learned from their mama and daddy. Since it didn't kill them, it's obviously the right thing to do.

But if the argument and the scenario is presented in such a way that it truly engages the feelings of the abusers, then I think we have a change coming in those people. I don't care how much they claim they're not going to change or how much they claim this doesn't happen. Once they are moved, the change is inevitable because you cannot live so divided within yourself, between what you know to be right and what you are in fact doing that isn't right.

E.B.: Why do you think people are so invested in being violent towards nonhuman animals?

A.W.: In thinking about *The Color Purple*, I should have included the mistreatment of dogs in poor communities, especially in southern black communities like the one in the book. Even today, in some of these communities, there is a real battering of dogs, in addition to a lot of child abuse and wife battering.

I think that people really pass on what's done to them. Therefore, we can only really change people by treating them differently. In that sense, you can understand how violence is not only obsolete, it's totally useless as a way of changing the world. The more violence you create, the more you have. Even what it accomplishes is illusory because you acquire something today by violence only to lose it over and over again. That's because people will always protest and the planet will protest too.

The planet is not helpless and its patience is wearing thin. I'm all for its patience to wear thin because I can't stand the abuse of the planet and the rampant lack of compassion for the Earth.

E.B.: What do you think is the artist's responsibility towards social change?

A.W.: To work for it, but also *to be* it. If you want a world where people are concerned about life on the planet, then you have to be concerned and work for change. But everyone is responsible for the whole creation and the artist has her or his part to do.

E.B.: At this point, what do you feel is your role in the animal liberation struggle?

A.W.: I wish you could see the place where I live when all the creatures are running around. Someone even saw an eagle here yesterday. I don't know what's happening, but I think that everything that ever used to be here is here! So I think coexistence is the direction of my effort and I'm still struggling with my vegetarianism.

E.B.: What is that struggle about and can people help?

A.W.: I get so much help from vegetarians, it's amazing! It's like being prayed through some kind of phase. Ever since people have heard that I was trying, they've been really rooting for me.

I'm not sure that I will ever be totally vegetarian. I guess about 10 percent of my diet is chicken and fish. I'm not sure that this won't always be so. Part of it is that I can't force myself anymore. I've nudged myself to the stage where I eat mostly vegetables, rice, and tofu. In fact, I was vegetarian for three months before I went to Nicaragua this past summer.

I'm still trying to formulate how I really feel about this. I feel in a sense that we are all eaten. That the earth is eventually going to eat all of us. What really bothers me about eating animals, in addition to being able to empathize with them, is that they can't get away. I think my reason for feeling that eating a fish is not as awful as eating an animal who is grown in a factory farm is that the fish can get away, at least in theory. Not being able to escape is the most awful thing. I know, in my soul, that to eat a creature who is raised to be eaten, and who never has a chance to be a real being, is unhealthy. It's like what I say in the essay about Blue, that you're just eating misery. You're eating a bitter life.

I have a friend up on the hill who has some chickens who run around and she gives me some of their eggs. So, sometimes I eat eggs. My struggle continues. But, I'm also just as concerned about the migrant workers who harvest the strawberries I eat. I read an article in the *San Francisco Chronicle* recently about two of them who are suing the growers they worked for because they were paid $20 a week for a six-day, twelve-hour-a-day week. They were housed in a shack with no toilet or bathing facilities, with eighty-nine other people. This is slavery.

F.B.: How has your reawakening to nonhuman animal consciousness affected your personal and professional life?

A.W.: I think the animals know that I have awakened to them and I feel an amazing connection. For instance, in my house in the city, animals come to the door and into the house. The other day, I was sitting under the tree over there and a bird politely came down and sat on my head.

Now, I am always aware that I'm truly coexisting in the midst of other beings.

E.B.: Are your friends already animal rights advocates or are you bringing this awareness to them?

A.W.: I think I'm bringing it to them. Generally, they are receptive. One or two of them have looked at me askance. People are so afraid to feel for themselves if the feeling is different from what they perceive the mainstream feeling to be. So I do have friends who just couldn't imagine what I was talking about—"You talk to these animals? Isn't that weird?" But now, of course, they talk to them too. So I don't give up on them, and I don't give up on myself either.

E.B.: The animal liberation movement is about compassion. Yet, compassion for the self is often the hardest to show.

A.W.: Yes, because we love to be perfect or even just vastly better now. But, as long as I feel I'm moving, I won't despair. I think this need of ours to be better than we are sometimes prevents change. It prevents us from acting.

For instance, I agonized a long time over whether I should write the article about Blue because I felt that I could only really take this position and express and share the way I feel about him as a fellow being if I was already a vegetarian. I kept asking myself how can I dare to presume to say this if I am not already at the point where I want to take people. I finally answered by saying to myself that I have the responsibility to share the vision even if I am not already in the vision. There's value in sharing the process. You want to encourage people by appearing as if you have it all together, but I frankly feel it's better to share that you don't because that's the truth and that's the reality. Nobody has it all together.

E.B.: Being vulnerable in that way often makes it easier for other people to begin their own process.

A.W.: Absolutely! It also makes it easier for them to share their process. I have gotten tons of cookbooks, letters, testimonials—I think I've heard from half the vegetarians in the world!

At times, I question my 10 percent of chicken and fish, but then I think it's okay because it is the truth. It's where I am and I'm glad to be there. Given my background of meat three times a day, this represents such a leap in consciousness.

E.B.: Was it hard to move away from that?

A.W.: Not really, although every month I would get a real chicken attack. I wrote about an incident when I was in Bali that is helping me a lot to deal with my chicken problem. One day, I was walking across the road with my daughter and my companion. It was raining and we were trying to get home. I looked down and there was this chicken with her little babies. They were trying to get home too. It was one of those times feminists refer to as a "click." Well, this was one of those human animal–to–nonhuman animal clicks, where it just seemed so clear to me how one we are. I was a mother. She was a mother. And she was trying to get those little brats across the street. They were not cooperating and she was just fussing and carrying on.

I feel I've been having a lot of help.

E.B.: What do you think about the argument that vegetarianism violates cultural traditions and rituals and, therefore, is racist or imperialist?

A.W.: You mean if people have been killing pigs forever, you should let them keep doing that and not mention that the pig has something to say? No, I don't think that's a good argument.

Slavery was an intrinsic part of southern heritage. Propertied white people loved having slaves. That was something they were all used to and they even fought a war to keep them. But that view did not take into account the desires of the slaves, who didn't want to be slaves. In the same way, animals don't want to be eaten.

E.B.: There seems to be an emphasis in the current animal liberation movement on male-defined philosophy and science, and on male academicians—even though women are the backbone of the movement. Emotions are for "little old ladies in tennis shoes," but not for a sophisticated movement that's to be taken seriously. However, in her article "Dominance and Control," author Gene Corea discusses the necessity of dismantling patriarchy and sounds a warning to women that we "betray ourselves in our work for the animals" when we adopt "artificial male language." Please comment.

A.W.: I read her article and I agree absolutely. I think the feeling that the animal rights movement and a lot of other movements are dominated by white men who have a very dispassionate, rational, linear way of approaching reality keeps away a lot of passionate Third World people who are really sick of that. That's gotten us where we are today, which is on the edge of extinction.

Who needs this? Who wants this? Who cares about trying to sit under that kind of tutelage—condescending, cold, cut off from feelings? Wherever I go, I take my passion. It's part of me. The whole thing is what you get. In any case, it's what I keep.

Think of it this way. During the enslavement of black people in this country, white women were required to look on the most savage beatings and also to administer some of them. White women were not supposed to care, only to take care of business—to see that "Suki" was beaten and "John" had his foot chopped off. This made the white woman's enslavement that much more profound. She couldn't even be herself in that situation.

A brave white woman looking at slavery would have had to try to see herself as one of the people enslaved. She would have had to know from her own suffering that there was a connection between herself and the slaves. She would have had to bond with the slaves and not with her husband.

That is what it seems to me we have to ask ourselves in bonding with animals rather than with the killer. What permits us to be who we are? I think the animals give us much more freedom to be who we are than people who are oppressing all of us.

E.B.: Why do you think that people who care about nonhuman animals are often called sentimental, and why does it seem that the word "sentimental" has a negative connotation rather than a positive one?

A.W.: The people who call us sentimental have destroyed great tracts of feeling in themselves, and what else can they do but say that we're sentimental? We are talking about people who have big holes in themselves that were probably punched out when they were children. Now when they meet other people who don't have the holes, they feel they have to say something. They have to project onto us.

I think some people think of sentimentality as negative because they associate it with women. To say that someone is sentimental, in the sense of being like women, is, of course, a positive thing. It means you still have your sentiments, your capacity to care.

E.B.: In your essay "Only Justice Can Stop a Curse," you wrote, "But if by some miracle in all our struggle the earth is spared from a nuclear holocaust, only justice to every living thing will save humankind." What's your vision of that justice?

A.W.: Obvious things like an end to hunger, an end to illiteracy. To put it another way, the beginning of health for everyone, food for everyone, education for everyone, respect for everything.

Part of what justice means for nonhuman animals is that there will just have to be fewer people, because I think the insistence of people to cover the Earth is itself a grievous insult to the nonhuman animals whose space is squeezed into nonexistence. Just because people can have three, four, and five children does not mean that that's the best thing for all creation. It definitely is not. Helping people to see that is an early project which has to go along with animal rights.

4

"Writing to Save My Life": An Interview with Claudia Dreifus from *The Progressive* (1989)

CLAUDIA DREIFUS: Your new novel, *The Temple of My Familiar*, has been published to mixed reviews. You spent eight years writing it. Surely, this must hurt.

ALICE WALKER: Well, you can only be hurt by the criticism of the people you respect. And failing that: the people you know. And failing that: the people who understand your life. Or care about your worldview. When people don't fit any of those categories, it's hard to be really *that* concerned. Yes, you would like to be understood by people. But I *do* understand that my worldview is different from that of most of the critics. I think most of the reviews have been by white men, you know, *real* establishment white men. And they are defending a way of life, a patriarchal system, which I do not worship. They are not working-class white males. They are not progressive white males. They are not the white males I have worked with in all the progressive movements and causes I have been active in over the years. I can't imagine any of these critics being at the pro-choice march. I can't imagine any of them blockading arms shipments to Central America. I can't imagine any of them being arrested at antiapartheid demonstrations. I can't imagine any of them knowing about or caring about the lives of black women, or of black children, or of black men. So there is no reason I should really care that they are angry.

C.D.: But they can hurt your work, your ability to reach readers.

A.W.: They can try. But what can I do about it? I can only persist in being myself.

C.D.: It's not just white male critics who get very angry at your work. When *The Color Purple* was first published, black male critics fell all over each other to denounce what they said was your negative portrayal of black male characters.

A.W.: My feeling was that the way some of the black males revealed themselves to be was far more negative than anything I would ever have even thought about black men. I would not have expected such pettiness. You know, they had no identification with the struggle of women! That's shocking in a people who, I had always assumed, identified with every struggle for human rights in the world. If you have in your cultural background Paul Robeson, Martin Luther King, W.E.B. Du Bois, all these people, how then can you really totally ignore a progressive movement like the women's liberation movement? So that when you read my work, you read it without any acknowledgment that my work, especially *The Color Purple*, is in the context of a struggle for liberation that women all over the world are engaged in.

What I did was to go on writing *The Temple of My Familiar*. But I just wish in general that people would truly read what you write, rather than launch attacks against you based on hearsay, based on what they think you mean. And I wish that men could have more of an appreciation of gentleness in men and not find it so threatening. That's part of the problem of men who can read *The Color Purple* and only find negative things about men in it. Because once the men in my book change from being macho men, [the critics] just lose interest in them, they can't recognize them as men.

C.D.: The striking thing about the men in *The Color Purple* is how much you permitted them to change, to grow. Mr. ___ starts out as a brute, but he ends up rather loving toward Celie.

A.W.: Right. They would have been bad if they had just remained macho brutes. But they don't.

C.D.: Do you think some of the attacks on you are really jealousy of your worldly attainments? You've got the prizes, the money, the fame—many of these gentlemen critics would like that stuff too.

A.W.: I suppose. There is nothing I can say about it except I've worked very hard all my life. I have not had an easy life. I did not start out writing to attain worldly goods. I started out writing to save my life. I had a childhood where I was very much alone and I wrote to comfort myself. I've been very suicidal at times in my life, for various reasons that I don't want to go into here. But I've had some really hard times. And whenever that has happened. I have written myself out of it. And it may look to other people like "silver-platter time," but to me, it's just been a very long struggle; so it was always just astonishing to me that anyone would be envious.

c.d.: When you say you've written yourself out of depressions, is that because you created characters to keep you company?

a.w.: No. It's because of the act of creation itself. It's like in Native American cultures, when you feel sick at heart, sick in soul, you do sand paintings. Or you make a basket. The thing is that you are focused on creating something. And while you're doing that, there's a kind of spiritual alchemy that happens and you turn that bad feeling into something that becomes a golden light. It's all because you are intensely creating something that is beautiful. And in Native American cultures, by the time you've finished the sand painting, you're well. The point is to heal yourself.

c.d.: More than many writers, you are known as a political activist. What do you get from activism?

a.w.: Well, it pays the rent on being alive and being here on the planet. There are things that you really owe, I feel. I think if I weren't active politically, I would feel as if I were sitting back eating at the banquet without washing the dishes or preparing the food. It wouldn't feel right to me.

c.d.: Did you go to the recent pro-choice march in Washington, D.C.?

a.w.: Yes. As someone who had an abortion before it was legal, it was very moving to be there with my daughter. Because I really knew what I was marching for. I knew that I don't want her to suffer the same kind of sadness, depression, and fear that I had, that many of us do.

c.d.: Tell us about the illegal abortion.

A.W.: It was really frightening. And also, I was brought up to feel that it was a heinous thing. I was nineteen or twenty, something like that. I was in an incredible moral struggle to decide. I wanted a life to live and there was no way I could support another person. So it was a problem.

C.D.: You weren't injured?

A.W.: Oh, no. No. It was quite nice. That part of it. A very nice Italian doctor whose daughter was at Vassar. He understood perfectly well why I, a college student, shouldn't have a baby.

C.D.: For many of the women who went to that march in April, it was an exhilarating experience. However, everyone noticed how few women of color attended.

A.W.: And the fact is that more black women have abortions than anyone else. You can't say they didn't come because they don't believe in abortion.

C.D.: Maybe there was a great ambivalence in the black community about the issue.

A.W.: Maybe so. You know, I don't think there's that much ambivalence about the issue. Maybe about being perceived as someone who is proabortion. But the reality is that nine out of the ten women you meet on the street have had an abortion.

C.D.: Your nineteen-year-old daughter has your name—not that of her father, your ex-husband. Why?

A.W.: I think she decided that she's a Walker. You know, I chose Walker. It was my name, but I also re-chose it, because I had a great-great-great-grandmother who walked from Virginia to Georgia carrying two children. She was a slave of white people. I always think of that walk in her as a Walker, as being totally heroic and wonderful. And so when I was deciding on what to name myself, after I had decided I didn't want to be called by my husband's name. I had to figure out what I really wanted to do with all these patriarchal names. This was back in the third year of my marriage when I decided I could not stand being called by my husband's name. So I went to court and had my name given back to me. So I decided I really wanted that name because of her walk, not because it was my father's name. So then [my daughter], really loving that history, decided that she wanted it as well. But also, we're very close.

c.d.: Your books are taught at hundreds of universities around the country. Yet there are many professors who complain their students should be reading Plato and not Alice Walker. There's a "back-to-basics" anger that writings like yours have become texts.

a.w.: Whenever you try to get inclusive, you get it.

c.d.: In your work, you've tried to go to other myths and histories than the ones that are standard. Do you think that's one of the reasons why you draw this kind of criticism?

a.w.: Of course. It's amazing to me that the white male establishment in literature and other areas really seems to believe that because they buy the myth that they have always been wonderful, that they've always done everything, and that the only thing worth knowing is what they produced—it's amazing to me that they think we should think it. We don't. If ever the emperor had no clothes, this is it. Whatever their worldview is, it is certainly not shared by me.

But this is entirely reasonable. I am not they. My life has not been theirs. My life has been one of everyone in the culture acknowledging that I, as a black woman, am the least respected person in the society. I'm the one expected to do most of the work and not complain, and a long list of other things, over hundreds of years. They, on the other hand, have been brought up to think that they are to rule, that their word is law. But just because they have the power to do that does not mean it is right or that I think they are great. I don't. I think any twelve black women anywhere in the world could do a much better job of running the world than they are doing. And I say twelve because if I had to create a structure for governing, it would never have one person at the head of it. To me that is really totally obsolete.

You have to have many more people in charge of things—and they have to be people who care about the future. This culture is one in which everyone is trying to get through the next four years—at best. And look where that gets us. It gets us plutonium in the drinking water and in the air. It gets us a trillion-dollar budget. At a time when people are starving and when they don't have medicines.

c.d.: What do you read when you have time to read?

a.w.: At the moment, let's say in the last month or so, I have read— these are wonderful books—I loved *The Great Cosmic Mother*, by Monica Sjoo and Barbara Mor. I loved Barbara Walker's *The Woman's Encyclopedia of Myths and Secrets*. I read a novel by a Zimbabwean woman, it's wonderful, it's called *Nervous Conditions*. Her name is Tsitsi Dangarembga. She's a young woman brought up in Zimbabwe in the home of a missionary uncle. The voice in it is rare. This woman has a sort of detached quality that is very rare in African women's writing. She's very perceptive. Then, another book I read some months ago is called *My Place*, by Sally Morgan, an Australian aboriginal woman, who is fabulous. I'm also reading, at the moment, *Lives of Courage*, about the South African women who are in the anti-apartheid movement. It's wonderful, because they are all kinds, all colors, and even all classes, which I didn't know.

c.d.: From *The Temple of My Familiar* and *The Color Purple*, one senses that color is a very important part of your life. In *The Color Purple*, you have a long section on the meaning of purple. In this new book, one of your characters, Olivia, owns a miraculous blue suit that works miracles only in a certain shade of blue.

a.w.: I think colors *are* miraculous. We live in a universe that is extremely creative and magical. We become happier as we appreciate these things in nature.

c.d.: And have we been cut off from appreciating them?

a.w.: Oh, yes. When we live in cities, which are basically artificial arrangements, we do forget, for instance, how miraculous spring is. I've been walking in Central Park today, and I've been so attracted by the fresh little green leaves that are such a beautiful spot in the center of this concrete city. But most of the people—and especially the children—in New York are so far removed from the magic that is inherent in nature, from spring coming to flower, to bloom. Even my daughter, who's been brought up around gardens all of her life, said to me last summer, when I was showing her corn I had planted and how tall it was, "Mama, tell me, does the corn come out of the ground—or where does it come from, on a stalk?" She was eighteen then. I was shocked. But I think if you're surrounded by buildings and paper and you learn about life through books rather than perceiving life itself, you don't know what inherent magic there is in creation.

C.D.: You used to live in Brooklyn, in Park Slope. Did you move to the West Coast because you felt too cut off from nature?

A.W.: Yeah. I bought a little house in Park Slope that gave me the largest possible amount of sky, and I had a tree planted in the front and one in the back. And I sort of thought these could represent sky and forest.

C.D.: A symbolic tree?

A.W.: Yes. Because I couldn't really live without at least a symbolic tree. I knew that much. But what I realized three months after I bought this house and moved into it is that it just wasn't enough. I don't want the symbolic. I want the real. So I moved. I moved to California, where there still are, thankfully, lots of trees, lots of sky, and lots of earth.

C.D.: Tell us about Olivia's blue suit. Her daughter, Fanny, takes it to the cleaners and it never comes back, so she makes another one for herself, but it is the wrong shade of blue and it makes her extremely tired every time she wears it. Where did that idea come from?

A.W.: I just made it up. Because it just seemed perfectly logical. All of us have had at least one magical garment that someone gave us or that we bought. And when we put it on, we just felt very vivid. And then, if you lost that and you tried to replace it with something else, it just wouldn't work. There was just no way. Because, actually, you were trying to make a material thing function as a spiritual thing. The first one actually en-spirited you because of the connection. It was made by someone who loved you. But then you get something off the rack, and it is not the same thing.

c.d.: One senses you have very strong feelings about handmade objects. Once, on *The Today Show*, you described a book almost as if it were a piece of sculpture or pottery.

a.w.: Well, I do. In my house, I don't have much furniture. But what I have looks like anybody could have made it. Anybody with a real aesthetic eye. Not fancy things. Useful objects. I love pottery, I wish I could make pots. I'm not very good at it. I value what has been made by people.

c.d.: Do you think the objects, after a while, encompass the spirit of the person who made them?

a.w.: Oh, I think they do from the beginning. When you respond to something because it's so beautiful, you're really looking at the soul of the person who made it. The spirit of the person who made it has gone into it; that's why it is so beautiful. It has all of her or his concentrated intensity and passion and thoughtfulness, and that's what you see.

c.d.: There's a New Age quality to your writing, to your ideas.

a.w.: What I'm doing is literarily trying to reconnect us to our ancestors. All of us. I'm really trying to do that because I see the ancient past as the future, that the connection that was original is a connection; if we can affirm it in the present, it will make a different future.

Because it's really fatal to see yourself as separate. You have to feel, I think, more or less equal and valid in order for the whole organism to feel healthy.

5

"Alice Walker's Appeal":
An Interview with Paula Giddings
from *Essence* (1992)

PAULA GIDDINGS: What made you focus on the issue of clitoridectomy in *Possessing the Secret of Joy*?

ALICE WALKER: I dragged my feet for a long time, because I knew my whole life would change once I published it. But I could not continue going on blithely, as if this weren't happening. As if this were not a part of what's wrong with Africa. Of what's wrong with us. I firmly believe that the reason AIDS spreads faster in Africa is because of these genital mutilations. And I think that if it continues, it will depopulate the continent—maybe not in my lifetime, or even my child's lifetime, but it will happen.

P.G.: There are those who will say that clitoridectomies are now only performed in isolated areas. . . .

A.W.: I love the people who say, "You're only talking about ten women, so what are you worrying about?" Of course, the point is that if it only happened to one little girl, that would be too many—but the estimation is that [almost] one hundred million women have been mutilated. One hundred million! Imagine that you're in Chicago and you could walk and meet everyone between there and the Atlantic Ocean. Then imagine that all of those people you met had had this done to them. That's what one hundred million would look like. Now tell me, how do you expect to have a healthy continent with this going on, when this is wrecking the very foundation of it? How do you expect healthy anything?

P.G.: The first thing I've heard a lot of men say is that this is done in secrecy by women and that men don't know very much about it.

A.W.: It's been happening for thousands of years, and they don't know? Some of the men have to take their wives to the hospital because they are so hard to break into, and they don't know? If we're going to lie about it, why don't we just say that we are a people who lie? Let's just be out front about it.

P.G.: Now, you know what the main thrust of the criticism against you will be: How dare this American judge us? What gives this Westerner a right to intervene in our affairs?

A.W.: Slavery intervened. As far as I'm concerned, I am speaking for my great-great-great-great-grandmother who came here with all this pain in her body. Think about it. In addition to having been captured, put in the hull of a ship, packed like sardines, put on the auction block, in addition to her children being sold, she being raped, in addition to all of this, she might have been genitally mutilated. I can't stand it! I would go nuts if this part of her story weren't factored in. Imagine if men came from Africa with their penises removed. Believe me, we would have many a tale about it.

The other answer is when Africans get in trouble, whom do they call? Everybody. They call on people they shouldn't even talk to—trying to raise money, appealing to people to fight their battles, buying guns from Russia and the United States. They [Africans] invite all of these experts from Europe and the United States to go there to say their bit about AIDS, to sell them condoms. So they can accept what I—someone who loves my former home—am saying. They don't have a leg to stand on, so they better not start hopping around me!

P.G.: What about those who say that this casts aspersions on the homeland?

A.W.: I don't really care where the child is who's suffering. I really don't. I just know that the child is suffering. That she's been held down and cut open. That she will never forget it. You know, you don't forget anything. You may not remember, but you don't forget. It's inexcusable, it's indefensible.

P.G.: It's hard to imagine living a life after being mutilated like that.

A.W.: It's such a shock to the system. You know everything you've been taught about African women, that they are "hot" and "lascivious"? It makes you wonder. . . . In Hanny Lightfoot-Klein's book [*Prisoners of Ritual: An Odyssey into Female Genital Circumcision in Africa* (Harrington Park Press, 1989)], she talks about visiting, in the Sudan, a place where at night all the women go in, like chickens. There are no windows, they lock the door—practically nail it shut—and then in all this heat they wrap themselves up in a way that is practically impossible to unravel. Then they huddle close together. There is no air. That's how they sleep. Because as bad as rape is anywhere, for them it is a matter of life and death. There, if you're torn open, you're subject to tetanus, to all kinds of infection and disease. Then there's the tearing—I mean you could bleed to death if there is no one there to repair you. So these women are completely controlled by the fears of being torn open without possibility of repair.

P.G.: What do you know about any movement against mutilation in Africa?

A.W.: As far as I know, there is not much of a movement, just woman after woman—either alone or with two or three other people—getting up and speaking out or writing about it. I think there have been periods when there was more of a concerted effort to stop it. After the British left, for example, there were attempts to raise consciousness about it, but it's the kind of thing that is so deeply engraved into the tradition that people slide back into it.

What I'm hoping is that this book will invite whatever movement there is to converge with all of the people who may now be aware of it, and together we may be able to do something.

P.G.: In *Possessing the Secret of Joy*, Tashi sees a psychoanalyst who tells her that "Negro women" can never be analyzed effectively because they can't bring themselves to blame their mothers.

A.W.: [Sighs] I knew that phrase would leap out of the novel. It explains the pattern of our repression, our self-repression. It has been extremely difficult to blame our mothers for anything, because we can see so clearly what they've been up against. It almost killed me to see women in Kenya and other places who actually have grooves in their foreheads from carrying heavy loads. How do you say, "Look what you're doing to me?" How do you criticize someone who has "made a way out of no way" for you? But we have to. For our own health, we have to examine the ways in which we've been harmed by our mothers' collaboration.

P.G.: That makes me think of something I recently heard about the reaction of a mother to her daughter, a college student, when the daughter told that she had just been raped. The mother said, "Oh, don't make such a big deal about it, all women go through that."

A.W.: That mother just put a nail in her coffin. And if the daughter's ever to rise again, she's going to have to get that nail out.

P.G.: There is also a comment in the novel to the effect that women have to minimize the pain that men give them so that they won't hate their sons.

A.W.: Yes. Perhaps that is why mothers protect them so, why daughters like the student you talked about are sacrificed—even when there's no actual son in the house. That's why we cannot continue this. We want our sons and we want our daughters. We can't raise sons who will break into a woman's body and just help themselves.

P.G.: How do we begin to heal all of that, Alice? I mean, do we all have to go to psychoanalysts? Can we do it ourselves?

A.W.: I doubt it. I don't think you can do anything without help. In order to see the back of your head, you need a mirror to look into. It doesn't have to be a psychoanalyst—it might be a novel. But it has to be some kind of healer.

P.G.: We tend to equate tradition with something that is positive, needed. But not all tradition should be preserved, should it?

A.W.: Ninety-nine and ninety-nine one-hundredths percent of traditions should be done away with because women did not make them. Like marriage, for example. Say you woke up one morning in a beautiful world and you had everything you wanted: you had your work, your health, you had your friends, you had good food, good lovemaking. Would you really look around and say "What do I really need now? I guess I need to get married." [laughs] Give me a break! But we think that way because we are in a heterosexist culture that says your life is incomplete without a man. It is the same with men. They are told that without a woman you can't have pleasure, you can't have joy. . . . And then there is the church, bless its heart, which has been so damaging. . . .

P.G.: You define religion as "an elaborate excuse for what man has done to woman and the earth."

A.W.: That's what organized religion is. Can you imagine a church telling you what to do with your body? Telling you not to masturbate, for example? It's your body! Or the church telling you what race or class or color to have sex with? It's none of the church's business.

I'm not saying that there are not some wonderful things about the church. But it is a reflection of a male-dominant tradition that has been reinforced by the slave culture. The church has to be taken apart and put back together in a way that is revolutionary.

P.G.: We've been made less than whole in so many ways, haven't we?

A.W.: Yes, there are so many people walking around who have forgotten to be whole persons. Just like they've forgotten what it is to laugh. We have canned laughter. I hate it, because I know what real laughter sounds like. Do you know that many of our children have never heard real laughter? Many people have forgotten how to love. We've forgotten to have faith in our own beauty. "Don't you know you're beautiful?" I ask people. "Can't you remember?"

P.G.: Is that in effect what Tashi is doing in this novel, trying to remember her beauty before society or tradition cripples her?

A.W.: Yes, and that makes Tashi a universal woman. I want people to see that there is not a big gap between Tashi and [a celebrity] who enlarged her breasts. She has been crippled. Why would you marry someone who wanted a woman with big breasts? Why not just send him a couple of breasts? That's what I would have done—I hope. I would have just asked somebody to make up two large breasts and put them in a box and send them to whatever-this-guy's-name-is, you know?

But collusion with this need of his is a sign of her crippling.

P.G.: In the novel, Tashi is surrounded by a loving community that includes an African American man, a European man and woman, and a young man who is both biracial and bisexual.

A.W.: I was never a separatist, but now more than ever before my own life is so multiracial, multiethnic, multisexual, multieverything. That's my life. And I'm glad of it, thank the Goddess. I think the reason that it's so wonderful is because sometimes your own oppression—let's say the relationship with your family—is so painful that if you couldn't do very much with it, you'd die.

But what you gain in that situation gives you another insight that you can apply to something else—and live. That's why we find ourselves connecting so deeply in these different communities, with all these different people. I just love that aspect of life. I love the people in my life.

P.G.: The idea of displacing pain makes me ask the question about black women's relationship to it.

A.W.: You can get addicted to pain. That's another thing that's *so* awful about the image of the crucifixion, you know? But you can also get addicted to joy! That's what I would do. [laughs] I mean, I am sure there is pain waiting in my life. The whole world situation is painful. But I am here to tell you that your joy can equal your pain—it can strip your pain.

And if you can have faith in a God that somebody else gave you and that you have never seen, you can also have faith in your own joy—something you've at least had a glimmer of.

P.G.: Have you always known this?

A.W.: I would have never gotten out of Georgia if I didn't know, 'cause those people were about to kill me. You just have to let joy be your guide. You know, when I was growing up, I used to escape from the house to the woods—there was tremendous joy there. And I said to myself, "One of these days you can actually have both. You won't have to run away from a bad place to a good place. You can have two good places." And that's what I have.

P.G.: What you're saying is so important: to be conscious of the world, of your own pain, and also of your own joy.

A.W.: Paula, I've never had a better time—weeping all the way, you know what I mean? You know the expression "unspeakable joy"? I have unspeakable joy even as I deal with my anger, sorrow, and grief. I don't have a big plan, a big scheme about all this. I have one requirement: that, because of this book, one little girl, somewhere, won't be mutilated. And that's plenty. That'll keep me laughing. I'll go home, I'll kick up my heels, and I'll feel that on this issue I've saved one child. That's enough.

6

"Giving Birth, Finding Form: Where Our Books Come From": Alice Walker, Jean Shinoda Bolen, and Isabel Allende in Conversation from Creative Conversations Series (1993)

JEAN SHINODA BOLEN: One of the images I had when I was invited to fantasize who I might have a conversation with, with you, I thought of the three of us as being really—you saw us walk in, we're all about the same size, and we're ethnically diverse, and we did not plan to dress in a color-coordinated way, but we have.

We have been sitting in the Grace Cathedral version of the green room, which is labeled "nursery," and we have been warming up by talking with each other, and one of the things that has come up is that we don't want this conversation just to be okay, we have a feeling/sense that many of you are here because you have creativity that wants to be born and wants form. And maybe something that we share with you will in some way help in your own birthing process.

The other thing that feels so very special to me is that I have a feeling that almost everybody in the room is related to all three of us, probably, certainly at least two, I mean people are related to authors of books in ways that really matter. It's like, when you write from a soul level, you share something of what deeply matters to you. You put it in form and you put it out there, and then a reader comes along. And often that reader comes along at a particular significant moment, connects with a book that has something in it that makes a difference. And so there's a feeling in this room of you are community, you are related to us.

We have a conversation about to happen, and we have not planned it. Not only will we have space for you to have questions, but there's something about being in the vessel that is this room, and being part of it, and picking up, perhaps as the currents of the conversation go, something of why you came and what you came to hear.

We have touched each other, our work has touched each other. We actually don't know each other well. We have already gotten a sense of where the conversation might go by raising such questions as the personal level out of which our work comes, and for me personally with my training as a Jungian analyst and psychiatrist, and being ethnically Japanese, there is a long tradition of really not being very personal. And certainly when I sit in my office, I'm focusing on the other people, and when I'm lecturing, I have a subject, and so this is a new form for me, and I am both excited by it and a little nervous, and so is Isabel.

ISABEL ALLENDE: I'm terrified, but I'm not terrified for the same reasons she is; I'm always very personal, and I don't mind being extremely personal, but this is the first time that I'm not reading. I'm, you know, English is not my language, and I'm always overprepared for everything. So I bring these pages, and I read, and I feel safe behind the pages. Well, this time I feel totally naked.

J.S.B.: And Alice has great trust.

ALICE WALKER: Plenty of it.

I.A.: Alice said, "You don't have to worry, these people come here and they will have to do the happening, not us. So you already know what your responsibility is."

A.W.: Right. So was there a question, Jean, did you finish?

J.S.B.: Well the overall question is where do our books come from? What is the model, being like the labyrinth in this cathedral or the birth process, what inseminates, impregnates, what starts the process, and what is it like?

A.W.: Well, I think with me it's different with each book, and that it's usually just that there is something that never goes away, you know, some feeling or something I want to understand that is always with me no matter what I'm doing. And I literally cannot lose it. And at the point I'm really knowing that I can never lose this, I then try to schedule a year in which to really look at it and really see what comes. Because it's so important to unclutter the brain, the mind. This society is so full of junk, and, you know, just stuff, that for me creativity is greatly impeded just by the chatter, you know, of all those things and the visual clutter of life. So I need to be able to see great distances, you know, just clear to the horizon for one thing, and a lot of time that is quiet and pure, that is not about which bills to pay or, you know, noise. It's just very important to have a space that is really really clear for whatever is emerging to come.

J.S.B.: Your last book [*Possessing the Secret of Joy*] was very uncomfortable.

A.W.: Yes.

J.S.B.: I would imagine you were not very comfortable living with this book and what brought it up and how you felt. Do you feel your way into the characters, does the experience feel, like, embodied and then it comes out? How was it for you to be with your last book?

A.W.: It was very difficult. There were days where I actually started the writing. First of all it took a lot, twenty years or more, for me to decide to write it, because I wanted to be sure that it would be in a form that people could feel and not really get away from, and also in a form that—

J.S.B.: [interrupting] It succeeded.

A.W.: But also that it would be in a form that wouldn't intimidate anyone either. I mean you could put it down, you could go for weeks without opening the book. But I learned about genital mutilation twenty years ago in Kenya, and it just was so completely beyond my experience at the time, because I was a student, that I didn't, I literally didn't understand what they meant. And then over the years I started to understand what that meant, and then what that meant to the women and the children when this was done.

But by the time I actually started, I was in such a state of grief that the only thing that sustained me was that I could go outside and just lie facedown on the earth. And somehow I got the energy that I always get from the earth directly. And I really understood, in a quite deep way, that the body of woman is the body of the earth, and it was the same kind of scarring, mutilation, control. You know, "If you're gonna have a crop, it's gonna be my crop. This is what you're gonna have. It's gonna be cotton, it's gonna be corn, it's gonna be soybeans." And the same where they cut the woman, and they sew her up, and they say, "If you're gonna have children, it's gonna be my child, it's gonna be a boy." But I have found in my work that I couldn't live without the earth; I mean, the people who think they could live in space, they're crazy. I cannot live without the earth. It gives me everything, including peace of mind. I mean, just by being under my feet, and under my body when I lie on it.

I.A.: I imagine that in the case of this book there was also a lot of anger that you have to transform to something else. I mean put boundaries to that anger and use it.

A.W.: Yes, but I still have it. I was able to use the anger that I had, but also to come finish the book and realize that I'm still angry, and that I'm justified at being angry. If you cannot be angry about something like this, I think you're dead. You know? And that is good, I mean it is good because it propels you on to do something more, and also to keep yourself really alive.

J.S.B.: Isabel, you've also talked or mentioned that your books have come out of the heavier feelings in your life, not the lighter ones. Is that right?

I.A.: Yeah, I feel that all my books come from a very deep emotion that has been with me for a very long time. And those emotions are usually painful. It's abandonment, pain, anger, death, violence, a lot of violence in my life. But there are also joyful emotions that go with the writing and all the senses, the sensuality of writing, the lives of the characters, the storytelling, all that is such an orgy. It's always pornographic, those moments that I spend alone with my characters in my bedroom in solitude doing whatever we want. It's great, almost those fantasies that I can never do with any men, I mean they are so limited. And then you find these guys, these characters in novels, that are just relentless, to say the least. So there's a mixture of both things, the love and the pain.

And sometimes I have a great idea for a book, like now for example, I've been planning my new novel. I always start my books on January 8. And it's not only superstition, it's also discipline. And I had everything planned for January 8 to start a wonderful novel that I know will be a success, it will be wonderful, my publishers would be delighted. It has everything in it. And I also would have a lot of help because my mom was going to help me with the research. But then when I turned on the computer on January 8, and I wrote the first sentence with an open heart, I realized that I was not going to write that book, at least not now, and maybe never. And the book that I have inside, like a pregnancy in my belly really, in my womb, not in my mind, is quite a different book from all the other books I have written before. A book that my publishers will hate, and probably, maybe, will never be published. But it's a book that I really need to write because it comes out of so much pain that if I don't write it I'll die. So that's what it is about. It's about separation, and death, and loss. So it's always a very heavy emotion, very deep, and very painful. However, the process of writing even if the thing is heavy is wonderful. It's wonderful.

I was talking today to a writer who says, "I'm always terrified that I won't be able to finish this book."

And I said, "What are you worried about? Writing is like making love; don't worry about the orgasm, just worry about the process. That's what it is about."

So just enjoy the process of writing and don't worry about the end. Unfortunately it happens sometimes.

J.S.B.: Well, I have yet to write anything fictional in the sense that both of you write fiction, but it seems to me, when I hear about your process that you really live with your characters; they seem to be quite real folks that communicate and move in and out of your psyche. And I think that I've ended up writing in a sort of in-between place in which I write nonfiction, but because I bring so much myth and metaphor, real stories from real people inform me about the meaning of the myth. And I do in my work and in my writing have to get into the place of what I am writing, and in an imaginative way, drawing upon some familiar experience that is like what I am writing of. It's the same process of intuitively feeling my way through my patients' stories, is to touch in with something that is like that, that then can kind of move in and expand into an emphatic understanding. If I can't feel what someone is telling me, I don't get it. And so I know when I write and maybe similar in some ways to your—I'd be interested in how similar it is—but like if I am writing about a character, a myth character, whether it be, say, Brünhilde or Demeter or Persephone, I move into that archetype, so that the first time

I wrote *Goddesses in Everywoman*, every single chapter was written in the style of that particular archetype. And so Aphrodite was beautiful and flowing, and Persephone was very vague, and Athena was very mental and logical and thinking. And then I had an editorial input that said, "Well, if you're gonna talk about how Hera is with marriage, you have to say what the other archetypes do too." And so then it required that I move in and think about, feel about how the archetypes would be. Think about women I knew who embodied this, what it was like. And there was a weaving kind of experience so that the women who were with each archetype were sort of in the room with me, and the part of me that was like them moved into it too. And so there was a kind of fictional quality that—

A.W.: Something that I always wanted to ask you, though—does it bother you that they're all separate and not all of these things in one? I always get really kind of confused when I'm thinking of this because they always feel like they're fractured, no?

J.S.B.: Well, you have different characters in your books, and each character, you have to get into them in order to express them. People tell me their dreams, I think about my own dreams, getting to each character. And so it's like through the pieces, I get what the whole story is. So I don't end up with that feeling.

A.W.: But I was talking specifically about the goddesses, that if one is vague, and the other, one is the hearth keeper, I mean, what about the one who has everything?

J.S.B.: [laughing] That's rather pretentious, Alice.

A.W.: But you know, what was interesting, I was thinking as you were talking was how when I create a character, what is always the crowning moment for me is when I am somewhere in the world and my character walks in the door. And then I think, "Well, yes, you know, I knew you were there."

I.A.: In my case it works the other way around. I don't think I make up the characters from my imagination. I'm always inspired on someone that has walked through the door before. And somehow I relate to that character very strongly because I can—maybe I had some experience in my own life that is related to the character. And when I see the person I recognize the things that I want to write about.

J.S.B.: Now I'm curious, because I know in your current book, that I know is coming out in May, that you've written about a woman I've met, who inspired you, and she's your friend. And how is it, how does that work? How does it work that you write a book and you take your character through the story and this is your friend who inspired it, and there is some of her, there must be some of her story in it; how does it feel to be one of your friends who ends up in your books?

I.A.: I think that you should ask her. I think she hates it, by the way. Really, I have two persons that served as models, and [from] those two lives I created the character in the book. But of course my friend is the strongest part of that, let's say the strongest goddess in the character. And she told me her life very generously, and I told her that I was going to use her, because I tell this to all my friends, that everything they say can be used against them. I am an insatiable story hunter. So they know from the beginning, they know. And so she told me the story and I added some stuff that she didn't like very much, and I asked her if I could use her name in the book. And at the beginning she said yes, and when she heard the details of what I was writing she said, "No, you better find another name." So actually I did. And this person is in this room right now. I'm not going to ask her to stand up. So that's the way it works with me; it's always real people and real stories that I somehow transform.

A.W.: Well sometimes that's true with me too, but I think there's just a special feeling when you imagine someone so real. It's as if you draw them out of the air, I mean it really is as if there are spirits, and that you then create them.

I.A.: But I think there is a prophetic or clairvoyant quality in writing, and it comes from the fact that one is alone for so many hours concentrated on something. And you start like living the story. I have found out that, I have found out years later that something that I had written that I thought was made up was true, was always true. And always the confrontation with that thing scares me very much because I feel that there is something going out, something happening behind my back that is awful or wonderful, I don't know, and that I can't control. And the best example I have for this is in my second novel; my second novel is based on a political crime that happened in Chile, they killed lots of people, but this particular case is fifteen persons that were killed in a place near Santiago. And this happened in 1973 during the military coup. The bodies of these persons were hidden in an abandoned mine, and they were found five years later when I was already living in exile. I could not return to Chile. And the trials in Chile were military trials, and all the information was kept secret. So it was very difficult to research. Oh, I got some information, not a lot. And the gaps I filled with imagination. I thought it was imagination, but I was very angry, and I was very much into the story. And I spent two years really dealing with this in a very deep way. The book was published, and years later, four years later, I was able to return to my country, and I had a wonderful welcome. I was staying in my mom's house. And then one day a man came to speak with me, and he said that he absolutely needed to ask me something. When I wrote this story one of the things that I could not explain was how the Catholic church found out about these bodies and could intervene before the police could stop them, and before they could close the mine. And I made up a story that a priest had heard this in confession, and had gone to the mine and taken pictures. And when my mom read the book—she's my editor—she said, "This is totally unbelievable, because in a country with a dictatorship, no one would dare go during curfew to a place fifty kilometers from Santiago, driving a motorcycle, open the mine, take the pictures, and come back with the proofs to the crime. Now, you don't do that kind of thing."

I said, "Mom, this is a literary license, so we leave it that way."

Four years later when this man came to talk to me, he was a Jesuit priest, and he said that he had heard in confession that the bodies were in the mine, and he went there on a motorcycle, and he opened the mine, took the photographs, wrapped them in his blue sweater as is told in the book, and drove back with photographs to the cardinal. And I had this cold thing in my stomach. And I thought "What is this?"

Like, he said, "The only person who knows about this is the cardinal, how do you know?"

And I said, "I don't know, I suppose I had a dream."

And he never believed me because he thought that somehow, that I had, the cardinal had spoken or something. And he couldn't understand why he had not been caught by the police. And so I feel that there is—when you say that the character walks through the door, you've met the character before.

A.W.: Yes. You know, I'm so happy to know though that in confession there's actually something really said. But really, seriously, I mean because I've often thought how much more forceful the church would be if people really told the truth in confession. And if they said something about what was really happening in this society as opposed to who they were sleeping with . . . you know, and things like that.

I.A.: But I think there is a lot of information that goes on in confession, but they're not supposed to, I suppose for a psychologist, the same thing, you receive information and you can't use it. I don't know, I'm not a priest, and my last confession was when I was like fifteen, and it was just about sex. At that time I was the last virgin in town probably, so it was a very hard confession.

A.W.: But you know, the other thing I was thinking as you were speaking is that when I was writing *The Temple of my Familiar*, that whole period was so amazing for me because I felt that I had really connected with the ancient knowledge that we all have, and that it was really a matter not of trying to learn something, but of remembering. And that propelled me right through that book. And some of the things in it, honestly, I just knew them. I just knew them. I didn't learn them. I found I knew them. And this was a great delight.

I.A.: I think that really we know a lot of things that come out in dreams or when we are silent, and with no noise around us. We, like, get into that knowledge somehow. And maybe that's why writers need so much time alone. And that is so difficult to get, harder and harder.

J.S.B.: I think there's something about being in the quiet and going in and seeing what comes up out of one's innards, but I also think there's something about how when people are with each other and speak the truth of their lives that you pick up on more than just the facts or the story they're telling. The book I'm writing now, in part, says something about a period of traveling with three other women on a pilgrimage. And part of the story is like *Canterbury Tales*, is that you must, as you travel to these places, tell the story of what is going on in your life to these relative strangers that are coming together to take this journey with you. And I was thinking on reexperiencing the journey, which is part of the treasure of writing . . . you get to reexperience and savor and have the experience in a different form than speeded by. And I was thinking when I was reflecting on the experience how I had learned, so I knew so much more than was ever conveyed of what the other women knew than by talk. And there was something about being in a car together, like a little car together, telling each other stories, going to sacred places, and having kind of a semipermeable ego boundary, which I think is what women often do with each other. We pick up each other's experience. But I think there's something about whatever the collective unconscious is that is between us and not just in our head, or not through time. We pick things up and feel them. And also I was wondering something about how writing takes being very comfortable being by yourself. It has a quality of richness and timelessness in the absorption, but it would seem to me that one of the things is that we all ethnically, you and I, Alice, in this culture are ethnically different than the majority culture.

A.W.: Not for long. Don't worry about it, it's their problem. [laughter]

J.S.B.: And [I am] assuming that Isabel, being Chilean and all, and that she would fit really well with her culture. I found that's not true either. There's something about—what is it about being a stranger, never fitting in, that has helped us to be who we are? And how is it you didn't fit in, and what is this not-fitting-in stuff that makes such a difference?

A.W.: Well for me it's been really very good, because I think that at a very early age I was separated. You know, something happened to me, as happens often to creative people: I was put outside of the family enough so that I could then watch it from a distance and start to see how it worked. And also to have a critical view. People who are just in there, who fit, never have that distance. And so it's harder, I think, for them to be free of whatever is molding them. So even though it is very painful because you feel this incredible distance from, for instance, your family, what finally happens is that you at least have an opinion that can be very different from their opinion, and you grow not to really care that it's very different from their opinion because it is yours, and because it has been earned. And nothing can take it away from you. So it is also a delight to realize that you—your balloon string may have been cut, and you may not know where you're gonna drift. But what a view, and what a great feeling, what sweeping movements in space. So there's just also a real freedom to express however you are. I have very little sense, or fear, or concern, really, about what other people think about certain things that I do, because I feel that this early being put outside has given me the freedom to not be bound by that. If I'm not concerned about what the family thinks, there's no reason why I should be concerned about people I don't know.

J.S.B.: What put you outside?

A.W.: Pardon?

J.S.B.: What did put you outside?

A.W.: Oh, an act of violence, when my brother shot me when I was a child. And the subsequent refusal of my parents and my family to blame him for shooting me. Rather, I was blamed for being shot. And that sucked then, and it sucks now.

So it takes a very long time, especially when you are indoctrinated as a child that this is the reality, for you to grow into an understanding that your reality, the way you have experienced it, is absolutely valid, and that you can go on on that. And you really don't need them, whoever it is, giving you their version as the only way that life can be perceived.

I.A.: I have the feeling that often, it's not the society that puts you aside. One is just born that way. And even if in my case, for example, I should have fitted in my family, and in my country, and in the life I had, but I never did. I was just born different, or born with this weird thing in my head that maybe [I am] always an outsider, and I always felt a foreigner in my home, foreigner in my country, in my school. My parents were diplomats, so we moved a lot. And changing schools, changing friends, saying good-bye all the time, changing languages and places, was also part of it. But I think it was much deeper, and it came genetically. It was something I had inside. And I still have it; I never fit anywhere. I feel very foreign here, and I'm glad, because it's justified for once. But before it wasn't, you see, because I even looked quite Chilean, but I wasn't, I didn't feel that I could accept the rules of the religion I was brought up in, the social class I belonged to, the family, my family; I never fitted. I was a feminist when I was like five years old. The first time that my mom said, "Sit with your legs crossed," I became a feminist. . . . I was really small, and I kept that anger in me, and that the feeling that something was terribly unfair and that I had to, like, exorcize all that anger and that pain and the feeling that I was different. And then when I grew up as an adolescent, people, girls, were always in groups, and had to look like the group, and be part of the group, and talk like the group. And I could never fit in. I was always alone. And so I think that the writing is like everything that I've done in my life, and I've done crazy things. I think it's part of that, the feeling that I am different, or I feel different, and allowed to do whatever I want. And if it's shocking, well, too bad.

J.S.B.: Well, I had a very similar experience of moving around because I was in kindergarten in Southern California as the Second World War broke out, and if you were Japanese, you were supposed to go to a concentration camp. My family didn't; my father got us out of the state . . . you could be a free American citizen once you were out of the state. But I went to something like six or seven elementary schools between the time of kindergarten and the fourth grade, and everywhere I went I was very much aware that we were at war with Japan, and I'm pure Japanese, and I had to be very careful about what kind of prejudice, what kind of experience I might have. And so there was a clear stranger in a strange land, and very often I was the only Japanese face in many of the places that I was in. And so there was that kind of being in the border world. One of the things that . . . worked for me was that it seemed like the school I had been in was ahead of the school I'd go to next. So I had my intelligence to move and ability to be successful in school even though I didn't fit in. In a social sense I could excel in something that mattered to me and was respected. But I also learned how to make my way and not make very many waves, at least on an interpersonal level.

When I got from about junior high school or high school on, I started to get in trouble with authorities because I took them on when it felt to me that something really grossly unfair was happening. And to this day it's much easier for me to lead a cause than to speak from myself and risk someone getting personally angry at me. And it seemed like part of my experience as a resident in psychiatry was to learn how to not be automatically disarming so that someone could have their own experience of anger at me.

A.W.: Aha. Automatic disarmament.

J.S.B.: Yes. But the point I'm making is something about if you do not fit in, that potential to start to individuate early happens.

I.A.: I think that most of the creative process comes from a very unhappy childhood. That's why I'm trying to help my grandchildren have that experience. I did not succeed with my children, they are very straight kids, but I'm trying to do that with my grandchildren. My daughter is in the audience here, she's turning green.

A.W.: One of the things that I often am asked is how I create and whether I do a lot of drafts. And I always say I don't. And they say, "Why don't you do a lot of drafts?" And I realize after years of answering this question that I don't because when I was growing up, my circumstances were so miserable, because of my brothers and crowded conditions, that I really had to do everything in my head. I mean, I couldn't leave anything lying around because it would be destroyed. And so I had learned to just go through drafts, drafts, drafts in my head before putting anything on paper. But just in the last five years, I realize that I have now reached a stage where I don't always do that. And it's such a different way of creating. I actually feel safe enough—primarily, I think, because I have my own house—that I can do like normal writers do. I scratch out stuff and throw it over my shoulder. But it's such a different way, and it's interesting to me that it takes so long to understand the reasons for one's process, why you have to go away, why you need such solitude, why you feel your head is the only safe place.

I.A.: It is important to know why?

A.W.: It was interesting, Isabel, really, for me. You know, it was just a very interesting thing, because it's like you've had your childhood, but you spend the rest of your life understanding it. And I think of it that way now because I'm not threatened by it. I'm far enough away, I always say I have the whole Rocky range between me and Georgia. So I'm okay.

I.A.: What happened with this nasty brother?

A.W.: Oh, still nasty.

I.A.: He still exists?

A.W.: Oh yes.

I.A.: Oh gosh.

A.W.: Yes, well, you know, that's his life. And he will have to handle his life as best he can, and I'm going on with mine.

J.S.B.: I think there is really something about . . . of course I'm in the business of helping people remember their childhoods, so I support the notion. However, what I have found is that as we remember pieces of our childhood, it's like getting pieces of ourselves, even or maybe especially if it's painful, and there is an emotional affect that goes with the memory. And you not only get your history back, and liberate some kind of energy that was used to sort of put a lid on it, but you free up some part of yourself that wasn't free before to feel the feelings. And so you go into the world with a little more of yourself. And I do think there is something about their lives being important to some folks and not to others. I think that for me, my parents really did support and love me, and help me to feel secure in the world. So I always knew I was loved, but I never got the sense that they were interested in understanding me. And so consequently there is something about my own quest to be understood and to understand myself that is part of where I come from, I'm sure. And it is also something that people do a lot more of at a certain point in their second half of life. So your time may come.

I.A.: Actually, when I came to live in the United States, when people asked me, "What is amazing to you or shocking to you in this society?" I'd always say, "Therapists." I'd never seen so many therapists for so many things, and specialized in different things. I come from a culture where you only go to a therapist if you have to go to an asylum, and there's no way out. And the rest you go to your mom, or to your aunt, or you just talk in the family and somehow you solve it. There's no money and no time for therapy. And I always thought also that the writing, my writing, first I thought I was [a] perfectly adjusted human being, that I had no demons, that I had functioned all my life so well that I didn't need that. And I also thought that the writing came from unresolved emotions. If I had been in therapy, I wouldn't need to write. And I always thought that *The House of the Spirits* was triggered by deep emotions, that if I had treated those emotions in therapy—I didn't have money to pay a therapist at that time—I would have never written the book. The book was like a long catharsis that I needed to do because I could not let those feelings out in any other way. So I always feared therapy. And now for the first time in my life, I'm in therapy. I am actually; the circumstances, it sounds funny, but the circumstances are really dramatic. My daughter died recently, a few weeks ago. And my daughter was in a coma for a long time at home. And I thought that I was coping with the situation very well, and then when it was over and we had scattered her ashes, then I realized that I had something inside me that was like a cavern, something empty and cold, and dark, that I couldn't live with that. And so all my friends around me started insinuating therapists, different therapists; you are the first one to be insinuated to me, Jean. And it's really amazing how Jean and I met. She says that there's no such a thing as a coincidence, and maybe it's true. That day, it was a terrible day, and I was really desperate and I was going someplace, and there was a traffic jam, and I was so uncomfortable that I, instead of just waiting, I tried to turn around. I turned around; I ended up without even knowing how in Book Passage in Corte Madera bookstore. And Jean was going to have lunch with a friend in Strawberry, and she decided that she needed to buy a map. So she went to Book Passage, also I had never met Jean, and we had been there at the same moment, and the same place, but not knowing each other. And then the owner of the bookstore introduced us. She had been telling me all the time that I needed therapy and that I should go to Jean Bolen. So when I appeared in the bookstore, and

Jean did at the same time, she couldn't believe her eyes, the wonderful chance of introducing us. And so she said, Elaine said, "Isabel, this is Jean." There are so many Jeans in the world. And I was so upset that I didn't realize that it was her. So I somehow said, "Hi," and I said, "How are you doing?" And I started crying, and poor Jean thought that I was totally crazy, that I needed electroshock. That my depression couldn't be cured with therapy, that I needed something really much, much more aggressive. So we ended up being friends.

J.S.B.: You have just slandered my profession.

I.A.: Well anyhow, I wanted to say finally that I'm going to therapy right now, I've been five times in therapy. And it's like opening a Pandora's box. All the demons are coming out. All the stuff that I think I didn't have in my soul is there. And I just can't—I don't know how, what I'm going to do. But all the anger that I didn't know I had, the pain, lots of stuff that would be wonderful if I could put it down into a book instead of paying a therapist ninety bucks an hour.

A.W.: It'll just be a different kind of book, you know.

I.A.: Yeah, it will be a Marin County book.

A.W.: Isabel, you could always move.

J.S.B.: You know, I think there may be something to the situation of when you don't have anyone to communicate with, when you don't have anyone who can understand you, and you take the time to commune with yourself and words come that you want to put down on paper. I think there really may be something to what you're saying about the abortiveness of some creative process that goes into journal writing and talking to your therapist. I think that that's true. And there is something about needing to know the difference about when you want to give form, I think, to something and leave your therapist out of it.

I.A.: But therapists have a way of getting in your life. . . . The other day I was asked how my sex life was. And I said I'm not willing to talk about that with anybody except my husband. . . . "Isabel, you're paying for this." And I say, "Yeah, but this I'm not going to talk about." And then I thought, "Well, I'm wasting my money here. If I'm not willing to talk about this."

A.W.: Well maybe you should change your therapist. Because that is a rather direct question, without sort of leading.

I.A.: Well it was formulated in a different way, not so blunt.
   Are you in therapy?

A.W.: See, no, this is how you do it. You see someone infrequently when you feel a need. You may do it for a long time, but you don't think of it as something that you're just hooked on forever. Because that's not the way I think it has to be. So yes, I have been, and when I feel that I really need an hour or two to talk with someone who really cares and who can really hear me, then I will ask for an hour or two. And feel that . . . I get what I need. If I need three hours that's fine. But it's not such a big . . . I don't feel it in any way as a threatening thing. I feel it as something, another wonderful thing, in the world that will help me understand myself better and feel happier. So, Jean, I think a great deal of your profession.

J.S.B.: Well I think it's an enormous privilege to hear the truth of people's lives and be a witness to it and help people through a particular time in their life where there's a sense of needing both a witness and somebody who's with you on a journey. . . . I use a metaphor about how each of us is a protagonist in our own life story. And whether you write . . . there's a point of, at what point should you be writing a story and which point should you be telling it, and not giving it form, just letting it come? It's sort of like those many drafts; that's unself-conscious. But when I was a resident . . . I remember 'cause I have a very strong liberal arts background, I started to realize that when people tell their stories about what has really happened to them and they have a vocabulary, it's prose. If it's because it's so true and the words fit whatever it was that really happened, and the details are there, and that really is prose. And people need to know that.

A.W.: And poetry is the more inarticulate emotion. Is that it?

J.S.B.: Well, it's more to the music.

I.A.: An angel passed. We say that in Chile when there is a silence. Do you say that here? An angel passed when there is silence in the room.

Two angels passed.

J.S.B.: Maybe there is a question.

I.A.: Maybe there are many questions.

Q.: My question is to all three of you, but it comes from a line in Alice Walker, in your book *The Color Purple*. One of the most important paragraphs, pages, in that book to me was what began with the words "Tell me what your God looks like." And I know that was written a while ago, and I guess what I'd love to hear is, tell me what your God looks like now.

A.W.: Oh, I'd be happy to. My God is the earth and looks like the earth. That's it.

I.A.: I don't know what my God looks like because I don't know what kind of God I believe. I don't believe in the God I was taught when I was a child, and I don't believe God has a shape or a form or a face or a name. I think that it is something that is like oneness or wholeness, or one spirit, and we are all like part of this spirit. And if I can really accept that in my heart I can see myself in every human being, in every animal, in every soul. And it's very hard because sometimes it's very easy to recognize oneself in the people one likes and very hard to recognize oneself in the torturer, the rapist, the criminal. But when one thinks in terms of one universal unique spirit, you are just representations of that. It's difficult for me to talk about this because I'm like beginning to explore that, and . . . I don't have any answers, I just have the questions.

A.W.: I would just like to add that actually I can now put my belief on a bumper sticker. "The earth is my God, and nature is its spirit." So there.

J.S.B.: Well, mine's a more complex answer. The book that I am currently writing, which is part of the becoming a more personal person in my writing, is about my own, it's about a certain segment of my life, but it clearly is saying what I guess I have been asked to talk about, which is that the experiences that have made a difference in my life, that put me on the course of what it is I do and what it is I believe, have all been mystical experiences. That underneath this professional kid, there has been a very strong direct experience of divinity that, when I was sixteen, made me convinced that—it wasn't a conviction, it was one of those ineffable experiences in which one feels graced suddenly. And in that moment of grace, so humbled, and out of that humility, having a sense of deep service. And for me at sixteen with all my liberal arts and debater, verbal kinds of abilities, the conviction was that I was so fortunate and that I could never repay; it was within a God context at that point in my life, so I could never repay God for the gifts that I had except by doing for others. And I had the conviction at sixteen that I should be a medical doctor with no talent in sciences or math. And it really was not a very easy task for me to surrender to that and do badly in college and those classes that I didn't do very well in, which were the pre-med classes. And that's when I made a sort of deal with God that said, "Well, maybe I mistook the message, but I'll keep on course and apply to medical school. And if I get accepted, I guess it was right, and if they turn me down, I guess I misunderstood what I was supposed to do." Well, that got me on this course that has led to knowing God and that—and I didn't know until I went into psychiatry that it was true—that I really had a gift for it, and that this was my lifework. So there is something about following that. And then I call myself an "episcapagan" because somewhere along the line in my second half of life, I really had the experience of a different kind of divinity that could only happen within a context of people. And I was in a time of considerable anguish. And a woman asked me how I was, and I started to cry. And she came over, and she held me. And I had this sense of us both being embraced by something that was Goddess, different. [It] wasn't transcendent God, which had been my experience before, it was something else. And that has led me to know something that I didn't know before that is the impetus for what was then the next phase of my life, which ends up getting somewhere close to where the divinity of the earth, and the sacredness of the body, and a knowledge that comes to women is part of it all.

Q.: I'd like to ask you, it's kind of like a two-part question: you both talked about the pain of creativity, you said that you were facedown on the earth, you talked about a book inside of you that's too painful to write. I'd like to hear more about that pain of creativity. And then another question, is there a time when you can write from a different place, not from the pain, but more of a centeredness, even from joy, and probably from the satisfaction that you were talking about, the satisfaction of a later time in a woman's life?

A.W.: Well, for me, just because what is painful is often understanding that what I'm writing about someone is actually living, millions of people. So that's really very painful. But to know that I can myself create a story which will show that pain and make people feel it, intuit it, there's nothing more joyful. So they're not really separate things. There are also times when you're not writing about something that is really crushing to the spirit and there's a great deal of joy just in being able to share one's sense of the unfolding of nature and the connection of people with the earth. I wrote an essay once about how when I was finishing *The Temple of My Familiar*, and all during the writing of that book, because I was so aware of our connection to animals, animals came from everywhere to be around me, to be with me. And I was just amazed; it was just so clearly a period when somehow what I was writing about, and mainly my deep feeling about animals that started to surface, brought into my life creatures of every kind. I mean some that had never, I think, been on this land. Well, maybe not in a hundred years.

I.A.: I have books and stories that I have written out of joy. *Eva Luna* is a book that I wrote when I realized how joyful and wonderful it was to be a woman. I always wanted to be a man. In the society I was born in it's much easier to be a man in every sense. It was much better to be one of my brothers. And then when I was around fortysomething I realized that I have done all the things that men do, but I had this wonderful privilege of being a mother, of being allowed to be emotional, of having this connection with other women that men usually don't have because they're competing. And so I realize all this, and that book came out of joy. But there is also a lot of anger in that book, and that's the anger of the injustice that women are done permanently. So it's a mixture of things, but the process of writing is always joyful. Even when you write about torture it's joyful. I think you had a question now.

Q.: You talked about a sense of entitlement when you have earned your creative right by having suffered and experienced alienation as a child, and this is something I do understand. I'm still finding that when I write about certain aspects that obviously are preempted by my life experience, I still have blocks where enormous guilt comes up that I am betraying and being disloyal to people who still don't understand what I have come through, and that my writing exposes what I perceive as the lie of their life. And I just wonder if you have any responses about how you deal with that kind of dilemma that comes up. I'm thinking specifically of, like, I'm writing a play which has a mother/daughter relationship and I have enormous guilt that I am really being disloyal to my mother. And even though I'm not writing about her, per se.

I.A.: Well, I can answer part of the question. There's always fear and guilt. I write a lot about relationships, and my mom is the only person who reads my books before they're published. And I sometimes feel the guilt, but writing is something that you have to do. You don't have a choice. And if you are offending people, and you are revealing secrets, it's too bad. You are helpless. You have to do it. And just go ahead and do it. I've betrayed my friends, my lovers, my husband, my children, everybody. And writing is about life and about betraying.

A.W.: I think of it in a slightly different way, which is that we really, especially as women, we must learn to be loyal to ourselves.

I.A.: But often to be loyal to yourself you have to betray others. In your writing you have to do it.

A.W.: But that's what I'm saying. Yeah, but if you think of it as being loyal to yourself rather than disloyal to your mother, I think this will relieve a lot of your guilt.

J.S.B.: Well, you know, it is really not about writing, it's about leading an authentic life that differs from what your mother expected you to do and say. And you don't have to do it through your writing, you have to do it through your life however you express it. And there is guilt. There is guilt at being different, at not meeting expectations; you feel guilty for being visible about something that our parents' generation would never be visible about, all kinds of things. And so I don't think that's about writing, I think that's about life, and that's about being willing to tell your story, what you perceive, and then wait for either lightning to strike or for the earth to sort of dissolve under you. And then you find it does not.

Q.: Hi. Each of you has spoken about the spiritual center from which you write, and I guess my question for each of you is what caused you to say yes to it rather than saying no? And just a small question for Alice because my daughter sent me here with a mission: she loves your children's book [Finding] the Green Stone, and I'd like to be able to go back and tell her something about the writing of that.

J.S.B.: I didn't know you wrote a book called Finding the Green Stone.

A.W.: I did. I think that the answer to the first question is that really it's a matter of necessity, and that you write to save your life is really true. And so far it's been a very sturdy kind of ladder, you know, out of the pit. About writing Finding the Green Stone, it has a kind of complicated, and I don't even know if I remember everything, but about thirteen years ago my mother had a stroke, and it debilitated her, and this is the woman who'd always been just this enormously energetic earth goddess, and so it's a great weight to even think about her incapacitated. But I started I think mourning for her, and somehow I at the same time was reading about a ceremony in some really ancient culture where when people die they have a green stone placed in their mouths to remind them on the journey that rebirth is always the next step. So the green stone as a symbol grew out of that. And I more or less dreamed the story of Finding the Green Stone, because I realized that you do, you come into life with your own green stone, your own vibrant life, your own heart, your own clear pure spirit. But this is sometimes damaged and destroyed if you're not very careful. And sometimes you do it yourself. And I wanted to write a story for children in which there is a character who does this to himself, who really mutilates his own spirit because of his really awful behavior. But I wanted also to show that we are healed in spirit in community, and so that is what happens. And that for us in this time, unlike any other time ever, we are able to be healed in a community that is incredibly diverse. So that everybody is our community.

Q.: Hi. I wanted to ask you about witnessing. I think that in some parts of the Christian church "witnessing" is a word that people use a lot to talk about their faith, but I also know that in my own life I've experienced both being a witness to other people's lives and changes, and seeing how I learned to witness my own that felt very hidden. I think actually that was something I read that Alice Walker wrote about; how do we survive really really painful awful times? And you said that there's somebody there that witnesses you and sees the shining spirit underneath it all. And that was a real gift to me because I started thinking of the people who had been witnesses in my life when others had not been capable of doing it. But I just wondered if "witness" was a word, being a witness and being witnessed, was a word that had any resonance for any of you both as writers and spiritual beings.

A.W.: Very much for me, but do you want to . . . ?

I.A.: Go ahead, take it.

A.W.: Well, I just really feel that if you're in a situation where something horrible is happening, and soul is being destroyed, spirit is being crushed, if you can't do anything else, you can witness it. And that is something that you do in your role as storyteller. You see, you take it in, you know this, you cannot not know it. And that's why in writing a book like *Possessing the Secret of Joy* I see myself very much in the role of witness. That if nothing else, I say that I know that this is happening. I know that these children are suffering, I know that these women are in pain. And I think that there is power in that because if you have ever been hurt in privacy by anyone, and you have a sense that no one knows this, and this is something that is yours alone to bear, you know how hard that is, it's a double oppression. But if you have just one person, a teacher, or a friend, or whoever, who at least stands beside you in this role as someone who just knows, then whatever the hurt is is shared.

J.S.B.: I feel really strongly about that also. I really think that one of the major functions of a friend or a therapist is being a witness to the life story of another person. And that when somebody that has had something happen to them that makes them feel beyond the pale, which often is true of women who as children were incested, for Vietnam War veterans who did things and saw things that shouldn't have happened, that if they could tell the story to one other person, and often there's a compulsion to tell it, and tell it, and tell it, and that's also why sometimes you need a therapist, because you are gonna wear out your friends. But that there is a community of human souls for which every other human being is an intercessor and ambassador, a healer, a means to bring that beyond-the-pale person into community, but only if they will tell the truth of the story of what happened and find that another human being can accept them and understand and not shun them for what happened to them. And that is what people do for one another when they tell the story and the story is accepted, received, witnessed. That's a major function of what we can do for one another.

I.A.: I also feel very strongly about this because I had the mission of being a witness twenty years ago. And that really changed my life forever. I was a journalist in Chile during the military coup in 1973, and a few journalists decided that our mission was to be the witness of what was going on, what was happening. And although we could not publish the information, we had to remember, we had to be like a living memory, the witness of what was going on. And I felt that when I left my country and went into exile, I had betrayed that cause in a very deep way. And for many years I was like in silence, and I felt that as a witness, I had failed. And everything that I had witnessed was inside me like a heavy load that I was carrying along. All these untold stories, these unwritten words, these emotions that were there without accomplishing what I had to do, and that was to be witness to this and tell the world what had happened. And I always thought that the only way I could do that was through journalism, and the fact that I was not able to work as a journalist made me feel like an invalid. And then one day I started writing books. And in my first book, in my second book, and every time I write, and every time I talk in public, this comes out again. And I feel like being a witness is still my mission in the world, and this is what I do when I tell stories. Before it was about torture, and about people who were desperate, and about dictatorship and abuse and violence. Now it's other things, but it's always about that. Storytelling is about telling other people's stories, and that's being a witness.

A.W.: I'd just like to add a little story. My first novel, *The Third Life of Grange Copeland*, grew out of the need to witness the murder of a woman when I was thirteen. There was a woman who was murdered by her husband as she came home on Christmas day with a bag of groceries that she had managed to buy. And I saw her body because my sister was the cosmetologist at the funeral home. And I would sometimes be there, and she took me into this room. And there was this woman, and in this little town they carry the bodies to the funeral home in wicker baskets. And then they actually had them, they put the head on an iron pillow, they called it. It was so much like what they said, I was amazed. But there was this woman; she had lots of children, one of them was in my class, and this person had really shot her face off. And it was so, I was so young, and it was just so overwhelming that I couldn't really forget. And also that she had one shoe still on, and that shoe had an enormous hole in the bottom, and in that hole she had put newspaper. And this shoe, this foot, this face, this woman just lived with me. Because who would know? They didn't do anything really to her killer. Who would know what this woman's life was, who would know that she had worked all that week as a maid for $7, that she had gone and tried to make Christmas for her children? And here she comes with this little bag of food, and then she's met with this. And who would know, who would know about this, who would care? But in the role of storyteller and witness, years later, I had to learn to be able to tell her story. I was able to do this, and it is a way in which I really think that you bring some peace to yourself, but also to the person that you are witnessing.

Q.: Most of us, I think, start our writing, birthing, creating process with what we see, and autobiographical experiences, and what we witness, and I'm interested in what is the process moving from that into fiction, and telling those truths through fiction.

I.A.: Well I began as a journalist, and I was supposed to be objective. I never was really, but you were supposed to be, expected at least. And I moved to fiction because I had a period of silence, like eight years, that

I couldn't write, and I couldn't do anything, I was just paralyzed. And then when I moved into fiction, I used all the techniques and everything that I used in journalism, I just moved it over to literature. And it worked very well. I could finally be myself in the sense that I could not be objective, I could be in the middle of the story if I wanted to. That I could not do when I was a journalist. So it was a swift change.

A.W.: I love the freedom of fiction. It really is just wonderful.

I.A.: And you can say the deepest truth with the lines of fiction. Somehow it comes out, that truth comes so much easier when you tell it through fiction. In storytelling all the hidden truths are there even if there's a lot of fantasy around it.

J.S.B.: The stories that both of you write are true.

I.A.: In a way they are.

J.S.B.: They're true to the human experience. They move people. They're true.

I.A.: Right, I agree.

Q.: She just asked my question. I'm very interested in that idea too, the difference between the fiction and the nonfiction. And do you decide, Alice in particular, because you write in many different forms, do you decide what form you're going to write in? Is it something you want to say, or do you find that when you're in that contemplative place it speaks to you in a particular way and then insists on being expressed in a certain way? . . . I'm interested in what that process is like for all of you.

A.W.: Well, a lot of it has to do with time. So that if I feel that something is going to be a novel, and that I want the freedom to explore it as a novel, I then know that I have to find a year to two years in which to be free myself so that I can be receptive to the growth of this. Poetry is quite different, it kind of strikes, and because it's short it doesn't usually take the setting aside of that kind of time, although time and contemplation is always good for whatever you're doing. Essays are usually, for me, things that strike me and that kind of grow over time, but I don't have to think in terms of just blocking out a long span of time. I can think more like a month or so, and not all together either.

J.S.B.: Well I thought the question was fiction/nonfiction and since I—

Q.: I'm just interested in what the process is like for each of you in terms of the form that you write in.

J.S.B.: Oh, the process for me is that I have a sense of having sort of cauldrons on my back burner. And I have a sense of a book that's forming, and I'm gathering the ingredients. And then when I am writing, if I'm writing from a deep place in myself, which is the only place to write from, . . . the universe lets me know that because synchronistic events keep happening, that the chapter that I'm writing needs just this poem, just this dream, just this whatever, and here it comes. And that happens. The actual doingness of it is—quite a number of years ago I asked a colleague who wrote a lot how on earth she did it with children. I had kids, she had kids, she was a psychiatrist as I was. And I wondered how did you ever find time to write, and she said, "Oh, there's no problem, I have insomnia." And out of that came a thought, which was I looked at my mother and she seemed to do fine without much sleep. What is this idea that I needed eight hours of sleep anyway? And I played with the idea, and my psyche got it. And I started to get up naturally, which I now always do when I'm writing, I get up somewhere around five because it's like an internal clock says, "Time to get up." And then I can get totally absorbed, and I write for many hours, lose track of time, and then go off and do my other aspects of my life, and when I come back it's like ready to go again. And I often have felt that the way I write is something to do with the discipline of seeing patients, that is, I see people once or twice a week, and they come in the door and I'm prepared to be involved in their story, and then they go. And unless there's something very troubling it stops until they come in the door the next week. I found that I could relate to my writing that same way, as an ongoing health process. So there's no warm-up, I don't have any time to spend thinking about "I'm going to write," sharpening pencils, or any of the stuff that I hear people do; I don't. I just sit down and I meet the experience.

A.W.: I would just like to agree with you that it is when the synchronistic support is there that you really know that you're doing what you should be doing. And it really does feel exactly as if you are just being supported in everything you're doing, just so that you can do it well. It's a wonderful feeling.

Q.: I know the experience, it's fantastic. It does propel itself, it creates a momentum. What about when that euphoria is not carrying you? You know, like, taking it all the way, what I have experience with is that in the process of bringing it to a final product, I burn out. And . . . when you're using the craft and trying to bring it into a final form, somehow . . . you get tired of it, I get tired of it.

A.W.: Well, just remember that it's about you, it's not about the thing you're making really. You're making something, but really you're making you. And so if the euphoria isn't there, go do something else that needs doing, you know, fix your whatever. But I think that if you love doing whatever it is, creativity is really wonderful. You want to create something that finally you hold in your hands, but actually maybe it's not about that. Maybe actually what you are doing is something else entirely.

C.D.: I'm curious since the subtitle was something about giving birth; I feel like I'm still being born as a writer, and I'm wondering if you could talk a little bit about your birth as writers. You're very accomplished right now, but I'm sure you didn't start out that way, and I'd love to hear how it happened and what you think can happen for other people in the process.

Q.: I don't remember very well. Actually, I think that I was telling stories all my life, and in a way I never thought that I could be a writer because it was such a big word. And women in my generation, in the place I was born, were not supposed to be creative, we were supposed to be good wives and help our husbands to be brilliant; they should be brilliant. And I tried hard; it didn't work.

A.W.: He was never brilliant, huh?

I.A.: He was never brilliant. Well anyhow, then I was a journalist. Which was like I was always, like, in the periphery of literature. More or less like literature, but we're not literature, because I never dared say to myself, "Well, I'm a writer," or "I want to be a writer." Actually, I wrote, I published three books before I could fill a form in an airplane and say "writer" instead of "housewife" or "journalist" or whatever. And then in 1981 we received a phone call from Chile when my grandfather was dying, and my grandfather was a very important character, very important person in my life. He was the male model that I had when I was a child, in my early childhood. And I couldn't go back to Chile and bid farewell in a way, and tell him that I remembered everything, that he would never die because I had everything that he had told me stored inside. And I began a letter, a sort of spiritual letter that I knew he would never receive, and that's how *The House of the Spirits* was born. It was . . . like writing in trance. I didn't have to think about it, it just came, voices, voices that I was hearing. And I just poured out everything I wanted to say. And most of it is the story of my family.

J.S.B.: Now, I think that writing . . . you have to have the idea that you can do something before you can do it. And that we give it to each other. I think that one of the major reasons why I write has to do with I kept running into everybody who wrote. And the sort of sense is, well, you know, when you first read books, you think that somebody who writes a book is really in some kind of special category. Then when you start hanging out with people who write books, you figure, well, they could do this, it's not such a big deal.

A.W.: Well, when I was—my mother tells this story—she says that when I was crawling, she would be looking for me and I would have crawled behind the house with the Sears, Roebuck catalog and a twig, and I would be busily writing in this, now. So I don't know what the model was for that, Jean. And then later I had this habit of talking to spirits, I called them, but just standing up on the porch and talking, and feeling or seeming to feel that I had a response. And I've since come to realize that in a way it was as if all the people who are now real in my life and in those chairs were these spirits who somehow I was trying to reach even as a three-, four-, or five-year-old. So it has always felt very natural, very organic, this way of reaching out.

I.A.: Excuse me, but this poor lady has been standing there for forty-five minutes; can she ask her question?

Q: Thank you very much. My question actually comes from the Buddhist tradition. Although I have written many things and been lucky enough to publish a few, I always, when I sit down at the computer, I always feel like I have never written before. I always feel like a beginner. And I always thought this was a tremendous liability. And then I read *Zen Mind, Beginner's Mind*, and I thought, "Well, maybe this isn't such a liability. Maybe it's great to start anew every time. Maybe it's okay that even though you can stack up the stories in front of you and say, 'Hey, I did that,' it doesn't help. That that's okay." And I'm just wondering if this echoes with you at all.

A.W.: Oh, it does very much with me. I always feel like this, and it's true too that you are a beginner always. And that's really lovely. And whatever you create after all is different. I mean, this is not true for every writer that we know in the culture, but we are easily bored by repetition, our own repetition and anybody else's. So it has to be you.

I.A.: I have been for eleven years, and I have a feeling that I haven't learned anything. It's true that every time I face a new book and I turn on the computer on January 8, I don't know anything. I don't remember the mistakes I made before, and I usually make them again. And it's always a new story, and each story has a way of being told, has a tone, a rhythm, a language of its own. And you have to be very respectful. So I can never use the formula that worked with another book.

J.S.B.: I feel the same way, because each time it is a new paragraph, a new chapter, and it is new if I am in the place of feeling and imagery. And out of that comes a dialogue where examples or metaphors come up as if from some other place other than my mind. If I write from a place that has been trained, I use big words, it's boring, I quit and go do something else. So that only in that beginner's mind of being totally engrossed and rather delighted when a right phrase comes up, it's an adventure. And that's when the writing is juicy versus when it's not.

I.A.: But anyhow I think that before we finish we should say that there is nothing to it really. Writing is not such a big deal. It's just sitting there and doing it, and it's very joyful and very simple.

A.W.: And also you do it in bed often.

7

"The Richness of the Very Ordinary Stuff": A Conversation with Jody Hoy (1994)

JODY HOY: What was it like growing up the eighth of eight children? How did being part of a large family affect you? You write of the black southern writer's inheritance of a sense of community; did the size of your family also play a part in developing the passion for community and connectedness in your work?

ALICE WALKER: Negatively, in a way. I was the last child and in some ways a neglected child, although this was not something that was deliberate: my parents both worked, and my mother and my father were very much partners in what they did. I have five brothers and two sisters, and we lived in very small, substandard houses from which we were often driven after a year by the landlord, who exploited the labor of the entire family. I was conscious of crowdedness and of not having enough of various things, although we always had lots of food, and my mother was a genius, she could create clothing out of all kinds of odds and ends that people gave her.

I think the reason I love community and I believe in it is because the African saying that it takes a whole village to raise a child is true—and part of the village certainly helped my mother raise me. For instance, the first clothing I received was not from my parents but from the woman who became my first-grade teacher. So I have a sense of the ways in which people in the community can actually shape lives. What is very sad in this culture, and more and more all over the world, is that people are often afraid to be a community to children because there is so little respect for elders. And, generally, respect has declined.

J.H.: Were you writing before you received formal training? Did your own method and style begin to evolve at that point, or did it come later? Where did it come from?

A.W.: My mother claims that I was writing with a twig into the margins of a Sears, Roebuck catalog when I was crawling, so sometimes I think it's a past-life activity. At other times I just think it was cheaper to write than to play the piano or paint, and that I was able to write about things that seemed far removed from my own misery but, in fact, reflected that misery. You develop what is called style by being as true as you can possibly be to the story you're telling and to give it all the time and space that it needs to be born whole. That's what style is, in a way; for me, that's what it has been.

J.H.: How did you transform yourself from "someone nearly devastated by childhood suffering" into "someone who loves life and knows pleasure and joy in spite of it"?

A.W.: How did I do that? I think I did that by working very hard. But the foundation for that was my mother's connection to the earth, and to wildness, and to landscape, and to natural beauty. Without that foundation in the natural world I would have found it exceedingly difficult to survive.

J.H.: You began *Warrior Marks* by talking about how important it is that we "adhere to our own particular way," "in being true to our most individual soul." Was there a specific moment in your life when you became aware of the choice to be true to your own soul, that you started living out that choice consciously? If so, what has been the cost, and what have been the benefits?

A.W.: I don't know if I can actually pinpoint a moment; in any life there would have to be many moments. For instance, when I was a student at Spelman, in Atlanta, I was there on scholarship and had struggled very hard to get there, yet I found it to be a fairly oppressive place. That made me terribly unhappy and I had to make a decision to leave, even though I didn't know where I was going. Fortunately, one of my professors recommended Sarah Lawrence (which I had never heard of) as an alternative to Spelman. I made that choice without any assistance or guidance from my family because they also didn't know Sarah Lawrence—actually, they didn't know Spelman either.

I think that life is a series of choices like that, and they just come one after the other. It's about all kinds of things—where you will live, how you will live. When I went to Mississippi to live with my husband in an illegal marriage, it was necessary to decide consciously that this was where I would be, and that if I couldn't be there, there was no point in trying to be anywhere else because, after all, this is one country. If there are places in it where you feel like you can't be—because of segregation, racism, bad laws—then it seems necessary to question one's citizenship. Mississippi's "antimiscegenation" law said I was not a citizen; at the time this seemed to me really unacceptable.

J.H.: Do you have any desire to return to the South, or are you settled in Northern California?

A.W.: I have some commitments there, but I have no desire to settle and live in the South. When I lived in Georgia during my formative years, and then when I lived in Mississippi, it was extremely violent, and for a long time that distracted me from the fact that the other part of it is often boring. It's enough to have lived there for all the years that I did. I don't really want to go back.

J.H.: In *In Search of Our Mothers' Gardens*, you said that, like Rilke, you came to understand that "even loneliness has a use and that sadness is positively the wellspring of creativity." Could you expand on that? And how is that reflected in your own life?

A.W.: I think suffering has a use, although at the time you can't quite figure it out. I remember having a very difficult time about ten or fifteen years ago, and I was very aware that I was suffering. I was reading *The Gnostic Gospels*, Elaine Pagels's book, and there was a quote from Jesus in the Gospels that didn't make it into the Bible (it seems to me that his best stuff was censored). He said if you learn to suffer, if you learn *how* to suffer, you will not suffer. It was such a mysterious thing to say, and yet I felt I understood it in the sense that suffering is inescapable, it's totally inescapable. So your task is to accept it as suffering, and to get to know it, and to learn it, and to learn how to do it.

One of the ways you can learn how to do it is not to inflict it on other people, unless you just can't help it. You can try to know it so well that it doesn't really surprise you and leave you flabbergasted or enraged. To know it, to learn how to suffer, to learn what suffering is, what it feels like, not to deny it, not to deny that it's happening, not to deny that it's happening to you and to make of it a companion—it's right there.

And true enough, when I learned how to suffer, which was mainly a matter of *accepting* that I was and that it was not to be escaped, I suffered much less! It was amazing—I felt an instant lightening of spirit.

There's another story in *The Gnostic Gospels* about how the crucifixion is symbolic, that it's not the most important thing actually happening there. What actually happens is that the spirit of Jesus at this point rises above his own tortured body, laughing. It's not that he's not being killed, it's not that he's not being vilified and turned against. But he has managed to see crucifixion as part of what seriously out-of-balance people can do to you, and to see the humor of it, and to understand that life is very long, time is very long, and you're pretty much very small, and even your suffering, whatever it is, can be seen in the context of what the whole world is going through.

J.H.: Is it possible to separate Christianity from patriarchy? Must one give up Christianity in order to free oneself from patriarchy?

A.W.: I think we should just kidnap Christ and go off with him; he's the best of the whole bunch. I say that having struggled for many years trying to deny him, get rid of him, or ignore him, because he is a captive of the church and they use him for absolutely everything. I feel myself to be a born-again pagan and quite happy in nature. And I feel a great love for Jesus as a teacher and as a very feminine soul, especially during that time. His tenderness, his caring quality always makes me think of someone who was raised by his mother. I mean, he's the son of a feminist. You can always tell the son of a feminist because generally speaking there is that ease that they have with women, and they seem to grip ("grip" is one of my daughter's words) things without having to have every little thing explained. You don't have to tell them that women don't like to be called "bitch" or "witch" or whatever in a negative way: they know this. It's a whole different sensibility from the sensibility of boys who are brought up with fathers in a patriarchal household. I love the sons of my feminist friends; they are very easy to be with, they're funny.

J.H.: In [an] interview, Marilyn French said that the true goal of feminism was to transform the world. In *Warrior Marks*, your colleague Pratibha Parmar said, "We need to be willing to transcend all our differences without ignoring them, to build new communities that bring us nearer to our utopian ideals, to continue to redefine our ideas about womanhood and feminist politics, and to embrace concepts of justice and equality while at the same time recognizing the complexities of our diverse identities." Is that possible? Are you optimistic about women's joining together to become a force for change? Do you agree with Marilyn French that we are living through the end of Western civilization as we know it?

A.W.: We're the only hope. Whether we can succeed is a question, but for sure we have to attempt it if we want to have any kind of world at all. The patriarchy has ruined the world; if it's not clear by now, I don't know what people need. And of course, yes, Western civilization, the world itself as we knew it, is no more.

When I was a child, I assumed that the world was pretty much stable, that it was endless, that it was ever generative. I thought that it was clean, that the waters were pure, that the air was pure—and a lot of that was true. But even then they were felling the forests at an incredible rate, so that now there are no big trees in Georgia except the ones that have been carefully preserved, like the giant oaks and the plantation tree boulevards.

I would only add that, for me, the alliance is between women and children: it is us. I think that children should be permitted to vote; I think that they have to have much more of a say in running the world and that a twelve-year-old child, boy or girl, is often much more compassionate, astute, and openhearted than the politicians who are regularly elected and who waste our money on extremely foolish things and who do damage every day.

Children have been disenfranchised, they have been ignored, but they are natural allies of women and of men who understand that the whole thing has to change for any kind of high-quality life to continue.

J.H.: Was it difficult raising your own child and doing your writing?

A.W.: Actually, [my daughter] was born three days after I finished my first novel, so she came at a natural break in the process of writing. I devoted myself to her for one full year, night and day, and then I enrolled her for half a day in the day care down the street. I could see the house from our yard, and I liked the woman who ran it. When we went to the Radcliffe Institute, she went to the Radcliffe day care, and I wrote and I took care of her. It was difficult—there were times when she was sick and it was very hard to get a doctor, and all those things—but I would have to say that I grew to understand the African woman who does her work with her child on her back, that this is all just part of life, this is part of what is. As long as you are not competing with some man who thinks that his balls are what can make you a writer, there's no problem. You just write as well as you can and you raise your child as well as you can.

Another way of thinking about it, which I really feel now, is that time is all there is, so there's no hurry either, there's no rush to do it. It's a very full life because a child connects you to the coming generations. Just from giving birth I felt a new understanding and respect for women. And then, because it is so miraculous, the whole process of conception, and pregnancy, and giving birth, and watching a child grow brought the miracle of life right up close where I could watch it every day.

When I look at my daughter, I sometimes see the little child crawling, or the little girl in the yellow jumper who's rushing out to play with her friends, or the eleven-year-old who has a crush on somebody. To watch a tiny being grow up until today she is much taller than I am, she's so smart, and caring, and such a good person—it's just amazing.

J.H.: You said some time ago, "I am preoccupied with the spiritual survival, the survival *whole* of my people. But beyond that, I am committed to exploring the oppressions, the insanities, the loyalties and the triumphs of black women." Would you add anything to that today?

A.W.: From *Living by the Word* to *The Temple of My Familiar*, I think in those books especially, I delved into my fascination with and interest in nature, and my interest in tracing my own spiritual ancestry all the way back to five hundred thousand years of wherever. It became really crucial to me to reconnect with the prehistoric, because the historic—for women especially, and for people of color—is so negative and so one-sided. And it truly is *history*—it just leaves us out, or we are shown in such mutilated ways that the depictions of us are not helpful.

So I started dreaming my way back and through all of these lifetimes on this planet. Just in the natural course of existence my focus has moved to include more than people.

J.H.: Do you have a familiar? And if so, what is it?

A.W.: What I was working on with *The Temple of My Familiar* was getting to the understanding for myself that your familiar is your own free spirit, and freedom is its temple. And that is what I have: that is my familiar. Frida [Walker's cat, named after painter Frida Kahlo] tries to be my familiar, but she just represents that part of myself which is the inner twin, the one who is free and is totally committed to being authentic, to being a free person. Your familiar is your own free spirit.

J.H.: In one of the essays in *In Search of Our Mothers' Gardens*, you talked about your aunts and your mother who worked on a farm and had strong muscles and would go out after working on the farm. "It is because of them that I know women can do anything, and that one's sexuality is not affected by one's work." If one's sexuality is not affected by one's work, what *does* affect one's sexuality?

A.W.: Well, one's passion, basically. I think it's not just in philosophy or even "life" that you follow your bliss, but you also follow your bliss sexually. I mean, that is what affects your sexuality—what you're attracted to and what you're drawn to and where your passion takes you. This doesn't always have anything to do with other people's notion of what *should* move you.

I was writing in *Possessing the Secret of Joy* about a pansexual person, someone who is turned on by waterfalls, and elephant rides, and horseback riding, and all of that. There was one reviewer who found this very funny, but actually there *are* women who are orgasmic riding horses and elephants and waterfalls.

I think of sexuality as something that, like spirit, has been colonized. It's the Bible again, that book that has done so much damage to women's self-image and their notion of what they're about. It says something like,

"Your desire will just be for your husband." In other words, if you're a woman, you're only supposed to be turned on to men. That's so limiting! It's hard to believe that people would limit themselves to men, or even to people. It's a world that is full of great sensuous experiences and it's like committing yourself to one religion or one way of thinking about things when in fact, the more we learn, the more mysterious the universe is. There is nothing that is solid, there is nothing that is hard, there *is* no hard copy. The universe is full of space, and full of movement, and full of flux, and full of change. That's the nature of what reality there is.

J.H.: I loved the section on Fanny and kissing in *Temple of My Familiar* and the wonderful descriptions of kissing. Kissing is fast becoming a lost art; one has only to look at American film and television actors, who are embarassingly terrible kissers. By resuscitating kissing in this country do you think we might succeed in bringing back intimacy?

A.W.: Oh, I think so! I am a great kisser myself; I love to kiss. Kissing is in many ways more a spiritual connection than making love because you exchange breath, and breath is the most ever-present, everlasting thing that you will ever have as a human being who is alive; it's very special. I just did a yoga retreat with a wonderful woman named Angela Farmer, and she was speaking of the breath as your most enduring lover. When you kiss, that is what you are offering, and that is what you are receiving. So it is a very high art and it's a very high expression of soul.

J.H.: You are one of the most respected writers in America today. Yet you have said, "To be an artist and a black woman, even today, lowers our status in many respects rather than raises it." What *does* it mean today to be a black woman and an artist?

A.W.: Well, in many quarters that's still true. Black women writers are constantly attacked, and for instance, during *The Color Purple* film and book, these attacks were fast and furious, with people organizing to picket the film. Most of my life I have been called various things. I find it very difficult to talk about people's criticism and vilification; I accept it as something that they apparently need to do and will do, but I find no pleasure in it. With *Warrior Marks* there are many African women and American women, black and white, who take the position that genital mutilation is something that is not my business and not my place to write about, think about, or campaign against.

When you say "respected," there are people who do respect what I do, and that's very good. But there are also people who hate what I do and who are very vociferous about it and have been from the very beginning of my career. I don't see that this is unexpected. I knew when I started writing that everything I wrote would be very hard, that it would be hard for people to accept, it would be hard for them to accept whatever lifeway I was indulging in, and that there would be criticism and that there would be hostility. At times this has been very painful, at other times it has been less so.

J.H.: In an August '89 interview in *The Progressive*, Claudia Dreifus asked you about the pain of getting mixed reviews, primarily from male critics, and said they can hurt. You replied, "They can try. But what can I do about it? I can only persist in being myself." Who are you these days? And where do you find the strength and courage to be yourself?

A.W.: I don't see that I have an alternative. I'm very happy to exist in this one lifetime that I have for sure as me. It seems ridiculous to try to live your life at any time as anybody else or as anybody else's version of how you should be. It's a waste of time, really, and as I said, time is all you have, so why waste it? I find it amazing that people do, that there are people who care more about what other people think of them than they care about what they think of themselves. It's almost something that I can't grasp because the pleasure of being who you are is very great; there's nothing like it.

One of the things that I've been attacked for is my insistence on affirming my mother's Cherokee grandmother and the Scottish-Irish whoever-he-was rapist who was my father's grandfather. Their take on this is that somehow it's a way of trying to get away from being a black person, which I think is incredibly backward. What people fail to understand is that the real pleasure of life is in what is unique. The world has such incredible variety; why not join it, be that different thing, that other expression, since that is what you are anyway, and love it?

It is such an affirming pleasure to rummage through your soul and to find the lost Scottish-Irish whoever-he-was and take him to task, and to rummage through your soul and find this great-great-grandmother, who apparently was very mean, and who had a story of her own which we may never know. How did she get into the family? And why is it that so many of us in my family either look very much like her or we have characteristics that are very much hers?

And then the African. I go to Africa every once in a while and I feel so tender, I have a tenderness for that strain of who I am, it just overwhelms me. It's almost like a puzzle, to trace one's emotional attachment to one's ancestry. Like why, why do you have these loves and these uneasinesses?

J.H.: It's as if you belong to the whole world.

A.W.: Of course I do, and so do you, and so does everyone. So why sit in a corner somewhere and try to be just one thing when you are all of it? I'm listening to a wonderful tape on Ayurvedic medicine and the science of life. Their way of looking at reality is that we are all made up of five elements—earth, water, fire, air, and ether—and that, literally, you have attributes that correspond to these factors. Even without having known their way of thinking about it, that is the way I feel.

I feel like that same microscope that looks at a leaf and eventually finds nothing but emptiness and some tiny little thing in there at the end of the magnifying process, some tiny, tiny, tiny little thing that you can't even tell is there except by its shadow—that's exactly what's happening in me, that's what's happening everywhere, and that is matter, that is what is here on this planet. It really helps to put things in perspective.

J.H.: Where do your characters come from? From what elements are *they* made?

A.W.: Imagination, and tiny bits or large bits of reality, love for certain people, and commitment to telling a story which, unless I told it, wouldn't make it. In the tape I made together with Isabel Allende and Jean Shinoda Bolen, I talk about my first novel and how, when I was thirteen, I saw this woman who had been murdered. Her husband had shot her, she was really poor, she had this one shoe left on and it was stuffed with newspaper, she had all these children, and her last name was Walker, although she wasn't related to us, to my knowledge. Domestic violence is something that today we have a handle on, although it's even worse than we thought. But back then, there was really no one to analyze this and put it somewhere where it could be useful. What it needed was a story to contain it and to make it possible to share it without bludgeoning the reader or the hearer. Over time I had to go to school and learn how to do it, but I finally did write this story. And so she's remembered.

J.H.: At one point you commented that your characters come through you, that they speak to you. I remember you said that when you were writing *The Color Purple* your characters told you to sell the house in New York and move to Northern California.

A.W.: Oh well, they just said they didn't like New York, and of course, they're me, you know. I love that Harriet Tubman and Sojourner Truth had this way of always saying, "Well, God told me that I had to pack up and cross the river, and that if I would just take these slaves ten miles he would take them the rest of the way." Every time I read those women I just love them more. It also is sad, though, because you realize that the spiritual colonization of people is so intense that most people cannot take responsibility for their own desires and their own will. So it was impossible for either Sojourner Truth or Harriet Tubman to say, "I just decided that I'd had it, and I was going to go and I was going to take all these people." In the same way you have a dialogue with the imaginary, and that's what happens. It's all you and you don't really forget that, but there's that wonderful, playful quality of knowing that you have dreamed up people who are walking around and who have opinions.

That's what happens too when you have long bouts of silence: it becomes such an echo chamber: You're dreaming people, you're creating people, they do surprising things, but it's only because you have given them that freedom in creating them. So it *feels* that way. I explain it as well as I can because many people think I'm talking about channeling, and I'm not talking about that at all. This is all hard work: it takes solitude, it takes money so you can do it for a year or so, it takes time and sweat—and sometimes wonderful swims in the river—but it's work. You open yourself to creativity really just by being receptive to it.

J.H.: When you write, how do you start? Does a book start with a character? Does it start with an idea, does it start with a story?

A.W.: It can start with any of that; there's no special way.

J.H.: And where do your images come from? There is one in *Meridian* which I still remember—"He cried as he broke into her body, as she was to cry later when their children broke out of it."

A.W.: By then I had had a baby and I had some sense of that break-age. I think that for many women the first sexual act, and sometimes later acts, are really break-ins; they're not something that the woman is particularly ready for or caring about. And I think some men, and maybe this is what's happening with this man in *Meridian*, some men are sensitive enough to realize that penetration is a kind of violation, it's an entering into a sacred space, and you are really blessed to have been invited.

J.H.: Celie, Shug, and Olivia from *The Color Purple* show up in later books. Was it your intention to create a kind of saga, a larger family, a community? Why did you do that?

A.W.: Let's see. I wanted to show what Shug and Celie were like later on in life. I felt like they founded a kind of womanist household, and they were a foundation for these children, Benny and Fanny, so this is a whole new beginning with this matriarchy. I also wanted to dis-cuss ways in which they did have strife with each other. But with Tashi, I never forgot that she was a character who had endured something very strange, painful, destructive, and that I kind of left her there, mainly because the book was going somewhere else.

I struggle with characters only because they are still with me, not because I'm trying to impose something on the work. I mean, if they don't come back to haunt me, I don't bother. There are people in those books—who knows, but I don't think they will ever show up again.

J.H.: What is the role of forgiveness in your work?

A.W.: Forgiveness is absolutely crucial to any kind of going forward, even though, as you know, it's extremely difficult because by now you think there are so many things that are totally unforgivable. But, in fact, they are so horrible that it becomes clearer than ever that you can only move beyond them by forgiving them. It's the stuff of which the soul is made; it is such hard work that to get there changes you completely. It's very difficult.

J.H.: In *The Temple of my Familiar*, the story of Zede and Zede the Elder has a happy ending, if I may call it that; the story of Suwelo and Carlotta has a happy ending; the story of Ayurveda and Fanny has a happy ending; the story of Lissie and Hal has a happy ending. There is all this tragedy in the book, yet there are also all of these happy endings. Your works are generally upbeat despite the dreadful things that happen to your characters over the course of their lives. One is almost always left with a sense of triumph at the end, including in *Possessing the Secret of Joy*. Do you do this because unmitigated suffering is too depressing or because you are by nature an optimist?

A.W.: I do it because they're not happy endings, they're plateaus. I think everybody has a plateau and then they start all over again. That seems to be the nature of the thing to me. You know, suffering is totally with us. It is completely a part of what is life, and yet, right alongside it, there is so much beauty and joy and happiness and understanding and peace and goodwill and good cooking and beauty, that it is again a waste of time just to focus entirely on how, when you are suffering, you may not ever get anywhere but there.

Also, in my own life, I feel that I so often get to the other side, and I get to the other side with the gift of whatever the suffering was, so I can't even regret it. Given that it has happened and there's no changing it, I have to say, "What is the gift of this? Whatever it is, what did I learn from this?"

If I had the power to design life on earth, maybe I would just make everybody happy all the time; but maybe I wouldn't, because sometimes people who are happy all the time and who don't go through these crucibles are really shallow, and you don't want to be with them for very long.

I am optimistic because that's my spirit, and again, I trace it to my mother, who was a warrior and very at home on Earth. You know, many people are really not at home on Earth. I wish they would just leave right now and stop using up our tax money to do it—get on a ship or spacecraft and move on out to wherever it is they want to go. Because there are earthlings who *feel* like earthlings and have no desire to go anywhere but to just be here and to really love and worship what is here.

J.H.: How do you sustain yourself within a specific work and for so long a period of time? What happens to your personal life over the time that you are involved in writing a book?

A.W.: I live in a world that I am creating, and I am usually very happy there, no matter what the story is. It could be a very sad tale, but I am very happy because I have survived to tell it. My partner has to understand that I need long periods of silence, so that he or she, depending on whom I am relating to, will have to be fairly quiet on long drives, for instance, or be very conscious that I am creating something. And while I am doing that, then they are free to be creating something too. I give myself over entirely to this process; I try to find a year or two to really look at whatever it is I'm interested in and to really tell the story the way it should be told. I love this; it is not at all a hardship. It used to be, but now it's a relief to say no to practically everything that anyone proposes—not to see people, and to just be very quiet and intent on what I'm doing.

J.H.: Have you always kept a journal? If so, what is the relationship between your journal and your published writing?

A.W.: I have kept a journal for maybe twenty-five years or more. It's a companion and a place to watch yourself grow and hopefully develop. It's very much like meditation: when your teacher is teaching you how to meditate, there's always a moment when they say, "There will be days when nothing much will happen and you will find yourself making your grocery list or thinking about laundry." And sure enough, there are those days when you sit there, and you try to meditate, and you can't stop thinking about what you're going to make for dinner . . . just trivia.

A journal is kind of like that: there are times when you just have that shopping-list feeling, and you're kind of jotting down everything. But then there are times when you make a breakthrough, and the breakthrough of course is what you've got to wait for, although you're not supposed to wait for anything, you're supposed to just be.

That moment sometimes comes when you back up in your journal, and then you have the breakthrough. There you sit (I usually write my journal in bed) and you flip back to, say, the first of the year (you're now in September or October), and lo and behold, you start to see the pattern of whatever it is that is a subconscious snarl. Then you see what you need to do to change it. I think that people who keep journals are a lot more lucid and a lot more clear about who they are and what is the essential me. That's what I think is really revealed in a diary or a journal.

J.H.: I read recently Toni Morrison's *Playing in the Dark: Whiteness and the Literary Imagination*. In her preface, she said: "For reasons that should not need explanation here, until very recently, regardless of the race of the author, the readers of virtually all of American fiction have been positioned as white. I am interested to know what that assumption has meant to the literary imagination." What do *you* believe that assumption has meant to the literary imagination in general, and yours in particular?

A.W.: It's meant a lot more hard work for those of us who are not white because you have to feel the story, whatever the story is, identify with characters who are usually very much on the surface not like you—you have to go for the heart and the soul. But again, it's one of those funny things: it really enlarges your ability to be empathic.

It's so curious about things that are obstacles—how they are so often things that cause you to grow in ways that you would not otherwise. Because, of course, Toni Morrison and all of us writers and readers, black people, Native American people, Chinese people—we have been reading all of these books. I loved *Jane Eyre*—that was my favorite book. Now on the surface, especially in the South, if Jane Eyre had come out of the nineteenth century and stopped at our house it would have been extremely shocking. The white people would have had a fit, they would have come and snatched her away, because it just wasn't done. This was classic segregation, so I was supposed to think that there was no connection. But there was every connection in the world because it was about the soul, it was about the heart, it was about courage, it was about being a real person.

I think all of us had that experience of being able to identify with what was really important. That means that if you turn it around, white people (you can see this with white women) in the last ten or twenty years have started to be able to do that with work which is not about white people, where they say, "Ah, this is the heart: my heart sees that heart, my soul sees that soul." That is why your friends and you read my work and you don't feel like it is written by someone who is so out-there that you can't relate, or that I would think or feel that you were somewhere out there that was impossible to reach. So that assumption which was meant to limit has in many ways enlarged capacity to feel for people at a soul level.

J.H.: The enlarged capacity to feel brings to mind one of my favorite writers, Albert Camus.

A.W.: Mine too.

J.H.: I felt that kinship very strongly in your work. Someone once asked him what his ten favorite (in the sense of most meaningful) words were. So many of those words are central to your work as well—"compassion," "justice," "love." Were I to ask you that same question, what would your ten most important words be?

A.W.: I think "love," "freedom" . . . I love this tape on Ayurvedic science that I am listening to because they are the first people I have ever heard who said that love and freedom are the same. There's usually that question, "If you could choose love or freedom, which would you choose?" And I would always choose freedom! But they say that they are the same, and I think that's brilliant.

Anyway: "love," "freedom," "justice," "compassion," "hope," "joy," "struggle." That's what comes to mind now.

J.H.: How does it feel to have achieved recognition as one of the most important American writers of the twentieth century and a Pulitzer Prize–winning novelist?

A.W.: I'm pleased. I was in Aotearoa, New Zealand, a couple of years ago with the Maori. They took me to one of their meetinghouses, and immediately, just across from me, was one of their seers, and she started to weep the minute I set foot inside the door. Of course I wanted to know why—had I stepped on something or whatever? It turned out that there was a message she wanted me to take to the Cherokee, my ancestral people (I can't tell you about that until I actually get around to taking it). But the other thing she said was, "So many people came through the door with you, you're just surrounded." That's why I'm pleased: when I walk through the door I'm surrounded by so many people that I bring in with me, and that feels very good.

J.H.: Are you fearless? What frightens you?

A.W.: I think the thing that frightens me most is that I won't follow through on something that I believe in.

J.H.: What have you not yet accomplished that you would like to do?

A.W.: I am dyslexic with manuals; I can't operate things. When I look at your recording machine, I know I want one just like it because I see how you operate it and I figure I can do that by watching and if you point out a few things to me. I have a Jacuzzi and I'm trying to clean it out for the first time myself. I've been on the phone with my friend Deborah down in the city; she had to tell me how to do it because I had looked at the manual and it gave me such a headache. I want to clean out this Jacuzzi, and I want to do it right. I want to get it really clean, and I want to put that polish on it that she says I should put on it, and I want to put the right amount of bromide in it so that I don't kill my guests who get in it, and then I want to get it running again. I have no idea if I'll actually be able to pull it off, but that's the kind of challenge that is intriguing to me now.

I have Oprah Winfrey's cook's cookbook and they have a recipe in there for crab cakes. I've been dragging this cookbook back and forth between the city and the country, picking up ingredients as I go because I don't have everything—I didn't have any baking soda, I didn't have any baking powder—but I'm going to get those crab cakes. I want to make that dish. I want to learn how to make really good pasta. I want to be able to give dinner parties for my friends without feeling so nervous that the food won't taste like anything, or that I will not have enough or something.

I want to do things like that that seem to me to be about creating a space where people can kick back, eat, laugh, tell stories, be comfortable, and by extension send that vibration across the world. Because really, what's important is not so much the frenzied activity that we all have been in—if we're not still in it—but the slowness of the daily and the richness of the very ordinary stuff.

8

"My Life as Myself": A Conversation with Tami Simon from Sounds True (1995)

TAMI SIMON: What are the beliefs and principles you live by on a daily basis—that guide your life?

ALICE WALKER: I try to be kind, and I try to maintain a peacefulness in my spirit. But I suppose the main thing I feel is a kind of internal drive to be my natural self. Because I feel to be the natural self is the truest form of gratitude for being and also of worship to what is here—the planet and the universe.

T.S.: It seems that by the time many people reach adulthood, they have lost touch with their "natural self."

A.W.: I think that what is required is silence. It requires listening to yourself and letting yourself lead, speak, and express. It is an internal flowering that is expressed externally. And also it's fluid; it's not as if you never change. It's more like everything else in life. It's always becoming and you never quite see it, but it's still happening.

Often in this culture people are programmed to think hierarchically: the blonder the better, the bluer your eyes, the whiter your skin, or the bigger and the taller your shoulders—the better. There is this whole notion that you have to be some other way in order to be right. Nothing in nature supports that view. So what people have to realize is, they are really just fine the way they are. Beauty and joy follow when you become more of who you are. And so the essential thing is not necessarily who loves you, or what group is accepting of you, or what group do you accept. But do you accept yourself, however you are?

T.S.: I know that in addition to being a poet and a writer, you are also a mother. I'm curious—is there anything you learned from that experience that you don't think you would have received from any other part of your life?

A.W.: Oh, yeah. When my daughter was born, three days before I finished my first novel, I was instantly connected to all the women in the world. Because I finally understood what an incredible thing women do in creating and peopling the world. You know, it hadn't really sunk in to me that women people the world. And that all the people that you see come out of women; they come out of women the way that my daughter came out of me. Through a lot of pain. And I realized that this is part of what is hidden—the heroic nature of giving birth, and the humility of keeping silent about this journey, which is harrowing. So I felt very much connected to my mother, who had done this eight times without any kind of anaesthetic.

T.S.: That heroism that comes with childbirth: how has that been hidden from people?

A.W.: I think by people not affirming it, and by the way they force women to lie on their backs to give birth so that the doctor can get the credit. In fact, the real normal way to give birth is to squat. And to let gravity help you deliver your child. And this is how it's still done in many parts of the world. But you know, there are no songs that I know of about "Now she is hugely pregnant. Now she is heavy. Now she has stood on her feet for nine months waiting for you. Now she is in pain. Now she is in labor. Now she is mounting the bed or the chair so that she can give birth to you. Ah, this is a woman of great courage. She would have to be, for now she will have much pain."

This is not a song that you hear, but this is a song we should be singing as women go into labor. Preferably in their own houses, or in some birthing space in nature where there are a lot of women around them. This is a ritual that I think would help us very much.

T.S.: Your most recent novel, *Possessing the Secret of Joy*, addresses the horrors of female genital mutilation, a practice that occurs in over thirty countries around the world. At the end of the novel, it's stated that "resistance is the secret of joy." Please comment on that statement.

A.W.: Just simply, that resistance to tyranny is the secret of joy. It means that the joy is in the struggle against whatever is keeping you from being your true self. You have to fight it. You cannot expect to have happiness in an intolerable situation where you are thoroughly oppressed and violated. There is no greater joy than being who you are, and what you are, and truly that. And to have someone come and say to you: "Well, you know, your body would be okay if you didn't have a vulva. Let me just cut yours off." It's not acceptable. You really have to fight it.

T.S.: What is your way of resisting or fighting back?

A.W.: My way of fighting back is to understand what I am fighting, and then in my writing to create a work that expresses what I understand. What is great about being a creative person is that instead of throwing a rock or a bomb or whatever, you can *create* something. And the creation of it is very healing.

T.S.: Do you believe in prayer? Do you pray?

A.W.: All the time. I think that for me the sincerest form of prayer is to express my being and my gratitude for being.

   Also, work for me is always prayer. I think of all of my work as prayer. In the work itself there is the speaking to the reader, but I'm also expressing all of the feelings that I have as to who I am. And that is the prayer.

T.S.: I know you are a student of Buddhism, and I'm curious what your thoughts are about the Buddhist concept of enlightenment or spiritual liberation. Do you think that this is a possibility for human beings?

A.W.: I do. I definitely do. I think it's all about being here and being happy we're here. Accepting what's here, including yourself. And knowing that there is no better place that you could be, if only you would get your stuff together.

I think "be here now" says it. And it's the hardest thing to do, of course, because there is that old imagination.

But imagine, if you could—I love sunflowers, so I'll say a sunflower—if you could just be like a sunflower, not complaining, just open, with your little seeds and your little yellow petals. And you're turning your face to the sun and following it around. At night you just stay there, quiet and content. Because where is true happiness? Your true happiness, or my true happiness, is in a peaceful spirit. It's hard for me to think that there's anything else that matters.

9

A Conversation with Howard Zinn
at City Arts & Lectures (1996)

ALICE WALKER: I would like to read a poem that I wrote over the last three days; it's called "My Teacher," and it's dedicated to Howard Zinn.

The first time I saw my teacher, he was doing what he perhaps does best. He was talking to another person. From the window of my humble room in the dormitory above the school's post office, I watched my teacher to be, as he leaned into the other person. Completely present, eyes, ears, even hair, alert. Totally there. In the raptness of his attention, the raptness of the attention of my teacher, I recognized a fellow subversive. The sweet and beautiful wife of my teacher wore sleeveless dresses in that repressive atmosphere, and was always home. The children of my teacher made music, and unintentional jokes. All around my teacher's house was merriment, because my teacher smiled and made jokes, even when life was very sad.

When the students that we were, where we were, rose against the local bosses, the killers of dreams, the reactionary cowards of that age, my teacher rose with us. When the country rose against racism and war, there at the front of everyone was my slim teacher. My teacher has heard the cry of the hungry, of the cold, of the imprisoned, and the humiliated. He has listened for the sobbing loneliness of the youngest soldier. My teacher has opened his arms to all. He has leaned forward into danger, never back. My teacher has written books that empower the spirit. My teacher has written the first true history of the United States. It is called A People's History, *because at last, we are all there. My teacher has taught laughter and subversion, and how to stay reasonably sane in a world gone insane. My teacher is a man with a modest style of living, and a lavishly appointed heart.*

My teacher is good. Therefore, I ask the Goddess of nature, of all bountifulness, to bless my teacher as he deserves. To light the sun so that he may rise each morning in its shine. To hang the moon and the Milky Way so that they might continually astonish him, and make him glow with joy. To let the grass grow tall, that it might brush his cheeks, as he walks beside the river. To let the trees grow huge, so that he might find a baffling amusement while attempting to embrace them. I ask the wind, especially, to always touch with gentle vigor, the sleek silver hair of my gentle teacher. That my teacher may remember that by all the students he has taught, thousands and thousands in his long life, he is remembered, he is revered, he is blessed, he is loved.

And now, I would like my teacher to come and join me.

HOWARD ZINN: Well. Now. Alice told me, as we were talking about what we would do, just how well organized this thing is. Five minutes before we came, we were talking about what we should do, and she said, "Well, I'm going to read something, and then I have a surprise." That was the poem. Do you really mean that?

A.W.: Yes, I really mean it, I mean every word. I do.

H.Z.: I really was her teacher. You may have gotten that impression. I also remember the first time that I met her. I don't remember the first day that I met every student, but this was Spelman College, Atlanta, Georgia, 1961, and I had been at Spelman for several years, but this is Alice's first year, she had just arrived from Eatonton, from out of, you know, the country.

A.W.: Deep country.

H.Z.: And we just found ourselves sitting next to one another at this freshmen's dinner or honors dinner—you were honored even then, God. Anyway, she was very quiet, but very dignified. Not like now. We talked a little, and then, as a sophomore, she took my course. In a little college you teach everything, things you know, things you don't know, and I was teaching a course in Russian history, and I thought I would jazz it up a little. It was art, literature, it had students read Russian literature, and Alice didn't say anything in class. And then the first papers came in, and she wrote this paper on Tolstoy and Dostoyevsky, and I read the paper—well, I showed it to a colleague of mine. This is sort of an inside thing about the academic world, I have a lot of inside things of the academic world, and this colleague of mine—as you can see, I'm not letting Alice say anything—I showed it to a colleague of mine, and with that professorial arrogance, he said, "She couldn't have written it." I never told you this, did I?

A.W.: No, who was it?

H.Z.: I never told you this? We're going to hear a lot of things we haven't told one another; even though we've seen each other over the years, there are things we haven't told one another. He said, "Somebody else must have written this." I said, "No, you're wrong. There's nobody around that can write like this." That was our introduction.

A.W.: And I took your class because I had been to Russia the summer before, and I was really right out of the country and really very young, and it didn't make a lot of sense, and I felt that if I came back and I studied Russian literature and history and a little of the language, which you taught too—you know, *mir y druzba*.

H.Z.: Nice, you remembered. You remembered all of the Russian language that I taught.

A.W.: Right. Please, thank you, peace and friendship.

H.Z.: It was amazing to me that you were doing all this traveling. You just came from Eatonton; traveling to Atlanta was something.

A.W.: I was trying to put some distance between me and Eatonton.

H.Z.: You did. You went to Russia, and at some point you went to France, and another point you went to Africa, and all this while you were a student.

A.W.: I really was very curious about the world, and I love travel, and I'm not so keen on it now because there's hardly anyplace that I would really like to go—except now I would like to go on the river in the Grand Canyon, that's the only place I can think of that I'd really like to go now.

H.Z.: Really? It's a big drop, isn't it?

A.W.: Big drop?

H.Z.: I mean, it's way down there. The Colorado River.

A.W.: Yeah, that river. But, at the time, I had never been anywhere, hardly, out of the state of Georgia, and most of my relatives had never been outside this little three-county area in Georgia, and it was wonderful to be able to travel and just bring back little things to show them what other people were like in other parts of the world. Those dolls, you know, that fit into each other, things like that. Shawls that had a lot of embroidery. It was good; I was always trying to bring the world back to my family and to my little town.

H.Z.: It must have been really astonishing to them, and you were only one of your many siblings who did that, right?

A.W.: Well, I had a sister [Mamie Lee Walker] who did it, but she eventually stopped coming back, so I guess I took over, that part of it, the one who goes far and says yes, there's land over there. You know, you bring back what you find. I love doing it, especially doing it with my mother, just try to make the world bigger for her.

H.Z.: You've been to Cuba a couple times—I think I may have told you I was at Vassar and saw Angela Davis, and she said she had just been to Cuba with you.

A.W.: We took $5 million worth of antibiotics, and it was very funny because of course they can use every little bit of that, it would go to all the hospitals and all the clinics, but when we were talking to Fidel later, he kind of pulled on his beard and said, "I think antibiotics are over-prescribed." I said, "Thanks, Fidel, that really makes us feel just dandy."

H.Z.: $5 million of antibiotics, just like that.

A.W.: It was very funny, though, and it's true, they are. It is true. In Cuba and Nicaragua now, and a lot countries, there is a lot of dengue fever, and there are all these other viruses and things, so they can actually use antibiotics.

H.Z.: I'm sure they can, though the Cuban medical system is a wonderful system.

A.W.: Well, it has been wonderful, it is not as wonderful now because it has suffered really badly, really terribly.

H.Z.: One of the things about people who go to Cuba, like you, Angela Davis, the Pastors for Peace, all sorts of people have been bringing things to Cuba, and then they come back—and I think one of the good things about it is they're trying to bring attention to this ridiculous policy that the United States has of starving the people of Cuba. I mean, on the grounds that of all the dictatorships and tyrannies in the world, this, Cuba, Fidel, is the one that has to be singled out.

A.W.: Well, it's Fidel, I think. Because of his attitude, the man has a real attitude, he's always had it, he's going to die with it, and they have to get used to it, you know. He is definitely who he is, and it's so wonderful to see. I have never seen anyone go through so many changes in being himself in a conversation, even. That's lovely. The second time I went it was right in the depths of the hard times, and you could actually see that people had lost weight. It was so hard to bear. It was very hard, too, to see people try to get from their houses to work on foot; this was also before they got a lot of bicycles. But then, the last time, it was much, much better, because they've really been working very hard to improve the transportation—and food too, food production, and they're doing something that's really wonderful, they're growing more soybeans, and they're making this incredible soybean yogurt.

H.Z.: Well, I knew you'd approve of that.

A.W.: I do. It's such a mess: because of the embargo they can't get the cattle feed, the cattle feed doesn't come in the country, so the children don't get the milk they're promised by the revolution. They are supposed to have milk every day until they're fourteen or something, and they had to stop having milk at age seven. So now they can use soybean products to bring up their protein.

H.Z.: This government has this thing about Castro; it seems to go even beyond ideology to a fanaticism about Castro. I have a suspicion that, aside from politics, they simply resent that he is so impressive, because they figure if you keep seeing him on television being interviewed by Baba Wawa [Barbara Walters], that people will compare him to Bush. I'm not giving a 100 percent endorsement to Castro—I want him to know that—but he is a remarkable figure, and I think they don't like that.

A.W.: I figure that Fidel's imperfections are about as big as he is, but still he is formidable. I'm not saying I know anything about his imperfections, I just assume that people do have their flaws, and you have to take that along with whatever else they have, but I often think about what a wonderful thing it would be if Clinton could be personable enough to try to learn from him. I think that he could learn so much from this person.

H.Z.: I'm sure Clinton would love to hear that from you. We'll see. Clinton is the man who got up at Nixon's funeral and said that Nixon had struggled all of his life for democracy and freedom.

A.W.: See, I didn't go to that funeral. Some funerals I don't go to.

H.Z.: I don't like to think about it. But you've also been to Nicaragua?

A.W.: Oh yes, I went to Nicaragua many years ago.

H.Z.: What I remember, shortly after you went to Nicaragua, you came to Boston, and you stayed with us—which is a real sacrifice—and you were going on a television thing. You spent the night, and in the morning this somebody came and picked you up, I don't want to say what came and picked you up, it's embarrassing, it came and picked you up for this television thing. We watched you, naturally, since you were our guest. And it was this interviewer, you know, one of those interviewers who had never read anything—not just not read anything of yours, not read anything of anybody's. At one point, she asked you where you'd been or something, and you said you just came back from Nicaragua. This kind of startled her, and she said—this was the only spontaneous thing she said—"Why did you go to Nicaragua?" Because Reagan and the contras were fully at it at the time, she said. "Why did you go to Nicaragua?" and you said, "Because I love the Sandinistas." And I thought, "That's Alice." How many people say that on television? You know, people say it secretly, but not on television.

A.W.: Well, she didn't know who they were.

H.Z.: That's what has struck me. I just want to make up a little for the poem. Just a little, but I don't think I've ever said to this to you, but since we're here alone—

A.W.: I know, you can't see them at all.

H.Z.: What I always really loved about you, Alice, was that even with all of that stuff, success, Pulitzer, all of that stuff, all of that, you never retreated from your political beliefs, and that's something you don't often see. That retreat is so easy. I'm not going to say anything good about you anymore.

A.W.: That's fine with me, but let me tell you something about you. Part of it is that you were my teacher. It meant a lot to have an example of someone who stood by what he believed. You know, you were out there all the time, and this is something that has meant so much to me, my whole life, and I really truly, deeply appreciate it.

H.Z.: We're going to have to start saying negative things. Let's talk about the film. The book. The film, the difference between the book and the film. How did you come by the title [for *The Same River Twice*]? I always wonder how people come by titles, because I always have a tough time.

A.W.: *The Same River Twice?* It's just a way of dealing with the reality, you know, you look at a river, you think it's—well, this is very old, everybody's heard this—but you go to a river and it looks the same, but actually it's completely different from moment to moment, so it's impossible, then, to step into the same river twice, even though you step into the same river twice. And you yourself change, so you're not the same river ever, and of course this is one of the great things about being alive, and that's how you tell you are alive: you are a different river. So when I came to work on this book, I was thinking how this is revisiting something that was very difficult ten years ago; what did it mean? I was looking for meaning for myself, in a way also to move into a different river with it, and ultimately go on to a different river altogether.

H.Z.: You couldn't judge the film simply by the book, because it was a different river. A lot of people made that mistake. *The Color Purple* had such an impact on people—here's another thing I never told you.

A.W.: Is it going to be negative?

H.Z.: Not to you. I was in Hawaii—I like to drop these places, I just happened, like you, "I just happened to be talking to Castro." You have Castro, I have Hawaii, and I was sitting in the student cafeteria, and a student was just introduced to me, and she was reading *The Color Purple.* Well, I couldn't let her go on, I didn't rush to say, "That was my student, I taught her how to write that," I didn't say that.

A.W.: Right, the language and everything.

H.Z.: I didn't say that. The only thing I said to her was—and this was very strange—"Do you like that book?" And she said, "It changed my life." Really. But anyway.

A.W.: I think that was very nice.

H.Z.: Yeah, but you must get a lot of letters like that, that say things like that. But, given the impact of the book, it was a real risk to do a film, so hard to have people satisfied with that film, and you had a hard time being satisfied with it.

A.W.: Oh yeah, I had to accept that it was a different film—you know, it was different. There are so many ways of thinking about why you decide to collectively do something rather than stay in your solitude, and for me one of the things that happened was that I was always thinking, growing up. Eatonton was totally segregated, and the theater was totally segregated, so white people would be down below and we would be up in the gallery, where the broken seats were. And I had never seen a film that had black people in it, in real character roles, where they were actually real people—you know, they were servants and maids and stereotypes and caricatures—and so I never ever thought that one of my books would become a film, never, it just never occurred to me that that would happen. And so I think when Steven Spielberg appeared, there was a part of me that really saw it as a magical thing, you know, and it presented kind of a challenge about whether—it's a great risk of course, because I didn't know Steven yet—but there was something about this person appearing, openhearted, good-hearted, very intense, loving towards this book. So I don't think I would have said no, just because of my own circumstances, of my childhood, and because it seemed to me something that just appeared that was very positive.

H.Z.: Well, you were taking a risk, but you say at one point in the book [*The Same River Twice*] that Steven Spielberg said that his favorite film of all time—you don't want me to say this?—was *Gone with the Wind*. I'm sorry.

A.W.: And that his favorite character was Prissy. Maybe he was joking.

H.Z.: So generous of you to let a guy whose favorite film was *Gone with the Wind* do your book.

A.W.: Howie, it was not like that. He mentioned this when we were almost to the end of filming. He waited; he was waiting. It was true, I felt like, Oh, my God, you know, this is really—I do have this saying that I have made up my own self, that it is always worse than you think, you know. But I think it turned out okay. It's still not the script that I wrote myself, and it mattered to me to have it as a record, because what happens to us, I didn't even know, but when you write, when you write a script for these people at Warner Brothers or whatever, they actually take the copyright and own it, and so I actually had to go through some small changes to be able to print my own script. And I didn't really know what had happened to it, or that people had been reading it, until I was down in L.A. giving a lecture, and some film students came up, and they started trying to engage me about my script, which they were being taught by, I think, Peter Guber, in his film class; he's a producer. So I realized that my script was actually out there, and I would really like to have it somewhere that people could actually see this is my script, and this is what I wrote about, and this is how I envision a film made about my book. I think that one of the reasons the film that we have is so far from my script is because people down in L.A., in Compton, were very upset about the lesbianism in my script, which they hadn't seen. But they decided to go after Steven and Quincy [Jones], and they made threats, and they wrote letters, and they had little clubs all over the country. And then, of course, on opening night, they picketed the movie.

H.Z.: Your mother wasn't happy about the lesbianism, was she?

A.W.: Well, my mother was a Christian—a Jehovah's Witness when she died, and before that a Methodist. And she had actually learned, through her religious indoctrination, that this was a bad thing, and that somehow it meant that you were not quite right. And she had learned that very same thing about Jews. My mother had never met a Jew in her life. So when she met the man I was going to marry, she stood there completely perplexed trying to figure out, "How do I greet this person? I've never met a Jew before." Then she remembered where she had seen a Jew before, and it was in the Bible, and she took his hand, and smiled at him, and she said—can you imagine what she said to him?—she said something very upsetting. And of course, I, you know—

H.Z.: You don't want to say?

A.W.: It's very hard. My point is, here's a woman that was very open, very loving, and had no way of knowing hardly anything outside of her community unless you told her. Which was one of the reasons I was always going off and bringing stuff back. Her religion actually told her how to look at Jews, and how to look at lesbians, and how to look at the world, and it was a very narrow way of looking at the world.

H.Z.: Lucky you didn't have a Jewish lesbian.

A.W.: The thing is, though, my mother came to visit me, and she met my lesbian neighbors, and she adored them. Because they were living exactly the way she had lived when she was in her happiest period, in the '30s, and to meet women who actually grew their own food, who lived in the house they built themselves, who raised goats, who had animals, she was just in heaven. So I had to, again, bring her from this little town all the way out here, and to share this experience with her in her last days. That period, she was so happy with me and my lesbian friends, that was the last time she was actually able to walk. After that, she really just declined.

H.Z.: I remember in the book, you tell about how when your family was in really bad straits—maybe they were always in bad straits, but this time they really were in bad straits, giving out the surplus flour. Do you want to talk about that?

A.W.: Yeah, but that's not in this book, Howie; which book are you talking about?

H.Z.: I'm sorry, that's *In Search of Our Mothers' Gardens*.

A.W.: Then this was during the Depression, and she was refused flour. So, in order to feed us, she had to borrow or barter.

H.Z.: Yes, but before that, I have to remind you about your own story.

A.W.: Well, that's because you've read it more recently that I have.

H.Z.: Yeah, I guess so. People don't go back and read their own stuff; they don't know what they've written. She was refused the flour because she was wearing this nice dress that the white woman who was giving out the flour resented. The dress had been given to her by your aunt, and this woman handing out the flour thought, you know, this is outrageous, that she's coming here for this flour and that she should have this nice dress. Of course, what this put me in mind of—and things are always putting me in the mind of—the whole business of welfare and the stories of welfare mothers, and "Oh God, look, they have a TV" and "Oh God, look, they have this," and "Look, they're wearing clothes."

A.W.: And it's all envy. My theory is that racism is all envy. In my mother's case, this was absolutely true. Here she was, a really good-looking woman with spirit, and she had gotten these secondhand clothes and she was wearing them. You know the experience—this woman can wear a dress, I mean my mother could wear a dress. So she was there, and she still needed the flour, but this woman had this attitude that if you're going to look better than me, I'm not going to give you anything. You know, I was listening to your *People's History of the United States* on the way down to San Francisco, and I can see that is part of what's been happening throughout our history, just this envy of what native people have had and what people of color have, and it's very clear that racism in a way is a mask for this desire to have what other people have.

H.Z.: I guess I never thought of it as envy, but I guess it's connected with that in that these are people that don't have much, and people who don't have much are vulnerable to prejudice and racism. And I guess it suggests that, very fundamental to getting rid of racism—maybe not sufficient, nothing is sufficient; well, it takes a lot—but one of the crucial things is dealing with the general impoverishment of all working people, like black, Latino, and so on, because it's their deprivation that leads them to fight one another, all to the benefit of that top one percent.

A.W.: The ruling class.

H.Z.: The ruling class?

A.W.: Is that accurate? Because I am trying to find a phrase for that one percent, you know, a word, a name, so we don't always have to get into color or whatever, but something that is really accurate.

H.Z.: I use the word "they."

A.W.: "They." No, Howie, I'm trying to get away from the word "they."

H.Z.: They have done this to us, they control the media, they run the—

A.W.: It seems to me that we need a word, we need a phrase—

H.Z.: "Ruling class" is two words.

A.W.: Still, it really kind of gets it. What I don't like about it is—there's something about it.

H.Z.: Well, it's been used a lot.

A.W.: But not recently.

H.Z.: You're bringing it back.

A.W.: Well, maybe not. Not if you can come up with something better than "they."

H.Z.: Maybe somebody in the audience will come up with something.

AUDIENCE MEMBER: The entitled?

A.W.: But they're not entitled.

H.Z.: Maybe he means "the titled."

A.W.: "Thieves," maybe.

10

"The World Is Made of Stories": A Conversation with Justine Toms and Michael Toms from New Dimensions (1996)

MICHAEL TOMS: Alice, what prompted you to start writing? What are the origins of your writing?

ALICE WALKER: I think a lot of different things. One was that I grew up in a very large family; I was very lonely and we always lived in very poor and small housing. I needed to be outside of the house in order to think. My head became the only sacred safe place to be most of the time because of this large family. And not a very gentle family, either. So I think I carried over that need to make a space for myself, make a world for myself. I also used to talk to spirits. So that carried over; so that every crisis in my life as a child I met with some form of written creativity.

M.T.: I think I remember your writing something about how your poetry only came out of crisis situations or sadness.

A.W.: Sadness, yes. That's not true anymore, but it was certainly true for a number of years. It really saved my life.

M.T.: You recall where you wrote about your experience in, I guess it was your last year of college, at Sarah Lawrence, where you were contemplating suicide?

A.W.: Yes.

M.T.: And you were writing poetry.

A.W.: Yes. Yes. And it saved me. It was about a time I was contemplating suicide because I needed an abortion. I was too poor, really, and too alone to have a child. There didn't seem to be much of a choice, really. There was no one, for instance, to say, "I'll take care of the child and feed it and clothe it and send it to school." Of course, there was no one to say that about me, either. Also, it seemed to be a very untenable situation and so I started writing poetry as a way to give thanks, because eventually I was able to have the abortion and I continued with my life. The poetry was a way of acknowledging the sadness and the circumstances but also saying that I survived and my creativity survived and I would continue.

M.T.: And you were taking the poems as you were writing them and you were stuffing them under, I think it was Muriel Rukeyser's door.

A.W.: Yes, Muriel Rukeyser had a little gardener's cottage on the college campus, right there in the middle of the campus. She was my teacher— a formidable and wonderful woman. I put the poems under her door. That was the beginning, really, of my publishing, because I really didn't know how to go about it and she did and just gave my poems to an agent and the agent gave them to an editor at Harcourt Brace Jovanovich and they're still my publishers.

M.T.: Yes. Muriel was one of your mentors, wasn't she?

A.W.: Yes.

M.T.: Who were some of your other mentors?

A.W.: Well, in Georgia, my high school teachers and my first-grade teacher. I went to an all-black school in Georgia, and I had many wonderful teachers who cared about me and my family and knew the culture and cared about everything. It wasn't just about teaching for them; it was really about nurturing and bringing us up in the best possible way with good values. Then at Spelman, where I went before Sarah Lawrence, I had Howard Zinn, who was—and still is—this incredibly funny, irreverent, wonderful radical history professor. And Staughton Lynd, who is also a really great historian and political activist. So these two men were very much a part of my life at Spelman.

JUSTINE TOMS: Can you describe how that was, how they mentored you?

A.W.: Well, I don't know if I would say they mentored me deliberately. You know, it was more a case of my recognizing in them great qualities of leadership and kindness and just following, learning from them in that way. But they didn't just take me under the wing, so to speak. There were too many other people who needed the same thing.

J.T.: Did you ever go back and see your first-grade teacher again?

A.W.: I see her all the time when I go back. Miss Reynolds. I never learned to call her by her married name, either. She has always been Miss Reynolds and always warm and kind and loving—and she still is.

J.T.: I know in much of your writing you include a lot of storytelling, and there have been times—I know in one of your more recent books, the most recent, *Possessing the Secret of Joy*, you have a moment in there where a man is dying and someone, one of the characters in your book, is sitting with him as he is dying and is sharing a painful experience and it is being written by another. And when it's truly written this man dies, then, really much more peacefully. I think you're really capturing something here about storytelling and witnessing each other. Can you speak about how that is in your life?

A.W.: I think the world is made of stories. I see this more and more in my own life. I was just in Australia, for instance. I spent some time in the bush with aboriginal women. We just talked about each others' lives and the stories. They were very curious to know the stories of my culture, and I was equally curious to know the stories of their culture. And what we discovered was just that they knit. There's a place at which they come together. It's when your stories knit, and when you look into the eyes of a person whose stories you're sharing—they're sharing yours—it's when you look into each others' eyes and you see "aha" in the eyes that you can let go and you can move on to whoever else you need to talk to. It is the same with this character. He has chosen this man to give the story to. The man, Adam, doesn't even want it. And this is so true to life, isn't it? I mean, how many more horror stories can we bear to hear? But he finds himself really hearing the story, and the story sinks in, and this man who is dying has enough wisdom and human feeling to see it sink in. I mean, he looks and he sees; that story just sinks right through the eyes and down into the heart. And it's there; it'll be there until Adam dies.

Then he can die. He's done it. He's passed this on. This is what the world is made of. It is made of people passing on their stories; dying, but not until they've done it. It's interesting, because I always feel when I finish a book, whatever it is, that it is perfectly fine to leave then. I'm sometimes amazed that I'm still around to start another one. But there is a feeling of completion that is just inherent in storytelling. When you finish the story, something does end.

J.T.: So, in listening to each others' stories, it's like an exercise of keeping the heart open. How does one keep their heart open hearing sometimes very painful stories and hold that? How do you do that for yourself?

A.W.: Then you come to the skill and the craft of the storyteller. Not to mention the theatrics of the storyteller. It is not just about you keeping your heart open, it's about the storyteller being good enough so that your heart is going to open whether you want it to or not. You know? So if you can just bring your body there and have your ears, and just anything, anything else at all that connects you to this person. In Adam's case, he is connected to the person because he's been on this AIDS floor taking care of people. He can't really just leave this man to die alone, because he's interested. He becomes interested in alleviating some of his suffering. Then the storyteller does the rest.

M.T.: What about the difference between storytelling and advice? You've written about that.

A.W.: What did I say?

M.T.: Well, you said that advice didn't have the strength and power of storytelling.

A.W.: Oh, exactly. You know, to really do your job well you have to— that's where theatrics come in. You embellish things, you make them, you fix it so that people have something that becomes a part of them rather than something that is plastered on them.

M.T.: So it's easier to identify with the story, to put yourself in it?

A.W.: Yes, because you don't really feel that it's implicating you personally. There's a distance. It's a beautiful verbal weaving that you can admire. It's only after you've gone home that you think, "My goodness, I'll never be free of that design."

M.T.: You know, I grew up with radio; the radio was like a storyteller coming into my home. I think now with the children exposed to television, the average preschooler has seen six thousand hours of television, and it's not the same thing. The storytelling is so important for developing one's imagination, particularly in a young child.

A.W.: Exactly.

M.T.: And that's not happening anymore. What's your view of television? What is your opinion of television?

A.W.: I'm not fond of it. I'm not as hostile to it as I was, primarily because I've learned how to use it. I can give myself two hours a week to watch television, and whether I use those two hours or not is up to me, but I can do that. I could watch two hours of news, say, or I could watch some really exquisite movie or special or something. I think, though, that for many people, there is no real sense of how to use it. They are addicted, pure and simple. They will watch anything that comes across the screen. This has had an incredibly damaging effect not only on children in general—and on people in general—but for black culture and Native American people it has been absolutely destructive. Not only do they get images that are not their own, but they get images in which they are pigeonholed in positions of weakness and just very bad ways.

M.T.: And others, Jerry Mander pointed out that in northern Canada their whole culture has been decimated by the influx of television coming in and basically, it has brought with it the material world and the outside world in a way that the young people are wanting to leave. . . .

A.W.: They probably think they're poor, because they don't have the houses . . . the cars, the refrigerators, and the motorcycles and all of that.

M.T.: Yes, and these are people who lived in longhouses in the communal way and shared things. Their whole culture is being changed radically.

A.W.: Yes, I've seen that happen in Bali. I've gone there over the years. It's been so upsetting; now so many people have TV. The first time I went, you would see a television set every once in a while. It would be under a tree, and they would be watching a puppet show on it, the same little puppet show you could watch off of it. It just leads to a kind of hardness in the faces of the people, because they take a much more cynical attitude about life. It doesn't—well, I can't say it doesn't ever, but it rarely, in sort of mainstream television, it's rare for it to promote values in keeping with community and struggle and solidarity and spiritual development.

M.T.: Since Bali has come up, Bali is of interest to us. What is your feeling about Bali and why have you gone there and what have you gotten from going to Bali?

A.W.: I went there many years ago just because I heard of it. I heard how beautiful it is and the people. I wanted to be in a place where the art is still inseparable from life. Where everything . . . Also where art and spirit are together. And people don't even think for it to be otherwise. That appealed to me, because in our culture things are fragmented in such a way that it is very difficult to go about your business as an artist, as a spiritual person, as a political activist, as a mother, as one thing, one being. And all these things are just part of what you do. They're not even part, they're just mixed so that you can't separate these things. So I went for my third visit about a month ago, about a month and a half ago. It's changed a lot. You really have to dodge the cars in the streets of Ubud. I was happy, though, to go out into the countryside and find the old Bali, still. But I often, wherever I go, I watch the faces of the people and this was the first time I felt and saw that cynicism, that look of smartness that I never associated with Bali, with the people of Bali. I also saw more unhappy children. The first time I went, I really never saw a child who seemed to be unhappy. Now, there may well have been unhappy children, but they certainly seemed pretty okay. This time I saw children who were hawking wares and obviously working because they were being made to do that. I noticed that the dancers in these dance programs have the saddest eyes, and I cannot believe that they dance because they feel like dancing. This is so hurtful to the spirit that I couldn't really go to any of these things. I gave up trying to watch any performances. I just had a much better time going out into the rice paddies and watching the people deal with the rice, because they seemed to be doing what they had always done.

M.T.: So you didn't think they were doing it out of a calling to ritualize the sacred. I mean, there wasn't that sense of performance.

A.W.: By now it is a performance. I didn't feel anything particularly sacred. The people looked too sad.

M.T.: Ah, interesting. Well, this is really kind of endemic in many cultures around the planet, where other cultures like the West, Western materialism, that kind of thing coming into heretofore what we would call primal cultures, native cultures, ancient cultures.

J.T.: One of the themes I pick up in some of your books has to do with children, and I know, in one of your current books, you say there could be (it's a quote from one of your characters; I think this is from *Temple of My Familiar*) there can be no happy community in which there is one unhappy child. That really struck me, and that's a theme that I pick up here and there in all of your writings. So maybe you could talk to us about the children and your feelings about children.

A.W.: I think a society that ignores a crying child is a doomed society. You don't need more than one child crying. I think that's why some ancient cultures have rules about how a child is always carried. I think, in Bali, until the child is two years old, or what seems like a very long time to us, but it's a period. I remember the first time I went to Bali. We lived in a house that was looked after by a family, this Balinese family. It was true; I watched them holding the baby. There was the mother, the father, and the grandfather. And that grandfather held this little boy. He was out chopping weeds and doing all the chores around the house, but he never let that child set foot on the ground. It was the most remarkable thing. So that the Balinese child traditionally is a very well-adjusted child because there is that feeling of being part of whatever's going on and loved and valued. They would also, all of them, sit with the child and be with the child, even though the child wasn't talking at that point. I just saw this little boy this last trip. He is big and he was carrying—he and his mother were going to the temple, and they had these offering trays on their heads. He just seemed really in sync, in whole. So I do, I feel that it's not enough to just think that your child is okay, the world is fine. I feel very badly about the way, in a racist culture, that white people can think, "Well, my child is okay and my child is well fed, well clothed, well housed, and is going to a good school and right across the track there are children who are starving, miserable, sad. There is no way to think that these children can be separate forever. Because the children who have nothing will always be trying to get what your child has. And then your child will be called upon to try to protect what is his or hers. A better way of doing it would be to try to make sure that all children are happy. And well cared for.

J.T.: It just seems to me this is a wonderful political platform if everything was run by that, what you just said: is it good for the children? Anything that we decide, poetically, if we say "Is it good for the children, all the children?" It certainly helps to separate what should be done and what should be—

A.W.: Okay, if you and I started a political program, I tell you what we could do, just for instance in Anderson Valley. We could go around to every household and we could interview the children. We could ask them, "How do you feel? Are you happy? What makes you upset? What makes you ill?" It doesn't always have to be that children are mistreated physically, although they often are. They have many many things to tell us about how they are treated and they really are the measure of our success. If we lose the children, we've lost. And we've just about lost the children.

J.T.: It's true.

M.T.: I'm reminded of an essay you wrote (and you may think differently now, I don't know) about having only one child.

A.W.: I think the same.

M.T.: You think the same. Tell us about that.

A.W.: I think that the planet being finite and resources being limited and things like that, from an ecological point of view, there is no reason why people should have more than one child. Two, if you really stretch yourself. That way you would at least have a replica of each other. But my feeling is that one way of relieving the planet of this burden that the population is, is to limit the number of children people have, because when you have a lot of children . . . especially in the West. I think the Western notion is often that it's just people in the third world who should limit their children. The truth is that this country, and countries like Australia and New Zealand and all these colonized places, really exist because of overpopulation by white people. Deliberately trying to have more people than the native population. But what that has meant, given the high standard of living of Westerners, that is why the resources are just gobbled up. They're gobbled up by people who have ten and twelve children or even six, because every child has to have a house, a car, a refrigerator, a whatever. I think that just in terms of survival of human beings, people really must voluntarily decide to limit their families. China, of course, has tried to do this by edict. I think maybe other countries will have to do something. But there are too many people on the planet. That is a much more serious problem than many people are willing to recognize because they feel a need to have children to prove something about themselves. My theory is that if you love yourself, the more you love yourself the fewer children you will have. Because really there's no need; also if you really care about children you don't have to have your own. There are millions of children you can look after.

M.T.: In that essay you referred to the impact of a child on your work. Could you talk a little bit about that?

A.W.: I was worried that I wouldn't be able to function as a writer and the kind of writer I intended to be and I was: very committed and needing long hours of intense work, to write novels especially. But I discovered that with one child, I really was okay. I had some rough times—that whole first year, for instance. I found it very hard to be that suddenly split person. I had been twenty-one or twenty-two years (or however old I was, maybe twenty-three or twenty-four). Anyway, I had been completely single-minded in terms of my work in college; completely single-minded political activism, right on whatever I was doing. Then, I suddenly had this little baby and she was just as primary as any thought I'd ever had, totally. Not to mention seductive and a miracle. So I was just really very much aware that I had suddenly become two people and this was really—it was going to be a juggling act. But after that, I did what mothers often do; I found a good day care right down the street. [My daughter] was always very bright and liked people, so she was happy, so we managed. Now I think she's the best thing that ever happened to me, just because she really taught me to love.

M.T.: Children can do that.

J.T.: I am reminded of the child within. I think also that you have spoken again of Muriel, the mentor in college, how she always brought the child to the classroom. How important is that?

A.W.: Oh, it's very important. When you go to most college campuses and if you listen in to most of the courses, you would never know children exist. You would never know there were people even sitting in that classroom who are looking at their watches, trying to figure out how quickly they can leave the class and go pick up a two-year-old or three-year-old. This is real. I mean, this is real life. I think the reason the children have been excluded is because if they are included, everything has to change. And it should. It should be a child-centered society. Obviously, they are the future. They are us. On and on and on. If they're neglected, we won't make it.

J.T.: Going back to the women's issues and talking about your being in Bali and telling stories together. I'm reminded of something you've written. This was after reading some writings that women from India had written. You said each woman was trying to be free, trying to be independent. She was trying to relate to the people she loved in ways that were not self-destructive. I think you've said a mouthful right in that one phrase.

A.W.: I was talking about a writer whose work appeals to me. That is the work of women now. Usually we have to relate to people in such self-destructive ways. We are able to assist them or support them or be with them only because we have given up on being for us. It is crucial that women don't do that anymore.

J.T.: What are some of the ways you are doing that in your life that are working for you?

A.W.: What specifically?

J.T.: In ways that you're relating then, without being self-destructive ways, that you are relating in being yourself.

A.W.: By not being married. Because for me marriage is so alien to my sense of how I would have done it. It is such a patriarchal construct and the vestiges of slavery are still so clear on it but . . . I did it, I was married. But I did it partly because it was illegal to marry the person I married. So that was a great challenge to me. But I have in my life . . . I relate to people without being bound to them by anything other than my love. I've found my love for people is the strongest thing I have and it doesn't need any other support.

J.T.: This reminds me and takes me into something I read about animals. Again, going back to your book *The Temple of My Familiar*. Talking about when women lived with animals and when they were living separate, men and women were living separate, and they would come together in a new sort of way. This really stimulated my imagination. Can you speak on that?

A.W.: As a friend said to me once, "Alice, imagine what it would be like if people came together only out of desire." It would be a very different world. Because you wouldn't have to follow somebody else's notion of how you should live. Everybody really is different. We all do require different things. We don't all require in the same form. We are different contents so we need a different form. What I like to think about is that people should devise: if marriage is great for you, that's fine, but I don't think that you should just accept it as the way it's done. Every June you see all these fifteen- and sixteen-year-olds in their little bridal gowns and they're getting married (well, maybe they're a little older). I just know that not one of those young women has had anyone to sit her down and say, "Now, look. It's true that people have been marrying for thousands of years. The wife usually goes and whatever, the husband does this. But, you know you don't have to, you don't really have to do this. There's no reason why you have to." Just talk to the young about different possibilities.

J.T.: In my experience, too, there are more and more people who are much older that are not married. As they get older they are really enjoying their lives in relationship, not necessarily in marriage.

A.W.: I guess I still remember in my genetic memory having been owned as somebody's slave. I just resent any form of ownership, any one of claim on me. Because I feel myself to be a free person and a free spirit. That is completely compatible with me.

J.T.: How about dreams informing your writing? I know you've said that you've used dreams, that they're very important to you. How have you used them in your writing?

A.W.: Sometimes if the dream is a part of what I'm working on, it's right in my writing. I just put it in because that's where it belongs. If you spend the kind of time I spent writing *The Temple of My Familiar*, time itself becomes dreamlike and you can hardly tell, in a way. I was really tapping my ancestral and sort of ancient memory because it represents my visions of the world and of time. So I would often dream parts of the story and I would often have visions of parts of the story, even when I didn't know what they meant. One of the first ones was the scene between the old man in the nursing home and the younger man who comes to talk to him. I was putting out the garbage one day and that just flashed. I could see it clearly. But I had no idea what it meant or where it went in the novel. It was much later that (actually at the very end of the novel) I finally saw, oh, yeah, this is where this goes. And the same has been true of dreams. Dreams are very . . . as you know, they like to give you . . . they're not entirely coherent, they're not logical. But they're true. The truth is in you. The truth is what you find in the dream. So it takes a lot of working with images over and over. Sometimes you never really know. But when you're working with a book like *The Temple of My Familiar*, where it's about vision, I did know enough to recognize that all of these things belong to this vision, even though I wasn't always entirely clear what it was exactly.

J.T.: How do you sort that out for yourself then, to find the truth of the dream? Do you have some techniques that you use or some, I don't know, scales you've developed in working with your dreams?

A.W.: No, I think life is the one. Life is what tells you what your dream is.

J.T.: Do you write them down? Well, of course you do write them down.

A.W.: Sometimes I don't. Sometimes I just mull a dream over.

M.T.: Well, one of the things you've done and obviously been pretty disciplined—I would say ruthless or relentless—about is minimizing your input from other sources. That's something that would help your inner life, I would think.

A.W.: What do you mean exactly, Michael?

M.T.: Well, what I mean is that I think you said that minimizing your input helps self-knowledge. It's almost like putting, shutting out. We're barraged in this culture so much, just the media images that are coming to most people all the time is enough to send you over the wall. So one almost has to take responsibility for minimizing that. Just as you said you limit yourself to two hours a week of television. Most people don't do that.

A.W.: And two hours, I find, is often too much. But I do give myself that, because I feel it really is a fabulous medium. Often there are incredible things. But, yeah, I do, I had to learn that, because I know that I am here in this form once, I believe, as far as I know. And I want to really be here. I want to be here completely as myself, as much as that's possible. I don't want to be here as somebody else. I don't want to be here as a composite of stuff that comes over the media. To do that would be to miss it, to miss being here.

M.T.: Miss who you are.

A.W.: Yes, but also to miss being here as who I am.

M.T.: Sure. Right.

A.W.: And that would just make me grieve.

M.T.: Yes, good point.

J.T.: This is reminding me of another quote I want to bring in. It's a quote that we've used on New Dimensions. It was, again, from *The Temple of My Familiar*, Ola saying you must live in the world today as you wish everyone to live in the world to come. That can be your contribution. Otherwise the world you want will never be formed. Why? Because you are waiting for others to do what you are not doing.

A.W.: That's true.

J.T.: It really moved me because sometimes you feel overwhelmed with all the input; but then if you just take it just one step at a time, saying, "I can do this, this is close to me. This I can do with my neighbor. This I can do in my own household," it's somehow hopeful.

A.W.: Right.

M.T.: I don't want to be presumptuous to try and compartmentalize the body of your work, but it seems to me the thread running through a lot of your work is a thread that does provide, does kind of provide, a grounding of hopefulness, of optimism. I'm wondering if someone coming from your background, from the Deep South, poor Georgia sharecropper farmer, how you were able to overcome not only that background but the cynicism that pervades our society. So many people, as you and I both know, feel disempowered, feel helpless, hopeless, "There's nothing I can do to change things." Somehow you were able to crack that code or jump over that wall. I'm wondering if you could talk a little bit about that.

A.W.: Well, among other things, I had a great mother who, around those shacks, planted the most incredible gardens ever. So that, in poverty,

I was surrounded by beauty, from birth. That beauty has sustained me through many many crises. I was also part of the Civil Rights Movements and changed my own part of the country, my own part of the world. So that has made me understand that change is possible and that people can do it. Also, that people can change themselves. I've never lost faith in people. I sometimes feel very sad because the people who have had the power to do so have been incredibly destructive to all of us and to the planet. But I've never lost faith in the people who didn't have that kind of power, who didn't do that kind of destruction. I also get—I mean the reason I'm here in this, here on this hill, and the reason I worked very hard to get out of the city, is because I get energy from the earth itself. I get optimism from the earth itself. I feel that as long as the earth can make a spring every year, I can. As long as the earth can flower and produce nurturing fruit, I can, because I'm the earth. I won't give up until the earth gives up. Of course, that's why where we are now is so sad, because you just start feeling the earth has pretty much had it with this species. And for good reason. We have to exert all of our love and all of our energy to try to convince the earth that we haven't forgotten that she is, it is, home. I know that there are some people who think they come from heaven and are going to heaven, but I don't believe that. I'm from earth; I go back to earth. I'll always be here.

M.T.: There is a saying attributed to Jesus. He was asked, I think it was in the Gospel of Thomas, by one of his disciples, where is heaven. "Lord, tell us where is heaven." He said, "Heaven is spread before you. You just don't see it."

A.W.: I know, and you think, "Why can't people see that they're in heaven already? And why must they believe they must turn it into hell?" To fulfill the prophecy of another part of the Bible.

M.T.: That's an interesting question. I don't know why.

J.T.: Going back to your idea of bringing beauty. We often don't put a priority on that. We put a priority on things that are utilitarian, but beauty is kind of the last thing. And yet, you're saying, what you just said is that sustained you. You are doing what you're doing today because your mother took the time to bring beauty to your surroundings, physical beauty. I'm very moved by that. I feel it is truly the truth and somehow—do you have any idea how we will be able to bring that more to the fore and bring that more into our lives?

A.W.: Fewer shopping centers, for sure. And fewer buildings. Just fewer. I'm always amazed that somebody thinks the measure of health of the economy is building more buildings. I can never understand why they think like that. It is a pure colonizing idea. Spread and conquer. That will really have to change. If it doesn't change—if, in fact, the developers and all these other people keep covering, paving over the earth—we don't have much of a chance.

J.T.: What you're saying—I'm just getting this new flash—we all disapprove of colonization. We look back in history and we see the mistakes of colonization, and you're talking about something that's going on right now under our noses, so to speak. That is still that same energy.

A.W.: That's how you colonize the earth. You just take it over with shopping malls and buildings.

M.T.: One reason is that the science of economics is very limited. It doesn't include human values and quality of life as part of its equation. The same is true of how we measure progress; it's called the gross national product. It doesn't include human-scale process.

J.T.: Or to say if we could measure the health of the children we would know the health of the nation. We don't bring that in.

A.W.: That's right. If you had healthy children you would have a healthy nation. And if you had beauty everywhere, you would have a people who have mellow spirits. I have been in ghettos. Thank goodness I never lived in one, because even though I had to live in shacks, they were just in the middle of the most incredible splendor, so I never confused myself with the poverty. I always identified myself with the grandeur, the beauty. But in ghettos, nobody should be surprised that people take drugs. If I had to live in the ghetto, I would take it by the ton. Anything I could get. Because I couldn't stand the ugliness.

J.T.: And that lack of community. There's nothing that brings people together, in a loving way.

A.W.: People have traditionally had the church. But it's problematical, because people are beginning to see that that is an institution, like marriage, that they also have nothing really to do with. It's a concept that is given to them. They had worship; everybody's had worship because it's innate. You would worship if you never saw a church because when you go out this door you see a California poppy and you see the orange of it; you worship that. You worship the spirit of the creation that goes into that. You look at a tree; the same thing. Everybody has that. But the church, and especially its patriarchal construction, makes it difficult for people to feel accepted in their church, accepted for who they are, as diverse as people can be. So I don't think people hear the sermons with quite the same ear that they used to. That's a structure that's more or less—not lost entirely, but fading.

J.T.: Some of Alice Walker's many writings include poetry. We'd like to share with you Alice reading from her book *Her Blue Body Everything We Know: Earthling Poems, 1965–1990*.

A.W.: This is a poem that I wrote some time ago, called "If There Was Any Justice."

If there was any justice
in the world

I'd own
Van Gogh's
Starry Night.
Not the tall
linear one
I
have
always
coveted
but the wide
horizontal one

on which the paint
is desperate
praise.

It would hang
over the headboard
of my bed
so that
every night
before falling
asleep
I could look at it
and then above
it
through the skylight
at the heavens.

If there was any justice
in the world
I could have saved up
for it
and bought it
for the cost
of a fancy dress
or a modest
house.

Vincent
would have wanted me
to have it. Of this
I have no doubt.

How he would smile
to see how

every night
I journeyed
through the cosmos

on the wings
of his brush
My dreadlocks
connecting canvas to
moon.

He probably
would have given
me
the painting
If we had been
neighbors
friends
or
bar room
aficionados
and I had offered
him a watermelon
or homemade
wine.

If there was any justice
in the world
I'd also have
that last
painting he did
of the reaper
and the
wide field
of wheat
and the crows.
I'd have the
Sunflowers
All of them
of course.

Whoever
has the

poor taste
to hoard them
could keep the
ugly portraits
of Madame Whosis
& Dr. Whatsis
but there are
a couple
of garden scenes
I would also take.
Vincent
knowing I
value flowers
& orderly
disarray
would have wanted
them
to be mine.

If we had met
in the presence
of these
paintings
he couldn't have missed
the wonder
the reverence
the stark
recognition
of shared life
in my eyes.
My delight in him
spirit   eye
& hand.

As the world
rushes madly
to its end
and one imagines

the *Starry Night*,
lonely
as Vincent
himself
in its vault
bursting
suddenly
into flame
like a bit of
star
or a bit
of rubbish.
And the same
tired assassins
whose blindness
drove
him insane
seeking at last
to destroy
all
the beauty
beyond
the vault
that
he labored
so
to make
them see
&
seeing

save.

M.T.: There are many children, particularly young adults and even adults in many cases—there's this kind of phenomenon we have of this increasing violence in urban areas and things like drive-by shootings, totally meaningless kinds of violence. Part of it is this disconnection with one's fellow creatures, one's disconnection with one's brothers and sisters and other living things. And also the disconnection with any kind of roots or family. A lot of your writing, in some sense, honors your ancestors. Maybe you can talk a little bit about the importance of your ancestors and your own connection to roots, because it seems to me that's one of the things at the core of some of the problems we have.

A.W.: I've always honored my mother and father . . . I could be critical at the same time, but I honored them and do honor them for all they were able to do to bring up eight children, under incredibly harsh conditions, to instill in us a sense of the importance of education, for instance, the love of beauty, the respect for hard work, and the freedom to be whoever you are. But beyond my parents, my grandparents, and my great-grandparents—and by now I have gone very far back to May Poole, who lived to be 125 years old and who was my four-"greats" grandmother—but beyond May Poole, I have gone back in *The Temple of My Familiar* to reconnect with the very first ancestors, as far back as I could push it. I think that one of the fallacies of modern thought, or postmodern thought (wherever we are), is that somehow the ancient people—the ones who lived and died, and thank goodness, because now we can put up a shopping center—that those people were somehow less than now. In my view they're really the same.

M.T.: Might even have been better.

A.W.: No, I'm deliberately not going to say that, but they probably were. But the point is that, if you can really understand that your most remote ancestors were probably just fine, you can feel a whole lot better about yourself now. So, if you go back five hundred thousand years and look at the people then, what were they doing then? They were raising their children, and hunting and fishing, and telling stories around the fire; and darn, pretty soon you can see that their life was not that much different from yours, in the basics. There's no point in thinking that just because people didn't make the catapult—or they didn't make some technological thing or other that people now will think of as an advance over the slingshot—it's no reason to think that they were less human. I have, in my work, delighted in dreaming my way back and remembering my way back to these ancient, ancient days in which I feel quite at home and have no quarrel with. So I'm at peace with my ancestors—all of them. It means that when I go about in the world, they're really with me. When I went to New Zealand, I spent time with the Maori. That's what they all said when I went to the Marae, their gathering site. They have this wonderful ceremony where they speak for you and they introduce you to the group and everything. They consistently said about me they always saw all of my people around me. And I said, "Right," because they're all around me. They said, "Yes, you came to the door with many many people with you." They could just see them. They had a seer, a woman who saw my Cherokee history (I can't talk about it because she gave me a message to give to the Cherokee nation, which I have to do and then I can talk about it), but she started to weep; she just started to weep; from what she could see. It's lovely to be in a society where people are still in touch, so in touch, with the kind of vibrational life of the person in front of them.

M.T.: The invisible world.

A.W.: The invisible world. It was such a relief. I felt seen and affirmed in a way that I had never felt.

M.T.: Our society doesn't honor the invisible world. It stresses the visible. It's part of our scientific revolution, as it were. It, in some ways, suppresses the sacred.

J.T.: There's a whole movement to work with native cultures and their science, which is just what you speak of: being able to see what we call the invisible world. But to them, it is not invisible at all, but to see that which is not apparent. And so they're meeting with physicists of our culture and shamans of other cultures and finding that there's a commonality there that they're coming together. Although language makes it difficult, because sometimes it's difficult to speak all of this.

A.W.: I don't know. I don't think they get it. Mainly because of the kind of arrogance involved in how they can't really believe it unless they can prove it using their tools. It's very prevalent. Some of this really has to do with just having faith and just being open to what you experience yourself and having faith in your own experience.

J.T.: This is where our culture comes in with experts. We have been so "expertized"—we can't trust it unless an expert says it. Recently,

I was listening to the news. There were some earthquakes in Northern California up in Eureka. There was some seismic expert saying, "Oh, there's no connection at all between that and what's gone on in Palm Springs in this other part of California." I don't trust that anymore. There's something in me—maybe I've done New Dimensions long enough to realize it—I don't trust that anymore.

A.W.: It's because they don't believe it's connected. If that's not the fatal flaw of the Western world, I don't know what is. It's this feeling. I think it's all connected. If you do something in Eureka, if something happens in Eureka, of course you feel it in Fresno.

J.T.: Or you do a test, a nuclear test in Nevada; it's going to have its effect someplace else.

M.T.: They were having that series of underground tests in Nevada and there was that whole series—slew—of earthquakes that occurred on the eastern region of the Sierra a couple of years ago. I remember calling the geological survey and asking them, "Seems to me there's a relationship here." But "scientifically" they would say that there's no relationship, there's no connection of the plates.

A.W.: The thing is how basically—I won't say uneducated, because often people have had a little bit of education—un-college-educated people often are so far ahead of the scientists. The case in point, I think, is that, for years, the people in Georgia have been talking about how the sun had changed, because they could feel it on their skins. These were people who had worked outdoors almost all of their lives. They were just talking about it: "I'm burned. I can't go from here to there and suddenly it hurts. It stings." This was long before anybody said anything about the ozone. They also kept saying that they noticed a real change every time they sent up a missile.

J.T.: You mean, like a space shot?

A.W.: Right. They said, "Every time this happens, the weather changes and the sun is different." Well, even now, you don't hear anybody saying that the fuel, the fire from the fuel, as they go up through the ozone, has burned it. People don't talk about that, except maybe Helen Caldicott.

I don't know if she even does it. I just feel that, eventually, somebody will mention it. And they will mention it at the point where the Pentagon has even run out of money, when we've stopped feeding this fantasy of going off somewhere. Or it'll just peter out somehow. Then they will say, "We don't want that because actually it was burning up the ozone, every time these things went up." But people have been realizing this and they are really, in my opinion, the experts. Because it's about their lives. If people who go out in the sun all the time—it's their experience—tell you that suddenly the sun is burning me, it gets worse every time you send up a space shot, this matters more to me than some scientist sitting, protected from the sun by several stories of stuff built all around him, opinionating about, "Well, no, it's all fine, it's just a tiny amount of it and you'll never notice it." He would never notice it, because he's not in the sun.

J.T.: That just brings us back to the earth, doesn't it? In our culture here in the U.S. we continue to think of expansionist—oh, we'll move out into space. What you're saying brings in a new thought of, "Oh, maybe there is no other place but Earth, really. Maybe this is really it."

A.W.: There are a lot of ways of thinking about that, too. There is no other place for me, and for many Earth people. But perhaps the people who want to go, or people who have a memory of having been somewhere else, and it would be lovely if they—and they alone—could go there.

M.T.: We'll support their going there.

A.W.: I'll give a couple of dollars. I'm sure you will join in. You have to wonder why some people do colonize naturally. That is their nature. You do have to think about that. You go from country to country colonizing and eventually you try to go from planet to planet colonizing. Why do you do that? Not everybody does that.

J.T.: So that's really allowing them to be who they are, but not at the expense of the other people who choose to live it differently here.

A.W.: The problem is that they're spending our money. They're using Earth resources to go to some other planet. Now, I'm willing for them to go as far away as they'd like and I would be really happy. But two dollars is all I'm willing to contribute. I'm not willing to give them all my taxes to go to these far-flung places, which are of no interest to me. Rocks from the moon I don't need. I have rocks right here. They always talk about exploiting these places that they go to because that, too, is a pattern. They have exploited every place they've been.

M.T.: So much of the space program has been co-opted by the military. You don't hear about that a lot. You just hear about the pioneering, the exploration; you don't really understand the reasoning behind it, what's going on underneath that.

A.W.: "Pioneering" is the operative word. We have to look again at what "pioneering" means. What "settler" means. All of these words tell us a lot. They have been completely distorted from what they actually meant to the people who lived here before these people got here.

M.T.: I think the land we're on right now was populated by the Pomos. Each of these little valleys had their own little Pomo tribe. The story is that many—most—of these tribes had all different languages and they weren't able to communicate with one another. There'd only be a couple, a few tribespeople, who would take the trails over to the coast, or other valleys, to trade. Things would trade back and forth. But there was very little interaction because these people had everything they needed in their own valley. Why go to the next valley?

A.W.: Many people feel like that about this valley. Again, there are other ways of existing. I noticed among the aboriginal people in Australia that they, too, have many different—they have hundreds of languages. Hundreds of groups of people. I never knew that. It makes a lot of sense, if you really have your way and you want to live your way. You have everything your way, even your language. Not everybody needs to have a United States. You need to have a United States if you're colonizing a large territory and you need to have posts of control. Like the fort at every place.

M.T.: I wanted to ask you about your process of writing. Could you describe it to us?

A.W.: A spiral notebook. I used to use a yellow pad when I was married to a lawyer, because he would always have the long legal pads. But I like spiral notebooks, because they're portable, they have nice covers, and they're very inexpensive. I write in that. I often write in bed. I use the computer only when I'm transcribing from the longhand, a manuscript. That's about it.

M.T.: What about where you write and how you allocate time to writing. Do you separate yourself from other activities?

A.W.: I do more of that, yes, because sometimes, as with this book, I wrote it over a period of a year—*Possessing the Secret of Joy.* I was able to do that because I took a sabbatical from the work of political activism. I just said, "I cannot both write this and appear there and march there and do this and that." Once you drop a lot of other stuff, it's just wonderfully freeing, so you can really put all of your energy into the creative work.

M.T.: You mentioned also, you wrote about meditating, using meditation, when you're writing.

A.W.: I meditate when I'm writing every morning. Sometimes, when I'm not writing, if I haven't decided to write a book that will take months and months, I don't do the discipline of meditation because I really do feel I do it in other ways. But when I'm writing, it just is so helpful to—I think I do it mostly because I want to be pure, I want my thought to be pure. By pure I mean really just the best thought, that everybody in the book will have really my best and finest thought. Even if I am writing about a demon. That demon should have my best and purest thought about his or her "demonness." I think that writing is a great responsibility because you can mistreat a maligned character, just as you can people. That's a great responsibility. If you do it badly, if you do something or cause the character to be out of character, I would feel it almost the same if I had done something bad to a person.

M.T.: I know you've responded to this critique before, but I'd like to ask you about it. That is, in *The Color Purple,* there was some criticism that came out about your portrayal of black men. Could you talk about that and respond to that now?

A.W.: Many of my critics really preferred the old model of the black man, which they were busily trying to construct during the sixties and some of the seventies, which is of someone who is fairly cold, in charge, up against the whatever (usually with a gun in one hand and a woman who is of no importance in the crook of the other arm, not connected to anybody else and rarely connected to himself): the need to be a man in the dominator model was very much a part of what that criticism came out of. I wrote a book in which someone starts out kind of like that, with the old model of what a man should be, but who changes completely, who ends up sitting on the porch with his former wife, sewing. I think that there are men who will never forgive me for that, because to them it means that I have turned this man into a sissy—or into a woman, even though I go to great lengths to show that not every man who sews is a "woman," and I try to remind them that it's a very old African tradition that men sew. Also, that men in Africa don't traditionally wear pants. They wear robes. But this was lost on the critics, partly because of our history, in which, for so many years, black men were seen as kind of weak and always subservient to white people. There was a need for a superman kind of quality, which I never bought, don't like, and would never try to pass off as what I consider a real person.

M.T.: There was also a redemptive quality you incorporated in the character Albert.

A.W.: Yes, because I love him as much as I love anybody else in the book. If anything saddened me, it was that people who denigrated the depiction of black men couldn't see how much I loved this man. In fact, that if I didn't love him so much I wouldn't have taken the trouble to put him through all of the changes that he goes through to become the kind of person who can be talked to and who can listen.

M.T.: I just was reminded of something you wrote about how when you were writing *The Color Purple*, working on it, that you didn't like Brooklyn.

A.W.: I didn't like New York. I hated New York. But you know, it's because I'm so completely melded with all of the parts of myself, and these characters are parts of myself. That's why they come to me and not to somebody else. They are mine. They come out of me. When we got to San Francisco, they liked the beauty, but they didn't like earthquakes, and they were loud and insistent and that's how I got here in Anderson Valley. I knew that I needed to be in a place where they felt comfortable. I know there must be writers who can write about the "kind of characters" in *The Color Purple*, [in] a little apartment somewhere in an urban setting, but that's not me. And for *Possessing the Secret of Joy*, I started it in Mexico. Because, again, this setting, which I love, was just really a little too posh. I needed a third-world country; Africa was far, but Mexico turned out to be a kind of Africa of this part of the world. I needed to think about what it would be like to have this kind of procedure, this mutilation, in a setting where you didn't have medical care, you didn't have antiseptics, you didn't have anesthesia, you didn't have people who actually knew what they were doing, even.

J.T.: Tell our listeners what you're speaking of.

A.W.: I'm talking about female genital mutilation and writing a novel in which I discuss this procedure and its impact on a woman in the book, and the need to leave my quite wonderful house for writing in Mendocino and go to Mexico, where I was right in the middle of a poor— well, I didn't live right in the middle of it, but I was close to a village that reminded me of Africa. Because the thing about living in this culture, it is so easy to assume that everybody in the world has ample space and ample food and ample clothing. That's just not true.

M.T.: We were talking earlier, before we started the interview, about radio being the medium of storytelling. I think, since you've brought up about where you live, it might be interesting for you to describe where you live, for the listeners.

A.W.: What attracted me to this part of the world—Northern California—is really the resemblance to Georgia that it has. Georgia isn't this dramatic; it's more simple and plain. But there is the same kind of spaciousness in the out-of-doors, the same forested areas and the same valleys and sort of rolling hills. I lived in Boonville for a while, but it became too congested. I don't know if you've seen it lately, but there are many more cars and things. I just needed to be back up in the hills. This has been a very good place for me. A very good place for dreaming.

M.T.: Your ancestors like it here, too?

A.W.: Oh, yes, they're quite happy.

J.T.: This reminds me, in your new book, *Possessing the Secret of Joy*, you're talking about genital mutilation, and at some point in the book, you talk about circumcision for both men and women: in circumcising men it's taking off a piece of foreskin that's like a feminine quality in men; for women it's taking the masculine quality and it's taking this away from our, making us one gender, rather than, maybe, something else. Can you speak to that?

A.W.: Well, I was just thinking, as you were talking, that the one thing I loved about the Maori was that they were very much at ease about being people of male and female spirit. They have no qualms; they would just talk about being balanced and having a spirit that encompasses male and female. This description of the circumcision of men and the circumcision of women is actually taken from a very old culture, the Dogon, in Mali. That is exactly what it is about, that the foreskin, to these people, symbolized that quality, that female quality in the man, that they were asking him, forcing him, to denounce. So you take off this circle that is representing your woman spirit and, as a man, you cannot have that. Then, for the women, the clitoris, to them, signified the penis in the woman (and also signified her masculine spirit), but as a woman she was not permitted to have a masculine spirit. So, by excising the clitoris, the message to her was that she had to be in every respect a person with a feminine spirit. That a masculine spirit, or a masculine and feminine spirit, could not coexist in the same body.

J.T.: There is much mischief in the world today due to sexual identity and stereotyping sexuality. You may have hit on one of the major mischief makings.

A.W.: I hope so, because I think it would help people to understand that people are naturally bisexual, as they are naturally bispiritual. You have a male and a female spirit. You have a male and a female sexuality. It's because you have a male and a female parent. I think it's useful to consider this discussion in the book, because we need to know what ancient people have done to start this duality that we have, that we are really burdened by this need to be sure that every woman is locked into femininity. And every man is locked into masculinity. Now, you could have that, you could have a really totally masculine man and a totally feminine woman, if you could somehow have parents who were both. For instance, if you and I had a child, we could expect, maybe, to have a totally female feminine person. But even then it wouldn't work because both of us had fathers. You know, the other sex never disappears. Why would it?

J.T.: Yes, that's the way it's set up.

A.W.: Right.

M.T.: Also the figure of a hundred million used to be mentioned.

J.T.: Even right now, today, in 1992, how many women and girls actually go through this circumcision?

A.W.: The estimates differ. The World Health Organization says 75 million to 100 million. Some people say 95 million; some say 85 million. But it's very high; the 100 million is the upper figure.

J.T.: You write about it in the book and I'd like you to share it with our listeners: some of the personality changes, the painfulness, of this mutilation and what happens.

A.W.: Well, first of all, I want to qualify this comment about the numbers, because there are three kinds of mutilation. One is clitoral; one is the clitoris and the inner labia; and the pharaonic, which is what Tashi has in this book, in which everything is scraped away and the woman is sewed up and has to be reopened with every . . . Intercourse often is preceded by being opened, often with instruments—knives and things. There's also the infibulation, which happens to this woman in this book.

It is just an incredible violation of the body and the spirit. There is no way of actually rectifying it. Intercourse is extremely painful and would not, I don't think, be recognized as intercourse, because it is such a battle and sometimes the men are actually wounded in this attempt to sleep with their wives. To have a child means that you have to be cut open again in order to have the child come out; I'm not talking about just the episiotomy; you have to actually cut through the sutures that have been made in the flesh of the woman. Often all of this is without any anesthesia and any antiseptic.

J.T.: Does this go on in the United States?

A.W.: It does. The people who come from cultures where it's done and settle here consider it part of their culture. It's like bringing favorite food or marriage customs. In fact this is a marriage custom. Apparently it is done in hospitals in Washington, D.C., and New York and Philadelphia. In London as well. And in France. Because the people who do it do it wherever they are. They don't say, "Well, we're going to America now, we don't have to do this." I think it's in this context in the West that you see how much it is about control of female sexuality. A lot of the people, especially from some of the Arab countries, feel that when the children get here they become too wild and too much like Americans. I don't know if you read about the people from an Arab country somewhere, where the child, a young woman, they thought she was too wild and they killed her. The mother and the father actually killed her. They expressed no regret because they felt she was beginning to be out of their control. So it is about deciding that your child will not have her own sexuality. If she is desexed she is much more malleable.

J.T.: This is legal, in hospitals? Doctors will go along with this?

A.W.: Apparently so.

J.T.: And if it's not, it's done illegally and it's done without the benefit of sterilization.

A.W.: But I think in this country it is mostly done by doctors. Now, this is something we will be looking into, as this goes on. As I can learn more. I've had a really wonderful letter from a group whose specialty in this country is female mutilation. It's a recent organization, but people are aware that it's being done. In London, it's the Somali community that has it done to the daughters. In France, it's the Mali community.

J.T.: In Africa, it's not done overtly; it's more underground. The tribal people are not for it, but it's more tradition.

A.W.: No, they are for it. Have you been aware of the story of Aminata Diop? She's a woman from Mali who ran away from Mali because her parents decided that she should have this done to herself. She ran to France. Her fiancé in Mali denounced her; her father denounced her, beat up her mother, threw her mother out of the house—banished her mother because the child had run away. She has been seeking political asylum in France . . . she's been there going on two years now. It's a custom and the sad thing, as with Tashi, what happens is that people think that the culture demands it, and if you don't have it, you're not really part of the culture.

J.T.: So for her, it was a group pressure to belong.

A.W.: More than that, though. If you're part of a tribe, and you have been completely overwhelmed by the settlers, whoever they are, you perceive yourself to be holding on to whatever you have that you are actually permitted to keep. You have to think about the cultures in which everything is taken: their masks, their everything. Everything. Then you have to imagine what things you could keep that nobody could take away from you, that would prove that you really are who you were. Then you get down to things like scars. Nobody wants scars. But you could get scars and you keep those. It's a very difficult choice she makes, and she lives to regret it. But it's one that you can understand if you've ever really thought about what happens to people from whom everything has been taken.

M.T.: Alice, one of the things you wrote about was Mother Africa dying, and as Mother Africa dies, the rest of the planet is dying. Could you elaborate on that?

A.W.: I think of Africa as the navel of the world, the birthplace of the world, the peoples of the world. Everything has been, she's just been used as a resource for all the other peoples of the world. They've just gone in and taken, for centuries, without feeling the need to repay and replenish, support, nurture. Now there are colonizers who will claim that they did that. But they did that only—what they did was to set up schools just to teach the people enough so they could work for them. You know, things like that, that's not the same as actually caring for the place. But Africa is so central to the life of the planet, as far as I'm concerned, that you cannot ignore it and let it die. You have to be very attentive because it is also a crossroads. It is also part of your body; I think that's the truest concept: that if Africa is your heart, and I think of how, from space, the photograph of the earth, Africa is the heart of the earth. It looks like a heart and it's right in the middle there. If your heart is dying . . . and you can even see from that shot how much of Africa has been used up. The desert, which used to be the breadbasket of Europe; the Romans, that whole area was planted. They grew food for Europe and for Rome. Now it's a desert. That is the way in which Africa has been used by the rest of the world. If it is your heart—even if it is just your arm—if it is dying, then you're dying. Because it's a part of your body. You can't turn away from any part of the earth. That's why every part of it is sacred.

M.T.: I just want to continue the Africa thing. You've written about your solidarity and compassion for Winnie Mandela and what she's had to go through, particularly during the time of Nelson's incarceration and the kind of persecution she suffered through and so forth. I wanted to give you the opportunity to speak to what's happening, the fact that Nelson and Winnie Mandela have separated. I want to give you an opportunity to speak to that.

A.W.: I feel happy that they're separating, because I think that they never had much of a chance to have a marriage. I prefer people to just honestly separate and go about being two whole people who still have some respect for each other. I prefer that than having people insist on putting up this united front that doesn't really exist. So that's really nice. What I worry about is that this charge against her (which has resurfaced with this announcement) that she helped to kill this young boy and that she's an alcoholic and that she has a younger lover, all these things. I think all of these things have been used to deflect attention from the fact that the new South Africa is really the old South Africa. It hasn't changed yet. People are pretending that there is some big major change—and there is some change. But we're still looking at a society that is extremely economically unjust, extremely repressive for black people. And a society in which the white people still maintain all of the best land, all of the best jobs, all of the best housing, all of the best food, all of the best fresh air. But somehow people have made this one woman . . . if she has broken and committed a crime, I think she really deserves all the compassion that we can muster. Because, frankly, personally I don't think I could have stood up to the things that she did, for so long.

J.T.: In talking about Africa, I know that you've written things about the goddess in Africa and about the original goddess. I know there was an article you wrote about Medusa possibly being the precursor to Athena. Can you talk about that?

A.W.: You have to take the very long view of history. If, in fact, the first people were Africans, if all of us are Africans, and if, in fact, worship is innate, and if, in fact, the ancient people were just as clever as the modern people, and if, in fact, you can say the woman's body, in the way that it gives birth and replenishes people, is a sort of symbolic earth in that the earth also gives birth and peoples the world with trees and flowers—they're connected, I think, in the psyche, in the ancient psyche. Then I think you can say that, of course, the ancient people of Africa were well aware of goddesses (which they still actually worship—Yemaya and other goddesses in Africa). I also believe that Medusa—the Greeks, you know, actually had a lot of interactions with Africans and learned a lot from Africa and wrote about their interaction with the Egyptians, who were Africans. For some people, it's hard to imagine that the ancient Egyptians were black. But all you have to do is remember that the ancient Massachusetts people were red, so that should help a lot. They tend to look at you as if Egypt was somewhere over in Germany. But in fact these were African people. So the Greeks learned from them. My feeling is that the African woman's hair was the Medusa snakes and the fierceness of the African woman warrior turned these people to stone.

J.T.: What would you say the snakes represented in the African culture? I know in the Christian culture, it's the bringer of evilness.

A.W.: Well, yes, it represents us: it represents women, and it represents black people. That's why it's always put down. But that is also why—because it represents earth people and women in all earth cultures, and especially in societies of women—the snake is revered.

J.T.: Do you use the goddess rituals in your life now? Thinking of Mother Earth, you said earlier that Mother Earth is really like the heaven, and, I think, in a feminine way.

A.W.: The earth, I think, is really all the goddess I need. But at the same time, I understand that what you are doing when you make goddesses (people do create gods and goddesses), you are making forms that represent certain realities, certain spiritual realities, material realities of the earth. You see this a lot in ritual culture, where they have goddesses who, if you talk to them, you pray to them, they bring you rain. Well, you can understand that what they're really saying is that there's a spirit, the way the whole thing works is very spiritual, and that the rain comes because you have a connection. Somehow the goddess is your connection to the forces up there.

M.T.: You write about acting out your vision and the importance of living your vision. Could you speak about that?

A.W.: I was writing about that in the context of *The Temple of My Familiar*, because it represents my great vision. The great vision is a Native American notion, or earth-peoples notion, that everybody has a great vision. It doesn't mean as great as anybody else's. It just means that it's the biggest one you've had. What happens is that, at some point in your life, you begin to feel and to see in yourself, in your own being, how it all comes together, how you're connected, not only materially but through time. You do have a duty to make this visible for other people to use, basically. But it's also very good for you and if you swallow, if you repress it, if you pretend you don't get the message, then I think things go very badly for you. That was how I wrote *The Temple of My Familiar*, feeling very much that, during that period of my life, I understood the way things are connected, and I needed to share that.

M.T.: Alice, I hope you keep going on sharing your vision and living your vision. Thanks.

A.W.: You're welcome.

J.T.: Thank you, Alice.

11

"On Finding Your Bliss":
Interview with Evelyn C. White
from *Ms.* (1998)

EVELYN C. WHITE: *By the Light of My Father's Smile* is your first novel in six years. What prompted such an overtly sexual theme?

ALICE WALKER: At the end of the novel there's a poem that says, "When life descends into the pit / I must become my own candle / willingly burning myself / to light up the darkness around me." Because there's no sense of safety anywhere, no place we feel we can go that's not polluted or poisoned, for a lot of people life has pretty much fallen into the pit. When I was working on my last novel, *Possessing the Secret of Joy*, I realized that sexuality is the place where life has definitely fallen into the pit for women. The only way we'll ever change that is by affirming, celebrating, and acknowledging sexuality in our daily lives.

Women must begin to write more truthfully about the profound mystery of sex. I think that race is also a mystery. Which is to say that neither can be fully comprehended except as deeply mysterious expressions through which we can learn profound lessons about life. It is almost impossible not to learn something about yourself in the sexual act. So it's important for women to be alert to the spiritual growth and self-discovery they can attain by paying close attention to their sexuality.

I was also thinking about how organized religion has systematically undermined and destroyed the sexual and spiritual beliefs of millions of indigenous people. There have been people on earth who didn't think about sex the way white, Western men do. It is very painful to think that the "missionary position," which reinforces patriarchal, male dominance over women, was forced upon people who once loved having women freely express their sexuality, whether they were on the top or bottom.

E.W.: Given the prevalence of patriarchal repression of female sexuality, what was the process you had to go through to get to the extremely erotic language in your book?

A.W.: I think the process started with wanting myself. Women have to understand that regardless of who does not want us, we have to want ourselves. Then we can begin to see and appreciate other women and the amazing possibilities of self-love and acceptance we can find in our union with each other. We can sit back and wait for men to love us until we are blue in the face, but since I loved women already, I decided, why wait?

There is also a place of humility that comes from really understanding that we have all entered this plane through the legs of a woman. And that it is a holy place. My love of women intensified during all those years I researched female genital mutilation and thought about women holding down other women and girls to destroy that holy and profoundly sacred temple. I feel this novel is connected to *Possessing the Secret of Joy* because, after writing about the debasement and sheer hatred of female sexuality, my spirit needed to write about the joy, the pleasure, promise, and growth. And I wanted to show how women can grow in a relationship with each other.

By no means am I saying that such a relationship is smooth sailing. It definitely isn't, but there are some incredible lessons that can be learned.

E.W.: What did you learn about yourself while writing the novel?

A.W.: That I am completely scandalous, rebellious, and stubborn! All my parts were telling me to write this book because it feels like a medicine for the times. Now, I could be terribly wrong. But with AIDS, we've reached a point where sex is scary for most people. We have lost the sexual spontaneity that most of us thought would be ours forever. That is a major loss. The youth are scared to make love and scared not to.

E.W.: With all the taboos about speaking openly of the sexual experiences of black women, was there also immense satisfaction for you in crossing this boundary?

A.W.: Yes, breaking out is probably what I do best. It seems to me that there is so much joy going on between women that is happening as we live, simultaneously, in a death-dealing culture. It is very joyful to write about this reality.

E.W.: This novel will probably turn you into a sex guru. Are you prepared for that?

A.W.: [Laughs] Yes.

E.W.: What is some of the advice you'd offer to women searching for sexual bliss?

A.W.: Self-love is the first and hardest rule to stick by. Women need to not abandon themselves in their quest for bliss and love. You can love yourself spiritually, physically—in almost any way that anybody else can. I think that anatomically this is the reason we're constructed the way we are.

There are many years when women get caught up in reproductive sex. It's my experience that in their late forties and fifties, women aren't that crazy about reproductive sex because it's generally too late for us; it's not that easy to conceive. But there's something at that point that I've decided to call evolutionary sex. It's a sexuality that can be with women, men, or yourself. It's about exploring and expanding your bodily love and spiritual awareness. That's a form of sex that is within the reach of everybody.

E.W.: You have an extraordinary reach and ability with characterization in your novels. Where did the characters in *By the Light . . .* come from?

A.W.: I do a lot of spiritual preparation, so the characters evolve from what feels like a state of grace. I also have a home in Mexico, and being there had a lot to do with it. Going there and trying to learn the language and meeting dark-skinned Mexicans got me thinking about African Americans and American Indians who came to Mexico to find freedom.

I was really struck at one point that, while I don't live in Mexico all the time, I'd done the same thing. I had been chased to Mexico to find peace and freedom. I'd always wanted to go deeper into what it means to be black and Indian.

In the novel, I create a band of people, the Mundo, who are neither African nor Indian, but a blend. The spirit I had to go by in creating this culture is essentially mine. It's a reflection of how I think things should be rather than how they've been. Because when we look at the mess the patriarchy has made of the planet, it's clear that we're on the wrong path. We know that matriarchal societies existed before. It's important that we start thinking about ancient future ways, because this way is not working.

On the other hand, it may be that the whole world is gasping its last breath. As one of the characters in the novel says about black and Indian people, the dominant Western thought has been that we're all vanishing. And it seems as if millions of us are being wiped out every minute. But that doesn't mean that the white men are going to be happy by themselves. Because what they'll have left is a planet that they've ruined, with no idea of how to heal it.

E.W.: In the novel, the ancestral spirit father witnesses and comments upon the sexual blossoming of his daughters. How did this narrative approach come to you?

A.W.: Again, it's my belief, based on my own self, that what women want most is to be blessed in our sexuality by our parents. As women, I believe we'd especially like to be blessed by our fathers. In that blessing, we'd like the father to know everything about us, just like when we were born, and to love us still. We want them to love what we love and bless what we bless. The only way to show that clearly was to have him witness the sexuality of his children. In the culture of the Mundo, whatever mess you've made during life you have to come back and deal with after you die. So in coming back, the father gets to witness his daughters' sexual behavior.

E.W.: Don't you think a lot of people are going to think this is heresy, given the sexually abusive role some fathers have played in their daughters' lives?

A.W.: Well, it's time for the fathers to deal with the hypocrisy of their own sexual behavior and to extend themselves to their daughters in a positive way. The worst fear many of these men have regarding their daughters' sexuality is that the young women are having a great time. And I'm here to tell you that many of them are. So get over it, and be there for them.

E.W.: Any words for the forces that might want to continue the tradition of trying to ban your books?

A.W.: Actually, I started to put a message in this one telling those people not to even let the children see it. It's okay with me. I know there are going to be people who will have a fit. But these are the selfsame people who every day for the last six months have been reading about the president's semen on this young girl's dress. The hypocrisy of it is astounding. When women get to be adults and elders, it's time for us to speak honestly about the issues that have been shrouded in hypocrisy and murkiness.

E.W.: Is that how you see yourself now, as an elder?

A.W.: In the ancient Cherokee tradition, you become an adult when you're fifty-two. I see myself as being between that point and the beginning of the elder state. I'm definitely in the place of speaking on these issues. There is nothing more important than looking at sexuality with honesty and openheartedness. Our children are continuing to get pregnant when they're very young. They're having unsafe sex—we know this because they're having babies. The HIV rate among young black people is climbing rapidly. I feel that the heart of our dilemma as a culture and as a people is sex. I think that many fathers have not known that they could have a positive role in sanctioning their daughters' sexuality.

E.W.: How do you think your novel will help such fathers?

A.W.: They need to know how deeply their daughters are wounded by their apparent incomprehension that their daughters have sexual feelings. I think young girls are hurt when they come to understand that just because they are female, their fathers don't believe they have sexual passions or interests. Meanwhile, they get to watch their brothers be encouraged to go out and sow wild oats and be affirmed in their manhood. It's a painful place for young women to be.

Because we live in a patriarchal system, most men haven't thought much about what they can do to deal with this, other than to try to keep their daughters home, to make them feel really bad for going out and having a sexual life. I think they should be made aware of the tenderness that is required from fathers in raising daughters. They should embrace the whole female child in a way that makes her feel affirmed in her body.

E.W.: Do you think the reason more fathers don't relate to their daughters in this way is because of the fears of being accused of sexual impropriety, especially because there have been so many instances of that?

A.W.: The fathers have to assume that these girl children, to whom they've given birth, inherit intelligence and can understand what is said to them. It then becomes imperative for fathers to talk to them about sexual matters and to be honest, loving, and patient. Fathers need to teach young women what is out there. The reason you see so many women become the victims of doggish men is because their fathers have not told them anything except that if you go out and do such and such, you're a slut and no daughter of mine. That is not helpful. At this late date, it also encourages disease and death.

My novel is really a call to fathers to stand with their daughters and help protect them in a world where they are vulnerable. If a child has a strong mother, she's very lucky. But barring that, she gets faulty information and easily becomes a victim.

E.W.: What role should mothers or the female partners of men play in this?

A.W.: Both parents should talk to both genders because what happens now simply upholds the patriarchy. The man gets to tell the boy to be the aggressor. The system has already told the woman that she is to submit. We need to break this. Parents need to understand that they made their children together. One is male, the other is female, but they are not that different spiritually.

All this talk about how a man can't talk to his daughter about menstruation . . . well, please. By the time men have slept with women for, say, thirty years, they've seen as much menstrual blood as the women have. So again, get over it. Don't try to hide behind that one.

E.W.: You recently made your fourth trip to Cuba. How was that?

A.W.: I first went to Cuba in 1978 with a contingent of artists, writers, and musicians. Some of the older white Cubans retained racist feelings that were conveyed to us with a certain condescension and stiffness.

We asked about the treatment of gay people in Cuba and were told that they weren't allowed to teach or become doctors. This was very upsetting. It was as if you'd met this really beautiful person who had one aspect of them that wasn't, and it just made your heart ache. But these feelings were something we knew we could work with them on, and we have. Gay people in Cuba aren't subjected to that discrimination now.

I remember the people of color being full of life. I've since returned to bring medical aid. I could see at one point how the economic embargo had brought poverty to the people and made them downhearted. It was the closest to defeat I'd ever seen the Cuban people, and it wasn't clear that they'd survive. But it was clear that if they went down, they'd do so with their integrity and dignity intact.

Recently, since I've made a commitment to defend Cuba and educate people about the revolution and the country's culture, I felt it was important to go to places I hadn't visited before. I asked writer Margaret Randall, who lived in Cuba for many years, to act as a translator for my partner, Zelie, and me.

We were treated so sweetly by the people. Wherever we went there were performances. We visited Che Guevara's crypt and met his children and widow. I loved seeing the extensive organic farms the Cubans have cultivated. They are good models for small, developing countries that want to maintain an independent food supply. I'm so grateful to see a place on the planet where there are people whose hearts haven't been shriveled by hatred or greed.

E.W.: The Cuban Revolution made great strides in creating equality for women. What are your feelings about what appears to be a reemergence of prostitution in the country?

A.W.: I think the young women are extremely naive. They have been educated and protected by the revolution from such things. Consequently, many of them have an arrogance about their own bodies that perhaps makes them think that they are immune to and exempt from AIDS. I am very afraid for them.

When I see older white men with these primarily young, educated women of color, it is hard on the spirit. The women are too naive and inexperienced to know that they are engaging in an ancient system that oppresses women. They think of what they're doing as a lark because it enables them to get a new tube of lipstick or some shampoo. But it's very dangerous for them.

E.W.: The governor of New Jersey has offered a huge reward for the return of Assata Shakur, who is in exile in Cuba. As you know, she was imprisoned in the U.S. in the 1970s for her alleged involvement in a shoot-out that left a state patrolman dead. What are your feelings about Assata?

A.W.: I take her word that she didn't kill the man. Cuba permitted her to have a life, but she is still unable to be with her family and friends. To put a bounty on her head is evil. Assata Shakur is a great human being. She should be left in peace and happiness. Any attempt to make her suffer is utterly demonic.

E.W.: What other passions do you have going on these days?

A.W.: I'm eager to learn more about the sovereignty movement in Hawaii. People should know that Hawaii is a country and should be respected as such. Because it was forcibly annexed to the United States does not mean that it is the U.S., except by conquest. A masterpiece on decolonization has been written by Haunani Trask, one of Hawaii's most famous and fierce Hawaii-loving poets. It is called *From a Native Daughter*. This book is so powerful it will change the way you think about Hawaii, and all lands seized by force, forever.

Besides that, I'm beginning to be very passionate about being a homebody. I'm not going to be doing any more lectures or readings beyond the ones I've already agreed to do. I'm going to curtail my travel after this book tour.

I've also become very interested in heirloom seeds. These are seeds that are not artificial hybrids but are open-pollinated, and that have been collected by people who are trying to preserve the seed pool. The seed companies are rapidly corralling all the seeds. By using heirloom seeds we make it possible for people to continue to grow fruits and vegetables without relying on the seed companies.

I'm also going to be initiating healing circles and women's and elders' councils on the land. These circles won't be designed to solve any problems, but for us to connect with each other and get grounded. Each circle will eventually connect with other circles around the globe so that, over time, we'll get a stronger sense of who we are, as just regular people, in the world. We're not going to do any conflict resolution. One of the things we may have to acknowledge at this point is that the earth could be entering its death struggle. We will have to try to be present as loving, compassionate earthlings.

I see the circles and councils as ways to share consciousness. This is an idea that many people are having at this time. It seems to be a spontaneous response to the situation we're in. Many people are aware that we are in peril and that there is no trustworthy leadership. It's important to comfort and be with each other during this time because so many people are alone. That really shouldn't be, but that's where this culture has brought us, to loneliness and isolation.

E.W.: I see a lot of isolation among so-called successful people, especially among African American women. How do you think this came to pass?

A.W.: We integrated into a system where loneliness is the norm. In the past, we became part of the industrial revolution, and now, in the present, part of the corporate era, both of which put money and jobs first. We've sacrificed community. That's what the circles can give back to us. We can "be" rather than "do," because we can see now that all the "doing" doesn't bring happiness. It just makes for exhaustion, depletion, loneliness, and fear. So it's time to slow down, sit down, and meditate. And join with others from a place of centeredness and calm.

E.W.: Does this come from your Buddhist practice?

A.W.: For the last few years I've studied tonglen. It is basically a practice of breathing in pain, fear, and darkness, and breathing out what you'd rather the world had. I'm concentrating on this one practice because it is useful in opening the heart. What's happening with all the heart disease is that people's emotions are getting locked in a tight heart. We need help from the ancient teachings to show us how to stretch and open our hearts.

E.W.: Is it ever frightening to breathe in the fear and pain?

A.W.: Yes, it gets very scary. One night I thought I was dying because I felt as if a herd of horses was running over my heart. I made the decision to just stay with it and keep breathing and relaxing my heart. I also accepted that they might just run over me and that I wouldn't get up. I'd die. As it turned out, my heart was okay. It opened wide.

There are many ancient practices that we should avail ourselves of so that we can address whatever constrictions we might have. Buddhism has been especially helpful to me because it affirms the necessity for quiet, compassion over anger, being over doing. It encourages people to accept life in its totality, not just the good parts.

E.W.: I'm sure there are those who look at your life and your literary career and can't imagine that there are many bad parts.

A.W.: The good parts are only really good because you have the bad parts. Otherwise, you wouldn't know the difference. You wouldn't be quite so appreciative of the good.

The bad times—and I've had my share—are almost invariably the places where I've learned crucial lessons. In fact, I'd say that the bad parts should be embraced more, even though you really don't feel like that when you're suffering.

After a while, you begin to see how the lessons come out of the bad, which makes you grateful for the pain you've endured. You learn to accept that one day you'll be famous, the next day infamous. One day you'll be rich, the next day poor. One day people will think you're great, the next day they'll think you're terrible. And this is just the stuff of life. Life is not bright, cheerful, and sunny all the time. The wise ones know this.

But this is the lesson that seems hardest for Westerners to understand. People think that when something goes "wrong," it's their fault. If only they had done something differently. But sometimes things go wrong to teach you what is right.

The way I see it, life is about growth, struggle, and trying to expand your love of self and of other people. Also to really try hard not to cause harm—to cultivate a way of life that is harmless. This is likely to take all your energy for your entire life. And if you harm some folks along the way, well, that's why the apology was born.

12

"On the Meaning of Suffering and the Mystery of Joy": Alice Walker and Pema Chödrön in Conversation from Sounds True (1998)

Judith Lief, Moderator

ALICE WALKER: About four years ago, I had . . . well, about four years ago, I was having a very difficult time. And I had lost someone really, really dear to me that I loved deeply. And nothing seemed to help. And I was talking with Tami Simon of Sounds True. She had come to do an interview. And after the interview, she said to me, "Well, have you listened to Pema Chödrön?" And I said, "No." And she said, "Well, I will send you a tape, a set, called *Awakening Compassion*." And I didn't tell her all my troubles, but inside, I was saying, "Please do, soon."

She sent it, and I stayed in the country on my sofa, mainly, and I listened to you, Pema, every night for the next year. [laughter] And I studied really hard, and I practiced tonglen. And it was tonglen, which is the practice of taking in pain and darkness, and just whatever awful thing you're feeling, and sending out whatever you would prefer, that helped me through this incredibly difficult passage.

And I wrote to you and I said to you, "Thank you so much, because it was listening to you and learning from you that helped me through this period." So I really, you know, want to thank you again, and also to ask you a question. The long way of asking it is that, in my experience, suffering is perennial. It always comes. And is there really a use? I mean, what is the use of suffering? I used to think there was no use at all. And now I know that there is. And I wonder if you would teach on that a little.

PEMA CHÖDRÖN: You know, these Lojong teachings that meant so much to you, I think the reason that I was so taken by those teachings is because they are based on using suffering as good medicine. Like, the metaphor is using poison as medicine, as if there's, like, a moment in time that reoccurs over and over and over again in every human life, of discomfort, extreme discomfort, called suffering. And what usually happens in that moment habitually with all of us—you know, it's, like, genetic—is that, at that point, it hardens us, somehow. It hardens the heart because we don't want any more pain.

A.W.: Yes.

P.C.: And the Lojong teachings say you can take that very moment and flip it. And the very same thing that causes us to harden, and our habitual patterns of suffering to intensify and escalate, can soften us and make us more decent, kinder people. So it's a teaching for people who are willing to cultivate their courage. It takes a lot of courage. But what's wonderful about it is, you have plenty of material. [laughter] You know, like, if it was just, like, wait for the moments of the high points, you know, then you might give up very soon. But suffering, you know, is like an endless succession.

And that was one of the main teachings of the Buddha, also, is that he called it *dukkha*, which is often translated as "suffering." But maybe a better translation, I think, is "dissatisfaction"—and sometimes, of course, it's intense physical pain, or emotional pain—that this dissatisfaction is inherent in being human beings. So, it's, like, not some mistake that you or I have made as individuals. And therefore, it doesn't really need to keep escalating. If we can learn to catch that moment, relax with it, it becomes the seed of compassion, the seed of loving-kindness.

A.W.: I was surprised, actually, that there is such a physical connection, that the heart literally responds to this practice. You can feel it responding. As you breathe in, what is so difficult to bear . . . there is the initial resistance, you know, which is the fear, the constriction.

P.C.: Yeah.

A.W.: I guess that's the period when you really have to be brave. If you just keep going and doing the practice, the heart actually relaxes. And that was quite amazing to feel.

P.C.: One of the things that I also like about this body of teachings is that, often, when we start out on a spiritual path, we have ideals for ourselves, particularly, that we think we're supposed to live up to. We're supposed to be better than we are in some way. And with this practice, you just completely take yourself completely as you are. And in fact, what happens, by taking pain and beginning to breathe it in for yourself and all others in the same boat as you are, ironically, or surprisingly, it heightens your awareness of exactly where you're stuck. And so, rather than, suddenly you feel like a magic makeover, that suddenly you're this great person, there's much more of an honesty, emotional honesty, about where you're stuck.

A.W.: Exactly. You see that the work is right ahead of you all the time.

P.C.: And then there's this word, *maitri*, which means then the loving-kindness and the compassion is for this self that is stuck. And then you have a sense of all the other sentient beings stuck, just like you; and so it also awakens compassion. And then, in the process, there is a kind of unstuckness that starts to happen.

A.W.: Exactly. Well, you know, I remember one day when I really got it that we're not, as human beings, joined together and connected because of our perfection; it's because of our flaws.

P.C.: Yeah.

A.W.: That was such a relief. [laughter]

P.C.: Alice has a dog named Rumi, right?

A.W.: Rumi.

P.C.: Yes. Jalaluddin Rumi wrote about all the shared darkness of human beings from the beginning of time, being a shared thing, and actually becoming something that opens up your heart and opens up your world. You begin to think bigger. And so, rather than it depressing you, you feel like part of the whole.

A.W.: Yes. Well, I like what you say about the darkness—beginning to understand that the darkness represents your wealth. Because that's true. I mean, in our culture, and in the world, there's been so much fixation on the light, as if the darkness can be dispensed with. And of course, it cannot. I mean, after all, there is night. You know? There is earth. So this is a wonderful acknowledgment of the richness.

So when I was listening to *Awakening Compassion* over and over—

P.C.: For one year, really?

A.W.: For a year.

P.C.: And then, when you wrote me the letter, I think you said, "Dear Pema," and you explained how you were lying on your sofa, and you were listening. By that time, I don't think the year was up yet, so I didn't get the whole picture. But then you said something like, "I write poems," or something.

A.W.: Yes.

P.C.: And then you signed it, "Alice," I think, or something. But at the top of it, it said, "Alice Walker." And I get a lot of letters, which you probably do, too.

A.W.: Yeah.

P.C.: You know, like fifty a day or something. So, I'm just writing back this answer. And then I said, "Alice Walker!" [laughter] And I think when I wrote back, I said, "P.S. Are you *the* Alice Walker?" [laughter]

A.W.: Yeah.

P.C.: "In which case, I am also a fan of yours."

A.W.: But actually, you know, when it gets to a certain degree of misery, you know, I think the Jamaicans are right to just call each other "fellow sufferer," you know, or "the sufferer."

P.C.: Right.

A.W.: Because that's really how it feels. And when you are in that place, it is just an incredible gift to be given a teaching. I mean, I never knew a thing about Tibetan Buddhism. And I always liked Zen poetry, and I read a lot of Japanese poetry. And I had never really felt that I had an affinity for specific teachings. I mean, I didn't know them well enough. And what I particularly treasured was that you were so real. And, I think it was in this set of tapes, where you talk about when you discovered that your husband was seeing someone else. You threw a rock at him. [laughter] This was very helpful. [laughter] Because, you know, we aren't angels; we aren't saints. And we're all down here, doing the best we can and trying to be good people. But we do get really mad. And so, this was really good, to have a very human, humorous, earthy, real person as a teacher. This was great.

P.C.: You know, it was when that marriage broke up—and that was one of those traumatizing experiences. For some reason—I don't know why it devastated me so much, but it was really a kind of annihilation. And it was the beginning of my spiritual path, definitely, because I was looking for answers.

And so, I had the same experience. I was in the lowest point of my life, and I read this article by Trungpa Rinpoche, which was the same kind of thing. Because this was called "Working with Negativity." That was what I was looking for—answers. I was looking for answers to my anger, which scared me a lot. I kept having all these fantasies of destroying my ex-husband and his new girlfriend. And they were, like, hard to shake.

A.W.: Yes. [laughter]

P.C.: So there was rage, and then there was also an enormous sense of groundlessness, and the fear that accompanied not being able to entertain myself out of this pain. Like, the usual exits, the ways of kind of distracting yourself—nothing was working.

A.W.: Nothing worked.

P.C.: So, when I read Rinpoche, what he basically said, he said there's nothing wrong with negativity. He said there's a lot that you can learn from it. But it's a very strong creative energy. And then he said the problem is *negative* negativity—which is, like, you don't just stay with negativity; you spin off into all the endless cycle of things that you say to yourself about it. You know?

A.W.: Yeah. I'm happy you said that. Because that was a new idea—that what gets us is the spinoff. You know, that if you can just sit with the basic feeling, and breathe that through, then you can free yourself. But it's almost impossible if you're just caught up in one drama after another, mentally.

P.C.: That's right. That's right.

A.W.: Which is what happens.

P.C.: See, that's essential with Tibetan Buddhism, the tantric Buddhism, Vajrayana Buddhism. For instance, because in Vajrayana Buddhism, they talk about how each of the powerful, negative—we call negative—energies, such as anger, say, and lust, and envy, and jealousy, these different energies, how they actually are all wisdoms in disguise. But you have to not spin off. You have to be able to relax with the energy.

So, for me, tonglen, that practice of breathing in, it was my entering into being able, for the first time, to sit with that kind of energy. Because it's so impossible. It seems so impossible to do so, to not spin off. For me, a lot of it was including all the other people, recognizing that so many people were in the same boat as I was.

A.W.: Well, pretty soon, you do recognize that, you know, everybody is in that boat sooner or later, in some form or other. And that's good to feel—that you're not alone.

P.C.: I wanted to ask you something about this. And this is a question about joy. So, it's all very well to talk about a poison as medicine, and breathing in the suffering, and sending out relief, and so forth. But did you find any joy coming out of this?

A.W.: Well, yes. Just not to be so miserable. And I think part of the joy-ousness is just to know that we have help. It was incredibly great to know that this wisdom is so old. It's very old. Which means that people have had all this pain for a long time, and they've been dealing with it. And they were foresighted enough to try to leave it for us to use. And this was very good to know.

I am often supported by spirits and ancestors and, you know, the people of my tribe, whoever they've been and however long ago it's been. So it was like having another tribe of people, of ancestors, come to the rescue, with this wisdom that came through you, and through your way of teaching.

P.C.: And these teachings, actually, they came to Tibet through someone who came from India, Atisha. And he actually, I think, he went to Indonesia—which must have been quite a journey—because he was attracted to them, but nobody was teaching them in India. So he journeyed and then came back to India, and then was invited to Tibet. And that's how they got there. And then, even in Tibet, they kind of went underground for quite a long time.

There's a story I'll tell about the teacher. He was called Chekhawa, Geshe Chekhawa. He was teaching this practice very, sort of, secretly. But he started teaching it to lepers. And the way it was working was, they had leprosy. And instead of the usual approach, which is to hate your illness, be ashamed of your illness, to want more than anything in the world for it to go away, they were being instructed to breathe in the leprosy of all the other lepers, so that the others could be free of it, and send out relief to all the other lepers.

And in Tibetan stories, usually they have happy endings. The lepers were all getting cured. So he was becoming quite famous. On the other hand, he was still keeping it very secret. But he had a really meantempered brother. And this brother hated Buddhism and was cynical, and was just, like, sour grapes about everything. But he began to wonder what was happening in there, with all these cured lepers. So he started listening at the door to what his brother, Geshe Chekhawa, was teaching in there.

And then Geshe Chekhawa began to notice that his brother was getting much nicer, and much kinder. And it began to occur to him that he was listening to the teachings. And, sure enough, he was. Then he thought, "I'm going to start teaching these to everyone. Because if they can help my brother, they can help anyone."

So, actually, they are emerging now, only recently. Trungpa Rinpoche first taught them to us in '79. And I remember then that, as students, most of them weren't ready for them, or ready for tonglen and this teaching. There were comments like, "I do the practice, but secretly, I hope it doesn't work." Or, like, "Who needs it?" basically. But gradually . . . I think the times are ripe for this kind of teaching.

A.W.: Oh, I think it's just the right medicine for today. You know, the other really joyous thing about it is that I feel more open. I feel more openness with people in my world—you know, what you say about feeling more at home in your world. And this is, I think, a result of going the distance in your own heart. You know, just really being disciplined about opening your heart as much as you can.

Now, the thing is that I find, Pema, is that it will close up again. You know?

P.C.: Oh, no. [laughter] One year of listening to me and your heart still closes up?!

A.W.: Well, but again, you know, it's like what you say, that it doesn't close quite. . . .

P.C.: Couldn't you have said that privately or something? [laughter]

A.W.: No, no, no, no. No, no. But it's like that room, you know, where you were saying how the ego is like a closed room. And that our whole life's work is to open the door. And that you may open it and then discover that you are not up to keeping it wide open for long. And it will close again. But then the work is to keep opening it.

P.C.: That's right.

A.W.: So I think it really is just like life. I mean, you do; you reach a plateau. You have an epiphany. You understand something. You feel slightly enlightened about something. But then you lose it.

P.C.: Yeah, right.

A.W.: And that's the reality.

P.C.: That's the reality.

A.W.: So it's not a bad thing.

P.C.: No.

A.W.: And I think, though, that what I'm learning, myself, is that that is when the practice has to be something that you continue. But that brings me to something else that I've discovered in myself and in my practice. Because I have been doing meditation for many, many years. Not tonglen, but TM and metta. And that is that there are times when I will go; I will meditate, really, very on the dot, for a year or so. And then I'll stop.

So, what happens? I mean, does that ever happen to you?

P.C.: Yes.

A.W.: Ah! Good. [laughter]

P.C.: And I just don't worry about it.

A.W.: Good. [laughter and applause]

P.C.: One of the things that I've discovered, you know, as the years go on, is that there can't be any "should"s in the whole thing. So even meditation practice can become something you feel like you should do. And then it becomes another thing that you worry about, or something like that. So I just let it ebb and flow, as it does—practicing, not practicing. And now I feel like somehow it's always with you in some way, whether you are formally practicing or not. And my hunger for it ebbs and flows. But the hunger always comes back again. And not necessarily because things are going bad, but just, it's a natural opening and closing, or a natural relaxation, and then getting more involved with something else. And coming back, and going back and forth.

A.W.: I was surprised to discover how easy it was to begin meditating many, many years ago. And what I most liked was just how familiar it is, that state, you know. And the place that I most love is when I disappear. I mean, there's a point where you disappear. And that is so wonderful, because I'm sure that's how it will be after we die. You know, you're just not here, but it's fine.

P.C.: What do you mean, exactly, you "disappear"?

A.W.: Well, it's just, you reach that point where it's just like space. And you don't feel yourself. The ego is not saying hello. And you're not thinking about what you're going to cook. And you're not thinking about what you're going to wear. And you're not really aware of your body, really. And I like that. I like that because, as a writer, I spend a lot of time in spaces that I've created myself. And it's a relief, then, to have another place that is basically empty. And so, I really appreciate that.

P.C.: See, I don't think I have the same experience, somehow. I always feel very present in some kind of sense. But I have less and less sense of who I am—which is, I think, different. It sounds different.

I realize that I don't have a strong sense of identity, as being something. And I think maybe that's more my experience.

But, on the other hand, there's a very strong physical sense of being here, at the same time.

A.W.: Yeah.

P.C.: But it's probably the same ballpark, I'd say.

A.W.: Well, I don't know. I mean, I live a lot of my life, especially when I'm out in nature, in a different realm, anyway. So that I feel that meditation, when I'm not in nature, is that place. And it is a place of really feeling the oneness. So that you're not kept from it by the fact that you're wearing a suit.

P.C.: Yeah.

A.W.: You know? I mean, you're just in it. And that's one of the really good things about meditation for me.

P.C.: And you're saying that—you know, you asked the question about, or made the statement about, the heart closing back down again. So you find that it sort of ebbs and flows from that to feeling . . . The heart closed down would be more like a stuck feeling, I suppose.

A.W.: Yeah, more like a stuck feeling. And triggered by these places in life that are bound to give you a stuck feeling.

P.C.: Yeah.

A.W.: You know. And there you are. And it's frustrating at times, because you think to yourself, "Well, you know, I've worked on this. And why is it still snagging in the same spot?"

P.C.: Yeah. I always call that how life keeps us honest. Because it seems like . . . my experience is exactly the same, what you're describing. And my experience of that is that it's sort of that feeling of what I would call just openness, and you were calling emptiness. The inspiration of that, and the feeling of being part of a much bigger picture of that, and not feeling isolated. And actually, it's a sense of profound happiness. That inspiration seems so important.

On the other hand, I'm sure it would turn into some kind of spiritual pride, or some kind of arrogance, or something. So, life just has this miraculous ability to just, like, just when you're beginning to feel like it's kind of going over the edge, in terms of "I've accomplished something," . . . smack you right in the face with a real humdinger. You know?

And so then that humbles you. And so, I think there's just this kind of natural balancing that happens, that keeps you human. At the same time, the sense of joy does get stronger and stronger.

A.W.: And, see, isn't that a good way to see it?

P.C.: Yeah, I think so.

A.W.: It is. Because otherwise, you know, there you are, thinking that you're just going to be smacked endlessly; and what's the point?

P.C.: Yeah, that's right. [laughter] Yeah. Because there's something about relaxing with the moment, whether painful or pleasurable. I teach about that a lot, because that's so personally how I experienced it—that the smile on my face, or the sense of gladness, just to be here, is something about that openness. When it gets painful, that's not like there's been some big mistake or something. It just comes and goes.

JUDITH LIEF: Do you think that there could be a danger in, when you're breathing in, or attracting more negativity, that you could become caught up in being a martyr, or to the usual image of the all-suffering housewife, or women, in particular, taking on these pains of their family more and more? Instead of being liberated, just becoming downtrodden? What is the flip between that and the approach of the tonglen?

P.C.: What do you think?

A.W.: Well, I think it's just knowing that you're not the only one suffering here and that that's what happens on Earth. There may be other places in this galaxy where people don't suffer at all, where beings are just fine. You know, they never get parking tickets, even. But, you know, what seems to be happening here is just really heavy-duty suffering.

P.C.: Yeah.

A.W.: And actually, I remember years ago, when I really was asking myself what's the use of all this suffering, I was reading *The Gnostic Gospels*. And you know, the part, you know—what Jesus said that they managed to censor from the Bible. And he said something that really struck me. And he said, basically, learn how to suffer, and you will not suffer. And this dovetails with this teaching, which is a kind of acceptance of it. This is the human condition. This is what happens down here . . . or up here.

J.L.: So, then, Alice, as an activist, your job is to take on areas of extreme suffering and try to alleviate that to some degree, I assume. So how has it affected your approach to your activist causes?

A.W.: Well, I think my activism really is for myself, you know. I see things, places in the world that I really feel I should be. Because I need, for myself, to feel that I have stood there. If there is something that is really bad, that is really evil, and it is being encountered by children, for instance, and there's nothing else I can do but be there, then that is where I should be. And it feels a lot better than just watching it on television.

J.L.: You mean physically going to the actual spot?

A.W.: Well, physically going there, or making some expression of concern, or sending whatever I can. If it's just, in tonglen, taking in the feeling of pain and suffering and then sending out mentally and spiritually happiness, you know, joy—tricycles—you know? Food. I like the feeling that this teaching supports of, when you have a really nice meal in a restaurant, you mentally and spiritually recognize that there are millions of people who don't have any food. And even though they're not . . . I mean, they might actually be right outside the restaurant these days . . . sending food, sending it or making a mental note about the disparity in the world and trying to equalize that as you're eating your dinner. You know, saying, "I wish that everybody in Ghana had some of this soup." Or, "I wish everybody in my hometown of Eatonton had this bread." So that's my response.

P.C.: It is true that people fear the practice for the reasons Judy is bringing up. Particularly if people have a lot of depression, it is tough going to relate with the suffering so directly, when there's already so much depression. But I have found in teaching it that if you always start with your own experience of suffering, so that you're feeling your depression, or whatever it is, and then, from that, you generalize to all the other people who are feeling what you do, that becomes much less overwhelming and more workable for people. Because it gives you a way to work with your pain that, instead of feeling like you're making it more, you're making it meaningful. So, it's sort of different.

Whereas, if you're only taught tonglen, that you should do tonglen for other people, then it's really too much for a lot of people. And for most people it's too big a leap, whereas if you start always with yourself as the reference and then extend from that, then you do find that your automatic compassion for others, without yourself involved, gets much more spontaneous and real.

In other words, you have less fear of the suffering you perceive in the world—yours and other people's. I think it's a lot about overcoming fear of suffering and realizing . . . The reason I asked you about joy is because I wanted a testimonial, you see. Because my experience of working with this practice a lot is that it's brought me a sense of, a moment-by-moment sense of, well-being. And I attribute it to the practice. So that's encouraging, you know, then, to people who are afraid to start. To know that actually relating directly with your suffering is a doorway to well-being for yourself and others, rather than some kind of masochistic thing.

A.W.: And I would say that that is also true for me, in this going to stand where I feel I need to stand. That is the way that I feel that I get to that place. Once I actually went to places like Mississippi, for instance, and actually stood with the people, and realized the suffering that they were actually provoking, just by demanding their rights, once I was actually there and sharing their danger, the danger that they were in, I felt this incredible opening and an incredible feeling of finally being at home in my world—in that world, even, which was what I needed to make sure I could be. I needed to feel I could be at home there. And the only way that could happen was to actually go and to connect with the people who were there.

P.C.: And then I think the other extreme is when, because we have a natural fear of pain, then if somehow that becomes our primary motivation, avoidance of pain, then, as you get older and older, not only do you not go anywhere that's scary, the world becomes scarier and scarier.

A.W.: Exactly. Exactly.

P.C.: That's the really sad thing, is the world becomes more and more frightening. You don't want to go out your door. And, sure, there's a lot of danger out there. But the other approach makes you more open to the fear, or to the pain that it evokes in you. So your will gets bigger.

A.W.: I also really appreciate the teaching on how fruitless it really is to always blame the other person. And I feel, in my own life, you know, I can see places where I have not wanted to take my part of the blame. I have wanted to just see what the other person did wrong.

Really, it's a losing proposition. I mean, there's no gain to that.

Because you never learn very much about yourself. You don't own all your parts, you know? I mean, there are places in each of us, places that are quite scary. But they have to be, as you say, made friends with. You have to really get to know them and say, "Hello there. There you are again." And it's just very helpful to do that.

P.C.: Yeah. You know, one of the things the Buddha pointed out in his early teaching was that everybody wants happiness, or freedom from pain. But the methods that one uses, habitually, human beings use, are not in sync with the wish. So the methods always end up escalating the pain. It's this kind of trying to run away.

A good example is that someone yells at you, and then you retaliate and you yell back. And then they yell back. And then, you know, it gets worse and worse. Whereas, you think the reason to not yell back is because, you know, good people don't yell back. But the truth is that you're just getting smart about what's really going to bring you some happiness.

A.W.: Exactly.

J.L.: I'm intrigued by the combination of the drive-all-blames-into-one, and situations where definitely, from a conventional viewpoint, certainly, it seems that there are bad guys and good guys. There are oppressors and oppressed, in situations where there's a sense of [a] righteous stand against a real evil. So, how do you combine that with taking blame and also combating oppression or evil that you encounter? How does that combine?

A.W.: Maybe it doesn't work there. [laughter]

J.L.: The statute of limitations.

P.C.: I think it does work there. I hope it works there.

A.W.: Well, why don't you. . . . You take that one, because I . . . [laughter]

P.C.: I think it would have more credibility if you took it. Could you take it and express my view, then?

A.W.: Uh . . .

P.C.: Well, here would be my question, then. Does it help to have a sense of enemy in trying to end oppression?

A.W.: No.

P.C.: So maybe that's . . .

A.W.: Yeah. Yeah. I think it's probably just, you know, about seeing—as Bob Marley said so beautifully—that the biggest bully you ever did see was once a tiny baby. And that's true. I mean, I have tried that, you know. On Ronald Reagan. [laughter] I even tried that on Nixon, but it didn't really work that well. But, really. You know, there you are. You're standing face-to-face with someone who just told you to go to the back of the bus, or someone who said that women are not allowed here, or black people, or whatever.

And what do you do? You know, that's the question. And what do you do with your spirit? I mean, it's your spirit that's being attacked. I mean, they could basically blow you away physically. But also, if they don't do that, it is your spirit. So you have to really look at them and see. I don't know what you do, Pema. But I always, at that moment, see that they are really miserable people and they really need help. And I think now, of course, that I would love to send them *Awakening Compassion.* [laughter]

P.C.: Yeah. Big deal. A chance they'd listen to it. But that's right. I mean, that's kind of a leap for some people, to actually see that the cause of someone's aggression is their own suffering.

A.W.: Oh, yeah.

P.C.: But on the other hand, you could also just realize that your aggression is not going to help anything in that situation.

So then, there's the situation. You're standing there. Actually, you *are* being provoked; you *are* feeling aggression. And what do you do? So that's when tonglen actually becomes very helpful. Because you breathe in, and you connect with your own aggression with a lot of honesty. And you have such a strong recognition in that moment of all the oppressed people who are provoked and feeling like that. And if you just keep doing that, something different might come out of your mouth, you know.

A.W.: Exactly. And, you know, war will not be what comes out. And that's, you know, I think that's really the hope.

J.L.: It seems to me that Dr. Martin Luther King had that quality. He wasn't a tonglen practitioner, but he *was* a tonglen practitioner.

A.W.: Yeah, he was, in a way.

J.L.: But it didn't stop him from making stands.

A.W.: Yeah. No. He was. He was a Southern preacher from a long line of Southern preachers. And, you know, a great pray-er, someone who could really get to that place of centeredness through prayer, and also through love. I think that the person who has a great capacity to love— and it often flowers when you can actually see and feel the suffering of other people—can also strategize. I mean, I think he was a great strategist. I think he often got, of course, very angry and upset, but, at the same time, knew what he was up against. So I think he knew what he was carrying, how much of the load he was carrying, how much depended on him.

I think, some kind of practice. And actually, what I'm thinking is just that it wasn't tonglen. It wasn't TM. It wasn't metta. But in a way, it was all of that. You know? And any practice that we do regularly, even if we fall off . . . I think of my falling out of meditation as kind of falling off the wagon. Falling off the meditation wagon. But it is really important to have some kind of practice so that when we do go out into the world to confront these more and more horrible situations, we can do that with a feeling of knowing that we are in the right place in ourselves, and also knowing that we're not bringing more fuel for the fire, more anger, more despair.

The difficulty of this is not really a deterrent. I think what I find is that the more difficult something seems, the more there is a possibility of—I think you say it really well—giving up hope. I mean, you sort of approach it with a feeling of already having given up hope, but that doesn't stop you. You know? I mean, that slogan, "Abandon hope," that you say we should put on our refrigerators . . .

P.C.: Give up all hope of fruition. Right.

A.W.: Yes. Right. And just do it, because you're doing it and this feels like the right thing to do, but not feeling that it's necessarily going to change anything.

P.C.: Right. One thing that I once heard Rinpoche teach, and it's been a big help to me: he said to live your life as an experiment, so that you're just always experimenting. So, you could experiment yelling back and see what happens. You can experiment doing tonglen, and speaking out of that, and see how that works. You know, in terms of your activism, or anything. In terms of the stakes getting higher and higher, like, what actually allows some kind of communication to happen? And you learn pretty fast what closes down communication. And that's the strong sense of enemy, I think.

A.W.: Of what?

P.C.: The other person feels your hatred.

A.W.: Hatred, mm-hmm.

P.C.: Then everyone closes down.

A.W.: But I also feel like fear . . . that what closes people up and down more than anything is just being afraid. And I can say that about myself, that the times when I have really been afraid to go forward in a relationship, or a problem, or whatever, that there is this fear. There's anger, and there's fear. And so, the practice of tonglen, or, basically, sitting— I mean, I think any kind of sitting and just being with your feelings, letting them come up and not trying to push them away or disown them—I think that's just incredibly helpful.

P.C.: Yeah. Yeah.

13

"I Know What the Earth Says": Interview with William R. Ferris from *Southern Cultures* (2004)

ON WOMEN'S LIVES

If you think of the early stories, it's true that the women end badly, but it's because they belong to the generation of my mother and grandmother, when they were suspended because they had nowhere to go. All of them couldn't be Bessie Smith or Billie Holiday, so they ended up doing all kinds of destructive things. Most of that generation didn't have any fame or glory. But notice that all of those women are much older than I am. They exist in an historical place that is removed from my generation of women. It's not until *The Third Life of Grange Copeland* that I got my generation of people. It starts so far back because I wanted to have a really good understanding of the historical progression. I wrote about those women in *In Search of Our Mothers' Gardens*. The women who have not had anything have been, almost of necessity, self-destructive. They've just been driven insane. And the ones who have managed have been the ones who could focus their enormous energies on art forms that were not necessarily recognized as art forms—on quilting, on flowers, on making things. It's a very human need, to make things, to create. To think that women didn't need that— that by having a baby you fulfill your whole function—is absurd and demeaning.

ON ENCOUNTERING ZORA NEALE HURSTON

When I was in Mississippi, there was a woman named Frankie Walton White who had read *Their Eyes Were Watching God*, and we were talking about it, and she loved it. And I got it, and I read it, and I loved it. That was when I connected really with Zora. The oddest thing is that in that same anthology that Langston Hughes did—where he put "To

Hell with Dying"—there's a story by Zora. But at that time I was so convinced that only men wrote literature that I had to read, that I read that anthology without really noticing. It's terrible, but I think it's true. Then I read *Their Eyes Were Watching God*, and it was so much my culture. I had never read a book that was so true to my specific southern black culture, full of music, full of humor, full of just—not righteousness—craziness. People living their lives, people having good times, people fussing and fighting. At the same time, as with my mother and father, they are absolutely rooted in the earth, in earth life. People in *Their Eyes Were Watching God* are really pagan. They are not bamboozled by religion as it is taught in the South. They are always poking fun at the hypocrisy. And the passages that are so incredible are, of course, when they drop a bean in the soil, and up comes this food. The Indians, too, the way they knew a storm was coming. They started leaving. The animals knew, they started moving. Only people were hesitating. Most of the people were not as connected. They had already gotten two or three steps removed from what is the natural rhythm of the earth, so they didn't know and so they had to sit there, be scared, and pray to the sky god, watching the sky god.

Now this is an aspect that I rarely see reflected in any review. Basically, it carries forward my sense of the transformation that many people have to go through to shed what is a deadening sky-god religion, whatever it is, in order to come back to their rootedness in nature as the source of divinity. That is why *The Color Purple* really is a book about learning to believe in your own god or goddess or divinity or whatever is sacred to you. It's not about what other people are telling you. You get rid of the Charlton Heston–type God, you get rid of Yahweh, you get rid of all these people that, while you are worshipping, try to convince you that you are nothing, and you begin instead to be a child of what you actually are, a child of—you are a child of the earth. That is why, at the end, Celie understands that if God is anything, God is everything. And so the birds, the trees she sees—she makes a long list of all these things. That is what this book is primarily about. It's about understanding that people may well need to have religions in order to further their social programs and their political agendas or even their spiritual desires, but essentially what is divine is in front of you all the time. You cannot separate yourself ever from the earth. I was thinking that if you understand that, you lose all fear of dying. You may be grass, you may be a cow, but you'll always be here, in fact even if they shoot you. I was thinking, "What would they do to me to really punish me for being an earth lover?" I mean they could shoot me to another planet, but because I'm made of earth, I could never leave. That is my home, that is what I am. I love this feeling of always being at home and always being with what is sacred to me, what is divine to me. It was a gift from my mother without her knowing because, before she died, she became a Jehovah's Witness, and part of those people's belief is that if your own child is not also a Witness, you don't speak to the child. Isn't it amazing? Imagine having that as your guiding light.

Because my work is grounded in spirituality rather than in politics, I am able to follow my intuition and my sense of being one with other people much more easily than I ever thought possible. When I write as I have done about these African children who are mutilated, I can do so without getting bogged down in all the cultural baggage and the political resistance of various African governments and African people. I really understand what they are saying. Some people have to do studies to know these things, but they have proved that things hurt if you hurt them. If you put a monkey in a cage and put electric shocks on one side and not on the other, they will try to stay on the side away from the shocks. So, if you can believe those children feel pain, and if you think that is not right, then you try to change that. My point is that there is a lot of opposition to people wanting to alleviate suffering by people who have a vested interest in continuing it, because it's their means of ruling, literally controlling.

ON CIVIL RIGHTS LEADERS

I have this theory, and I wrote a poem about it, that Martin Luther King, had he lived, would have become a violent revolutionary rather than a nonviolent one simply because he would have perceived that he had met an object, specifically, this country, that is not going to be changed nonviolently. I think his dedication was so intense that he would have tried other strategies. In the poem, I talk about his love in front and his necessary fist behind. I also mention that people who are crucified should decide not to be crucified—that they should do as much as they can, but then they should know when to stop, that they're much more valuable farming, or raising tulips somewhere, than they are dead—if they would only understand that.

A good example is Bob Moses, who was in Mississippi in the early sixties and who was rapidly becoming a legend. He was with SNCC (Student Nonviolent Coordinating Committee), and he was just wonderful because he knew how to go into a community and let people lead him rather than trying to tell the people what they needed. He would listen to what they wanted done and then he would try to help them do it, which is the true revolutionary way. But then the people started saying that this man was their Moses because they make these quick religious connections, and he decided he didn't want to be their Moses; he wanted to disappear. So he changed his name, took his mother's name, and he just walked away. The last time I heard anything about him, he was teaching school in Tanzania. I think that's brilliant. That's exactly what people should do.

After King's speech against the war in Vietnam, it would have been so lovely if he had known somehow. He had all these premonitions, but he was so into the propelling force of history, where you have to go right to the end and be shot. He never considered not listening to all the things telling him that the end was coming. He knew the end was coming. But wouldn't it have been terrific if after the speech "On the Mountaintop," ["I've Been to the Mountaintop"] he had gone back to Atlanta, said, "Coretta, get the children, we're gonna go to California. Let somebody else lead. I've had it." He was tired. Or think about Malcolm. Malcolm could have started a little farm in Detroit and been ready to come back another time.

If people think that's taking the easy way out, well, to hell with people. I think the symbols are wrong. I think the symbols have always been wrong. I think that the worship of death is really stupid; to hound people until they feel they have to be shot is just sick. We got to a point when people were saying, "Well, now it's time for King to be assassinated for him to be any good." Now, that's sick. Here's a man who had given every ounce of his energy, absolutely everything he had. And there we were just saying, "Well, he's screwed up in Chicago; he can't reach people in Harlem. The only thing left for him to do is to stand there and be shot." I've thought about it constantly. I would like for people to think they can have more than one life and that there are more ways to be committed than to give your absolute life's blood. Going to teach in Tanzania or Harlem or Mississippi, that's a commitment. I would love to have had Malcolm or Martin Luther King teach my child.

But the culture doesn't deserve those good people if violence is the only thing that will move them. If people are going to sit back in front of the television set and only be moved because you're dying, they don't deserve you. I think the culture is sick. The thing to do is to think of ways not to give in to the culture, to affirm what you believe to be stronger and more important. Great importance is attached to an assassination, as if people will rise up and great changes will happen. But that doesn't happen. People can forget overnight.

ON CHILDHOOD MEMORY

Flannery O'Connor said that anybody who's outlived her childhood has enough material to last her the rest of her life. I draw heavily on my childhood and what I knew and what I saw and felt. But after *Meridian* I have slowly moved away from that. I'm creating situations and characters that are really much removed from what I knew as a child.

I was very much into my community, but at the same time I had this sense of almost always knowing I was observing it. Even with things like my father's funeral I was very aware that, on one level, my father was dead and therefore that meant great, weighty stuff. But I was also very observant about everybody's reaction to everything and remembered with great alertness everything that was said.

I will always draw on my background because it was so rich, and I always recognized it as being rich. I really have liked it. Richard Wright, for example, found very little in his childhood to like and admire, and he often felt it was barren; I feel just the opposite. When I go back to Eatonton, Georgia, I get these new reverberations of things, new enlightenment; I understand on a deeper level. That will probably always be somewhere in the work. But *Meridian* was set almost equally in New York and Mississippi, and I think that means something. In my own life I have had the kind of mobility that has taken me not just all over the South but all over the country.

ON HAVING A CHILD

I would not have missed having a child. It was tough going at times, but I think children connect us to the natural world and the natural processes of life in a way that you can't really grasp. In the long labor and the sheer pain involved I felt like I was connected to women wherever they are and whatever condition they are in, in a way that I had never felt. It was a bonding with my mother, with her mother, with my great-grandmother. I understood as never before what it was like for women and what it is still like for women all over the world.

I thought about my mother. Finally, they gave me what they call a saddle block so that I didn't have all the pain at the end, but you know, she had eight children, and I remember her saying that the pain increased with each child, didn't diminish. They claim it diminishes, and she claimed that she had forgotten it, but I don't think so. So, I felt like, with [my daughter], I was given this information, this knowledge, and I think it just made me more humble in the face of what women go through in order to populate the earth. They provide all the workers, they provide all the teachers, and they provide the labor force that keeps everything moving. Which is why I think there should be a moratorium on birth until the planet has gotten back into a shape that really can sustain a high quality of life. I just don't see the point of everybody continuing to have children, even one. I mean I think that one is good, but I think it's really very thoughtless for people to continue to populate an overpopulated earth when they haven't attended to the earth so they can keep sustaining this.

ON REVISION IN HER WORK

There is much revision in my novels. I started *The Third Life of Grange Copeland* at MacDowell, a writers' colony in New Hampshire, and I worked on it through several winter months. Three years later, when I finished it, I had changed everything except one line, and then I changed that line. I have four or five complete drafts of that novel. Since *Meridian* was written in a different way—not chronological—I revised the sections a great deal. Do you know that I had a great fight with my editor because the original jacket was of a little black girl who looked exactly like a cockroach wearing a dress? They tried to sneak that cover over on me. We had this huge fight and I made them change it. Nevertheless, the novels take a lot of revision. They don't really write themselves, but a lot of them are just somehow formed. I might work on the dialogue to make it sharper.

The ideas for the novels come from wanting to understand something. With *Grange* I wanted to understand what happened in family life over a period of years. And I wanted to understand the concept of self-hatred and family hatred, the kind of destructive thing that

Brownfield exemplified. I wanted to understand Brownfield and also to understand people who could be Brownfield but were not. I wanted to know what made the difference. Everything starts from wanting to understand something, whether it's a person or just an event. For instance, the scenes in *Grange* when Brownfield notices that whenever a white man comes around, Grange's behavior changes completely—those scenes come from living in a culture that produces that kind of reaction. I have seen people change their behavior because there are white people around them. My father's behavior changed. He just lived in a culture that was intent on destroying him, so he built up defenses of various sorts.

In *Meridian* I started out being really concerned about some of the things that people did to each other in the sixties in the name of change, in the name of revolution. I wanted to see what qualities we were giving up in exchange for other qualities. Somehow part of it really understands the questions, not just understands the answers. Sometimes when you start, you just have the vaguest notion of where you're going, and you don't even know what things are important to work with. This has nothing to do with that, but it may show you what I mean. My regret is that Langston Hughes died before I knew what to ask him.

I live in a culture where storytelling is routine, where memory is long and rich. I was born into this huge family where everybody told stories, and it was my function to make some sense out of all of it, to write it down and present it. It's not just me knowing; it's what they've let me know.

ON LITERARY INFLUENCES

In college I loved Camus. He was just a beautiful man. I [also] really love the Russian writers. I'm a moralist. I'm very concerned about moral questions, and I have definite feelings about what is right and what is not. Russian writers have a kind of essential passion, and they can engage in that kind of questioning of the universe and of human interactions. They really care. I like that. I don't like writers who don't care. I think writers should care desperately. I just discovered the poetry of Anna Akhmatova. She's typical of the Russians in that she has passion and political sensibility. The Russians live completely in their world on every level. There is no worrying about how their political involvement will be perceived. This poem is called "The Last Toast":

I drink to our ruined house
to the dolor of my life
to our loneliness together
and to you, I raise my glass.
To lying lips, that have betrayed us
to dead, cold, pitiless eyes
and to the hard realities
that the world is brutal and coarse
that God, in fact, has not saved us.

Isn't that terrific? I think that is so true. God hasn't saved us. I really thought for so long that God had saved black people. I thought that we were really saved. However, we're not.

Victor Hugo was another influence. He was also a moralist and very compassionate and big. I like really big writers who have scope and who see things in a distance. I love Flannery O'Connor, but it was very upsetting when I read in some of her correspondence that she referred to black people as "nigger." The Brontës were influential. *Jane Eyre* was one of my favorite books. I loved that sense of life intensity that you see in Mr. Rochester. I love writers who make you feel the cold when it's a cold, gray day. There are people who influence you. And there are people you discover later on, and you know that you're on the same wavelength and that you would give anything to have had them earlier. That's where Tillie Olsen comes in, that's where Zora comes in, that's actually where Toomer comes in. I didn't read *Cane* until 1967, and I didn't read Zora until the seventies.

ON CHOOSING THE WRITING LIFE

I wanted to play the piano, and I think I would have been good at it. But piano lessons were fifty cents, and I tried very hard, but I couldn't raise it every week. Then I wanted to draw, but I wasn't that good. I think writing was just all that was left. I became really interested because of my oldest sister, "Molly," who left Eatonton when I was an infant. There was no high school for black people, so she had to go away. She's twelve years older than I am. When she was thirteen, she left to go to Macon High School. And she was a great reader. I was an infant, but she would come back, especially after she went off to college. She went off to Morris Brown in Atlanta, and when she came home in the summers, she would read to us. She would tell us stories. She introduced us to a new kind of aesthetic. My mother was part Cherokee, and she had that real Indian belief that basically you let things live where they grow. When you grow them, you don't cut them; you just let them be. But my sister, who actually looks very much like my mother's grandmother, very Cherokee looking, had gone to school. She knew that there were people who actually cut flowers and brought them into the house. This was a different way of looking at things.

My father and mother, even though they went through the fifth grade and the fourth grade respectively, loved education, really worshipped education. They were that generation of black people who would do anything to educate their child, and so they let my sister go because they wanted her to be educated. They read to us, things like the newspaper. Whenever books were thrown out by any white person they worked for, they were happy to have them, bring them back, and they would read to us. So we always had books in the house. I think that was unusual because many people like my parents did not have books around, or they did not appreciate them enough to take them out of the trash when someone was throwing them out. But my parents worshipped reading. They thought it was just the greatest thing. Of course, by the time I was [born], they were rather exhausted, and that's where my sister came in. She came back for the summers, and she would read. You know the song "God Bless Mother Africa"? When I was six or seven years old, my sister taught me that song. It's incredible. The ANC [African National Congress] was around then, trying to teach people what was going on in South Africa. She was obviously very moved by the struggle, and she learned that song, and she taught it to me. Those are the kinds of things that influenced me a lot.

I also had great teachers in the sense that they loved my family and me. They knew my family, they cared about me. I wasn't just another little face. My mother had to take me to the fields, and I would trail along behind her as she chopped cotton, or I'd fall asleep out at the edge of the field where she couldn't really look after me because she had to work. When I was four I went to school, and my first-grade teacher, who is still alive, gave me books for my birthday and gave me my first clothing.

When I was eight or nine or ten, I was writing, and I kept a notebook because my life has had its trials. I learned very early that this was a way to deal with pain and isolation. I also had brothers. They were very brutal in some of their ways, and they were brought up not to be gentle with animals or younger siblings. I learned that you could put things on paper, but a safer method was actually to just keep them in your head. So I have kept until very recently the habit of writing very long and complex works in my mind before I write them because I always feel that's the safe way.

ON THE SOUTHERN LABEL

I don't consider myself a southern writer. I think I'm dealing with regions inside people. The people are in the South, but I really just leave that up to other people to decide. If people can only understand the work by placing it in a context, that's fine. But I'm really trying to understand people and how they get to be the way they are. The region is the heart and the mind, not the section of the country.

There are many reasons I am still not at ease with the southern label. Part of it is that any kind of label limits. It tends to make what you're dealing with seem localized, when in fact your main focus is to find out why people act the way they do. Wherever people are, that's where you are. Also, when you think of southern writers, you think of white southern writers. I don't really have any interest in integrating southern writers. On the other hand, how can I possibly ever not be considered a southern writer since I am a southerner and since I write?

ON ZORA AND AUTOBIOGRAPHY

The only time I know of that an autobiography did not work was Zora Hurston's autobiography. An autobiography is very difficult to write. It's the hardest writing if it's going to mean something, and if it's going to be honest. The hardest thing in the world is to write down what you really think, what you're really feeling. The tendency is that you're thinking, "I am a rotten person," but by the time you get it down on the paper, it's, "Well, I'm not so rotten." Zora suffered from that.

She also had to placate this "godmother" of hers. This woman [Charlotte Mason Osgood] financed Zora's expeditions into the South to do folklore. She gave money to almost all the [Harlem] Renaissance people, including Langston Hughes. She really thought that black people were these wonderful, exotic primitives and that she could read their minds. She thought she could read Zora's mind. Zora would have a party with her friends and would say, "Let me call Godmother." So at five o'clock in the morning, Zora would gather her friends around and call Godmother. Zora would say, "Godmother?" and Godmother would say, "Yes, Zora?" "Godmother, do you know what I'm thinking now?" And Godmother would say, "Oh yes, you're thinking this, or that." And Zora would have a big laugh. It was really hokey and a sad example of how, in order to get work done, people have to do so many terrible things.

This godmother would not allow Zora to publish certain things that she wrote until godmother said she could. Her work was really controlled. In addition to her writing, Zora made films. They were on children's games, the Mardi Gras, and on some of the conjurers whom she met in New Orleans. Among the things that she learned from these voodoo doctors and conjurers was how to kill. She became a converted soul.

I don't know the nature of her relationship to Van Vechten, but supposedly she placed a spell on him, albeit probably playfully.* The problem with rich and poor is that the poor person can never forget that the rich person is rich. And no matter how hard one may try, it's impossible to forget that they have more than they need and you don't have enough. There was a lot of that in Van Vechten and Zora's relationship, although she kept saying, "I love you and it's not because I need anything. I mean, please don't think I'm asking for money." And she wasn't. It's just that he happened to be so bloody rich, and she happened to be so bloody poor. It's really hard to love people who have had all the advantages that you don't have. It's very difficult, and I can say that with a great deal of experience. Even with much effort, I still find it difficult to love people who control, who have everything. And it's so sad because no matter what they do, the feeling remains. They can be ever so wonderful, and yet this barrier rises like a ghost.

ON BELIEVING IN VOODOO

I believe in voodoo as much as I believe in any other religion. It works for the people who need it to work, and there are probably some definite medicinal qualities the people use. In Haiti, for example, the thing that Hurston discovered about the zombies is that they know this secret that they brought from Guinea, which apparently puts a part of the brain

---

* Carl Van Vechten (1880–1964) was a white American music critic, novelist, and photographer well known for his interest in the Harlem Renaissance.

to sleep and allows people to appear to die. But they're not really dead. They can be brought back, and they can be put to work, to just work and do nothing else. But the part of the brain that controls memory and speech and everything else is gone. I think that's entirely possible. I don't see why it couldn't be. All of these things can probably be explained. Zora talked about the way people would collect dirt from graveyards to use to destroy people. It's in *Tell My Horse*. What she discovered after taking some of this dirt to a chemist was that it's full of disease and germs. So if you went to the grave of someone who died of smallpox and took the dirt, it keeps its potency up to twenty years or so, and you could actually give a horrible disease to someone.

With my own mother I understand new layers of meaning in our relationship. She was devoutly Christian and went to the church regularly as a mother of the church for most of my life when I lived at home. Yet behind that, I think she was the most sincere worshipper of nature. I know that because I am also. And I know that what's different about the way that I relate to nature and to the earth is that I don't feel compelled to put a Christian face on what is essentially a pagan mark. So I just love the earth and love nature, worship it, and think of it as my source of life and any kind of life. I know there is a galaxy and a cosmos, but I think that if there is a divine intelligence that orders everything, it's too much for me to comprehend. So I'm happy to just love what I can feel. And I feel. And this I think was true of my mother in the sense that she had absolute faith in nature. But if you had asked her that, she would not have necessarily understood what you meant. But she did because I have seen her visit a house, and if there was a sprig of anything lying that had broken off of any plant, she would take it home, stick it in any little bit of soil, and would have absolute certainty that it would do well, and it did. That was her way. I grew up with a woman who was so connected to life and so much in sync with the source of all that there is. It was just wonderful watching her exist in the world, and this was true even though we were poor and we had to deal with people who hated us or couldn't really see us. There's no doubt in my mind that my mother was a great, great spirit, and I actually think of her as a goddess.

ABOUT THE BLUES AND B.B. KING

I love B.B. because he loves women. They can be mean, they can be bitchy, they can be carrying on, but you can tell he really loves them.

He's full of love. I would like to be the literary B.B. King. There's something about him that has remained true and has remained genuine. He seems to be authentic. Average people respond immediately to what he is and what he says, and I like that. That is the best kind of acceptance.

The blues can be very disturbing, actually. I love it, and I love some songs much more than others, some musicians more than others, but what's truly disturbing is how frequently when women are singing they are telling about abusive relationships. I'm struck by that time and time again. And then of course it makes me think about all the stories those women were trying to hint at that they were not able to say. You know, I remember once, Quincy [Jones] was talking, and he laughed and said, "You know, Celie *is* the blues." And that's so true, because if Celie were singing, she would be like Mamie [Smith], Bessie [Smith], and Ma Rainey, all of whom were abused. Those women were abused by men. I always feel so deeply when I listen to them, and then I think about how people took it for granted that your man would be this way. Of course you'll be abused. And so they weren't really heard, and they got used to it, actually dancing to this. It was like a spiral that was not going up but going down. People sing about this and then expect it in relationships. It was self-perpetuating. I doubt if any of these people had relationships that nourished them. They had relationships, instead, that prompted cries of anguish that were then used to entertain. The people who were entertained modeled themselves on what they were hearing, and it was just a very bad cycle.

What I love about the blues, of course, is the music and the honesty with which the people were trying to sing about what was actually happening. I hate the kind of music that was popular back then, and is popular now, where no matter what is happening, it is a kind of *la, la, la, la,* all sweetness and light, and you can hear that phoniness in their voices. You would not want to go across the street with those people because they are totally dishonest about their emotions. They don't know what emotions they were feeling. They are very unauthentic, but with the blues you feel like you are hearing authentic feeling and that people are struggling to find joy in life. I mean, look at Bessie. She's got all the vitality in the world. She is connected to the source, and she knows it. And the world, the rest of the world, is really trying to tell her that she's not anybody big, and there's all these little ways that this is done. Your hair has to be straight if it's kinky and you must wear powder, do something to your nose, whatever. All of those things are really designed to try to convince you that you are not what life and poetry are about. But Bessie used all of that power she had to affirm constantly that, "Absolutely, I'm what this is all about. I mean, I don't care what you are doing. I know what I am doing, I am here."

I know what the earth says. Life in earth says, *Be like me. I mean, I grow bananas, I grow strawberries, I have trees dropping nuts all the time, I have waterfalls.* I mean the earth says constantly, *I am not a poor person.* The earth says, *I have everything.* And so do we. That is one of the reasons, on a whole other level, why people who do have everything are constantly robbed of it. You know, it's like people come up on something that's just magnificent, and they just can't stop until they've stripped it and killed it. This is what's happening to the earth itself. And we are no different; we're the same. There's no such thing as mankind or peoplekind having the earth. I mean, please, have a little humility before all of this. Before all of this. Just one little red clover—you can't make that. So, we live in paradise.

14

Alice Walker and Margo Jefferson: A Conversation from LIVE from the NYPL (2005)

MARGO JEFFERSON: Do you remember the first things you ever wrote, first words, first poem?

ALICE WALKER: No. [laughter]

M.J.: Do you remember why you wrote it, or why you started to write?

A.W.: I think I started to write because I was in love with the feel of pen on paper, or pencil on paper, and that it was something that I could do in solitude, and it was something that seemed to feed me as a little child.

M.J.: You were the youngest of eight.

A.W.: I was the youngest of eight.

M.J.: So solitude—

A.W.: Was hard to find. [laughter] And very much something I *loved*.

M.J.: And where did you find—where did you write? Where did you go off?

A.W.: I went off behind the house. Well, actually, there's a story that my mother told. She said that when I was crawling, she would look for me, because apparently, you know, I had a way of getting away from them, and she would look for me, and I would have crawled to the back of the house and I would be writing in the sand with a twig or in the margins of a Sears, Roebuck catalog, and I think she said that that was, as far as she was concerned, that was my beginning as a writer.

M.J.: So she always took note of it.

A.W.: Well, I think she took note of it fifty years later, you know. [laughter]

M.J.: I think she *had* to take note of it fifty years later.

A.W.: It wasn't that way, she wasn't—

M.J.: You mean, she wasn't "Oh, my daughter."

A.W.: No, no, no, no, this was not the kind of family, actually, where there was that kind of thing happening a lot. Although my sister took notice, one of my sisters took notice, and *that* was enough, and my teachers took notice, and, as you know, you just need one person to *notice* that you're doing something and to say, "My goodness, that's wonderful, that's different, that's whatever," but at least they notice.

M.J.: I have to say, it took you as many years to notice your mother's garden as a form of art, right, in a sense?

A.W.: Well, in a sense, it took me a long time to really get it, to really get—

M.J.: Let me just go back. Alice grew up in Eatonton. I always want to call it Eatonville because of Hurston—

A.W.: I know, Zora.

M.J.: Georgia, on a farm. All right, so your mother and her garden.

A.W.: Well, my mother had this amazing ability to grow anything, and in fact, she'd also *can* anything, and my sister says this, my sister says, "Anything that could grow or that, you know, could walk around, my mother could put it in a jar," meaning, you know, she could . . . [laughter]

But she had this amazing ability and so her garden was something that was a work of art, and I have relatives here tonight, who I'm so happy they're here, because they remember this garden. They may not remember it in all the ways that I did growing up, but it was such a sanctuary, and I saw that when my mother, having worked in some other woman's kitchen all day, or worked in the dairy with my father all day, or worked in the fields all day, when she came home, and she kicked off her shoes, she went into her garden, and she was in, you know, *bliss*, she was in a place that only artists and extremely religious people and spiritual people get to. She was in this *amazing* state of grace. And *that* is why when I grew up, and I understood that, I realized that as daughters and, of course, sons too, but especially daughters, we are often looking for that, we are in search of our mothers' gardens, that place that lifts us very high.

M.J.: And that when you first wrote *In Search of Our Mothers' Gardens*, which was in the early seventies, you were also speaking very particularly about the garden as the way for a woman to find her art, her creativity, and, as you said at the time, Virginia Woolf said a woman needed at least a room of her own, and most black women, you know, had *no* space of their own, not a room, not necessarily anything, even a plot of land, and most black women did not necessarily have pen and paper of their own, or literacy of their own, so you were talking about art forms that live in the realm of the vernacular, the oral, what people call "crafts."

A.W.: Yes, and also, knowing that if we can understand these quote "crafts" as art, and if we can understand the fulfillment that comes from creativity, then whatever it is that we have that we do, *that* is our art, that is our sanctuary, that is where we become holy, and this was very important to talk about with people, because often people just say, "Well, you know, I don't know how to do anything, I don't have a gift, I'm not creative, I don't, you know." But I could see that in my community, these women who were making these incredible quilts, and you know quilts have now been shown and acknowledged to be a very high art form.

M.J.: With the quilts of Gee's Bend, just finally—they just finished off that notion that art and these kind of crafts are—

A.W.: Exactly, exactly. And that is what, that is one of the things we could bring to the culture. These overlooked areas of creativity that gave our ancestors so much joy, because art, as you know, is *joyful*. People often ask me, well you know, you write so many sad stories, aren't you weeping and moaning and groaning? Not at all. Even if I am weeping and moaning and groaning, the joy is just right there, because the whole point about creativity is that you can *do* it, that you're able to actually do it, that what you envision is something that someone else can see, can touch, can smell, can feel, and they can feel *exactly* and know exactly what you felt, and this is a kind of magic.

M.J.: What—I can't answer this myself either. What do you think is being overlooked now? You know, thirty, forty years ago, quilts were being overlooked. What are we taking for granted now?

A.W.: You know, that's something for everyone here to think about. I would have to ponder it. I would have to ponder it for a while, and *really* look at the culture, and look at my friends. I have many artist friends. What are they creating? I have a friend who not only paints huge beautiful paintings but she realized that she had never seen a frame that she liked. And so now when she paints these amazing paintings, she also makes the frame and paints the frame so that you get the whole thing at once.

M.J.: It's very beautiful. Whenever I teach that very troubled and troubling book *Uncle Tom's Cabin*, I always ask myself, "What are we missing, what are we as ignorant about as Harriet Beecher Stowe was?" I mean, she grasped many things, but she could not grasp that, say, black people had a civilization; they had to become good Christians. And I think, "All right, what are we going to look as foolish about, you know, twenty, forty, a hundred years from now? Will it be animals? Will it be nature?" Yes, I'm sure.

A.W.: I think it will definitely be animals, other animals, because we're animals, too. But I think that very soon, everyone, even if they don't change their eating habits, everyone will have to acknowledge that animals feel, and that they think, and that they are perfectly aware of what's happening to them, and that they are constantly trying to communicate this to us, sometimes through illness, so I think that in the same way that two hundred years ago, people looking at us, you know, our ancestors out there slaving away, and the ministers were saying that we didn't have souls, so it was okay to just basically grind us into the ground, in that same way, I think, people will see that the way that human beings abuse other animals, and the way that human beings think of them solely as food, I mean, I think that people will just think that that's really just unbelievable. And in fact, at least I hope this is what happens, because it's also true it could go the other way, where we just become beings who just *devour* mindlessly whatever there is, you know, people, we devour animals, the planet, and nobody stops.

M.J.: Well, warfare is a form of devouring.

A.W.: Uh-huh.

M.J.: People, it seems to me—my experience of you is as one of the first black feminists publicly to be called that [whom] I could, not only that I read, but that I spoke to in person and interviewed. I do remember, in those days, people would ask every woman of color who was also a feminist, "Well, how do you experience the balance of racism and sexism? Does one matter more? Did one affect you more? And I want to ask this differently, I want to actually ask you what you *remember* as your first experience of racial and sexual—it could be powerlessness, it could be self-doubt, it could be a sense that contempt was coming from outside or suddenly had sprung up inside you.

A.W.: Well, on the racial issue, I think that I noticed, from a very early age, that white people, when they came into the vicinity of my parents' basically shack, caused a certain *coldness* to just descend on the whole area, and it seemed to petrify my parents, so I noticed that they actually behaved in a different way, and this was extremely frightening to a small child. The other racial incident that was very marked for me was the reality that my mother, who I needed to be at home with me, had to go to work for these other people, white people, with white children, and that that meant that I was left unprotected at home, and this was a *terrible* situation. It was so—and it's so global, I mean this is what happens when a mother has to go somewhere else to tend other people's children and her own children are unprotected, and this is something that we should really work on very hard to stop, because our children need us, and we need to be with them, and it's a bind because usually our governments don't give adequate support to mothers, to parenting. In fact, every child that is born should know that it is going to be well taken care of, fed, clothed, housed, and educated, at the very minimum, and that its mother can be with it.

M.J.: And that it was wanted.

A.W.: And that it was wanted, yes. Now, the other question, about sexism.

M.J.: Yes.

A.W.: Well, I have to say that my father, who had started out, according to my mother—I wasn't there, early in their marriage—but he actually was a very tender parent, very tender with his children; he liked to bathe them and nurture them, much more than she did, this is what she says, but by the time I was a child, he had become very narrow and so he actually thought that there were certain areas of work for men and for women. For instance, he would not let his sons sweep a floor or wash a dish, because this was women's work. Needless to say, we fought. [laughter] Because it was absurd, you know; we grew up with men and women doing everything. My mother milked cows, my mother worked in the fields, and so it made me very sad for him, in addition to being very angry with him, that he started to narrow his perspective about women.

M.J.: And you perceived that as soon as the first chore.

A.W.: Exactly. I certainly did. I was not happy.

M.J.: Did your brothers lord it over you?

A.W.: Of course, of course they did, of course they did.

M.J.: Yes, how could a brother not?

A.W.: "Yeah, well, we don't have to do that. Yeah, we made a mess in the kitchen, but we don't have to clean it up, we're boys." I wish I knew where the rat poison was. [laughter] Those are the kinds of things that really go very deep when you are oppressed. It *is* a kind of oppression, and you actually see that they are preparing you to be oppressed in the bigger culture and in the world, which I *really* don't like.

M.J.: That's the thing. As soon as you take the small things for granted, you're prepared to take the larger things for granted.

A.W.: Exactly.

M.J.: Now, let me add the third element to the trinity, as I now call it, which is class. What was your first visceral experience of that?

A.W.: Well, we were poor, although we didn't really think of ourselves as poor, because we had—as my sister loves to say, "We had plenty food." [laughter] "How can you be poor if you have plenty food?" But we were, and the way you know that you're poor is if you can't afford health care. That's really it. If you cannot see a dentist, if you cannot, you know, go when you have an appendicitis attack, well, you're poor. I really *got* it when our cousins, who lived in Macon, [which is] a bigger town than Eatonton, would come and visit, and they had cars, and they could go to the dentist, and they could have health care, and I couldn't understand it, because we *worked*. We worked *so* hard. We had these huge fields to, you know, clear, and plant, and poison cotton; I remember being out there five years old with my little dipstick and my bucket. You have to do that to kill the boll weevils. See, you didn't even know about this.

[laughter]

M.J.: No, I didn't, but I'm a city girl.

A.W.: Well, somebody back there was not.

[laughter]

M.J.: I can sing Ma Rainey's "Boll Weevil Blues."

[laughter]

A.W.: Well, it didn't last that long for me either, because that whole system was changing, and it was changing basically because the land-owners, I know, the people who had grabbed all the land, had basically worn it *out* with cotton; it was a monocrop, they planted cotton until it just—the same was true of, you know, many places in the world, like Hawaii, for instance, where you can go fly over Hawaii and see all these huge plantations where there used to be pineapples, but they planted pineapples there until *nothing* will come up. So that is why eventually sharecropping, that whole system, collapsed.

M.J.: A land driver, like a soul driver. An antidote.

A.W.: No, the thing is, these roses don't have any scent, and that's a big problem. [laughter] And this is something that we should actually refuse. We should start refusing plants that don't have their essence, you know? [applause] I mean, the same way that you refuse to be with people who don't have an essence. [laughter] You know? Don't waste your time. [laughter]

M.J.: It's true.

A.W.: So this looks—it's got the red, and it's got the green, and it's the little spot of color, but this rose has no life, this rose has no essence.

M.J.: It's an accessory.

A.W.: It is, and this is—if we're not careful, this is what we will be, this is exactly what we will be.

M.J.: Or fruit with no taste, there is that.

A.W.: You know, GMO'ed food, you know, engineered food, we have to keep our souls, our grits, that just—ineffable thing that makes us *us*. You know, we don't need to all look alike and be the same size, you know; this brave new world, isn't it a nightmare?

[laughter]

M.J.: Yes, yes it is. I'm abandoning any notion of transition. [laughter] This is going to be a collage conversation, and that's just fine. Oh God, yes, yes yes yes. But you know what? Alice's first book of poetry, or first or second, was called *Revolutionary Petunias*, so you were already there. Now, you started off as a poet.

A.W.: I did, yes.

M.J.: How come—why start as a poet and what drove you toward prose?

A.W.: I love the succinctness of poetry. In fact, my early poetry, actually my very early poetry, was kind of long-winded, but I soon understood that that was not necessary, partly because I became enamored of the Buddhist Japanese haiku poets, Bashō and Issa, you know, poets like that. I liked the idea that you could say something, you could write a poem, and it would be almost like a snapshot of something. One of my very favorite poems is "Sitting quietly, doing nothing / Spring comes, and the grass grows by itself." Now, isn't that just *it*? [laughter] I mean, doesn't that just make you want to just, you know, abandon all the strife and stress of trying to get somewhere, you know, "Spring comes, and the grass grows by itself"? Do you remember that? How do we forget that? How do we forget that that is actually also what is happening, and that the *rushing* that we do—I came down—well, first of all, we got here last night, we checked into a hotel that was just a *nightmare*. It was so noisy. It was just impossible. So I got up early this morning, checked myself into a different hotel, went to bed, but even so, coming down to here, I noticed so many people, all of them moving very fast, and you know, it is just not necessary.

[laughter]

A.W.: Well, you notice, I lived in Brooklyn, not in Manhattan. Yeah, I did, I have lived in New York many times, and I enjoyed it very much. But even when I lived here, I worried a bit about the *speed* of things, because there is nowhere really to go other than where you are. It was much slower, I had a rose garden, I had roses that were hundred-year-old roses, and they smelled great, and right around the roses I planted collard greens, and they *also* smelled great.

M.J.: Now, did the smells mingle?

A.W.: Does it matter? [laughter]

M.J.: It would be interesting if they did.

A.W.: Yes, of course they did.

M.J.: Yeah, no, I like that idea.

A.W.: Good. That's the thing, you know, more things go together than you would ever imagine.

M.J.: There we go. There we go. Now what about living—could you live anyplace but in California now, within the U.S.?

A.W.: I don't think so; I really like Northern California, not Southern, but Northern, and I like it because it reminds me a lot of Georgia.

M.J.: Now, I'm going to wander back to your writing life. Okay?

A.W.: All right.

M.J.: Your first novel, *The Third Life of Grange Copeland*, which came out—Alice, really, you know, is—basically your whole career arcs the movement right from civil rights into the women's movement in 1970, and that was when the first little controversies began that would then—and you can roll your eyes, I don't blame you—that would then get larger. But the first controversy, as I recall, had to do with that old question of intragroup and self-censorship, meaning, if you belong—well, bluntly put, you got *some* criticism, which would recur, for depicting several generations of black men in torment, in various emotional and social ways, and that torment was taken out on themselves and on the women in their lives. It marked, it seems to me, it really split that world open, and—let me put it properly, because it's something I'm obsessed with, because it so hits you internally.

If you belong to an oppressed group, you are constantly aware of being stared at, and watched, and judged. Therefore, though you may be criticizing each other constantly, and though you may be criticizing the oppressor, there is a great deal of anxiety about when any kind of criticism of the group is *published* so that the outside world can see it. I experience this. The visceral feeling is "It will be turned against us," that's what one always grew up hearing. That's what I think was happening. How do you—and it climaxed with *The Color Purple*, and then it—I'm not going to worry about "climaxed," I'm just not—

A.W.: [laughter] Good.

M.J.: We just have to go on with it—and then still more when you wrote a book about genital mutilation. How did it look to you? You lived through it. How did it feel; *now*, with some distance, what does it look like?

A.W.: You know what an African man—I actually had many a time with African men, because they would say to me, "We do not have female genital mutilation. This is just something that you are making up out of your own distorted imagination."

M.J.: Are you serious?

A.W.: Oh, yeah.

M.J.: This was after it was also published?

A.W.: Yes, yes. And also, another one said to me, "We have a saying in our tribe," or "our group," "that to tell the truth hurts the people."

M.J.: This was a saying he had just made up. [laughter]

A.W.: No, no, no. Well, well . . .

M.J.: No, not necessarily.

A.W.: I'm just getting to this whole thing about people being afraid of what other people are going to do with the information that you give them, as if they haven't noticed.

M.J.: As if it hasn't already been said.

A.W.: Exactly, and as if it's not happening in every corner of the globe that I have been to. I just cannot understand this feeling that, if you attempt to heal yourself, there's something about that that's going to make you sick. No, it's true, you may get grief-stricken and sad and angry and sick in *that* way while you're dealing with it, but you're going to be a lot healthier after you deal with it honestly and look at it. You know, so when I'm writing about these so-called men who have suffered through the generations and done this, that, and the other thing, what was really different, I think, is just that I was showing what that behavior looked like from the perspective of the women to whom it was happening, who *matter* to me.

M.J.: And you were also showing what it was taking out of the men who were doing it.

A.W.: Oh, absolutely, and out of *us* collectively. You cannot batter and abuse and stand on half of your population and expect to thrive. How can you do that? I traveled all over Africa talking about FGM. And sometimes I would just very bluntly say, "Look at this village. Look at this community. There's so much sickness, there's so much pain. People are barely shuffling along."

M.J.: That walk that you describe. In *Possessing the Secret of Joy*, Alice keeps describing the walk that the Olinka girls and women have after the cliterodectomy is performed, and it is this painful little shuffling walk; it's what we associate with the abject shuffle of the dispossessed black person.

A.W.: And not only that, it's very painful. When women have intercourse, it's excruciating. There's no such thing as pleasure. When they give birth, they often have to be cut open again in order to give birth. I mean, this is as horrible as anything you can imagine. How are you going to sit and justify that? How are you going to sit and justify beating women and girls and forcing them to be subservient because they are female? You cannot do it. And furthermore you cannot expect to be a healthy people if you abuse each other in this way. It is impossible. So I accept all the criticism. I am so thankful that my ancestors made me really strong. You know, I'm really strong, and I understand that strength, having suffered a lot, but I am strong enough to take it, because we are worth it. We are *worth* it. And we are worth it; not only the men are worth it, but the women are worth it.

M.J.: You speak of healing oneself and what it costs, and it strikes me that a great deal of what stands in the way of healing is one's own shame and embarrassment of not only how you will be perceived by others, but of facing it yourself.

A.W.: Yes.

M.J.: What does one do with that?

A.W.: Well, I was shot when I was a child, and I was blinded in my right eye, and this was something that was so excruciatingly painful, and caused so much shame, that it took me so long to deal with it at all, but when I was able to deal with it, Margo, it just transformed the way that I could see the world, and I began to understand that it is when we can accept our own woundedness, when we can see the way that we have suffered, and just accept it, acknowledge it, and say, "Okay." And I've talked to people who have been raped, who have been cut in various ways, who have been shot, whose parents did this and that and the other thing or to child soldiers who have killed their parents. When you can at least say that this is what life has brought to me, you know, openly, honestly, then there is a possibility for some kind of shift and transformation, but if you can't do that, if you are sitting there holding on to all of the grief and all the sadness and all the shame, you will never move.

M.J.: What made it possible for you to deal with the scar, the wound from the eye?

A.W.: I think love. Love is what usually helps us deal with anything. I had this *amazing* brother who had basically tried to have my eye operated on when I was still in Georgia, but the doctor basically took the money and didn't do anything, so years later, like six years later, he asked me to come to Boston, and he took me again to the hospital and he had surgery performed. And the surgery was wonderful, and I loved feeling a lot more *sightly*, but what really did it was his love of me. This is the thing. If we can truly love our siblings and truly love each other, there is a possibility of transforming the most heinous, horrible things that happen to us.

M.J.: And that is, it seems to me, what you are going at more and more in each piece of writing. You are moving from the black American world of the early works in Africa, Latin America; you now speak of your American Indian and black ancestry. Did it start with those characters coming to you in *The Color Purple*?

A.W.: The inclusiveness or the healingness? No; here is one of the places it started. My ancestry is actually English, Irish, Scottish, from the Euro side; Cherokee, from the indigenous side; and African, from I think Ghana, because I get along really well with Anansi. Now, this is something, really, I want to share this because everybody in here probably is a mixture of something.

M.J.: Yes, we're a mongrel country.

A.W.: Yes, and so many people do not want to deal with that. There's one you don't like. This one did that. Well, I actually had that problem, I had the problem with the European ancestor, because they did some awful things. Part of my family comes from something that's still today called Grant's—Grant like Hugh Grant—Grant's Plantation. You know, and then there's the Walker section, that's the Scotch-Irish people. What do you do with these people, you know, what do you do with them? One of them was a rapist. He raped my great-grandmother when she was fourteen. This is where "Mister" comes from, you know, and it's been so sad to see that we are so ahistorical that we can't even recognize the behavior of the slave owner in ourselves. So I had to *really* deal with this ancestor, this white ancestor, because he's here, he's nowhere else but here. So I really decided that he had to have other attributes than rapist. And I know that he—and I now know this after many long nights and many struggles and traveling all the way to Edinburgh, where they just *adore* me. They sit there and say things like, "Well, Alice, the English are trying to bury their nuclear waste in Scotland. What shall we do?" I say, "Brother, I don't know." [laughter] Oh, my brother. But, anyway, so I decided, knowing the Scotch people, and I really grew to like them because of their poetry, I realized that, oh, this is an ancestor who must have loved poetry, even if he was run out of Scotland, and he probably liked music, because they do love to dance, and this is true also of the Irish, and to some degree of the English as well. You know, I had to enlarge my sense of who this intrusive person was. And then I had to think about how he came to Georgia. How did he get there? You know, was he like one of those little starving boys in *Oliver Twist*? I mean, was he Oliver Twist? You know, I mean, these are the connections we make.

And then there's my Native American great-grandmother, and what was her story? I learned very late in life because of my friend Wilma Mankiller—she used to be the chief of the Cherokee—but the Cherokee held slaves, you know, and so this was an ancestor who was part African, she was Cherokee, but she was part African, and then she came into our family through the Calloways. The Calloways are these people in Georgia who have big flower gardens. Now, gardens. And on and on like that. And then the African. The African got off the boat and walked from Virginia to Eatonton, Georgia, carrying two children. Now *there's* an ancestor.

See? And that's who's sitting in front of you, that's who's sitting here, and you look into who you are, that's who's sitting there, maybe not the same configuration, maybe a different configuration, but we have to really claim all these strands in order to be whole. I remember in the Black Power phase of the movement there was this insistence that you had to be just black, and they were saying things like that about someone who looked like Kathleen Cleaver, just really very, very light-skinned people had to be as if they had just come completely from Benin. [laughter] And this is *absurd*. We are people of color. I love Du Bois for giving us that phrase. Isn't it beautiful?

M.J.: Yes, I love it, too. Yes.

A.W.: People of color, you know?

M.J.: Intense and muted and every kind of, yes.

A.W.: And all my English and Scottish and Irish people, they are now people of color. And I'm sure they're very happy. [laughter]

M.J.: I hope mine are, too.

A.W.: Yes, they are, Margo, they are, listen, I'm telling you. When you free them, you're happy. Set them free.

M.J.: Oh, Alice, you've just reminded me of a painful story. In the height of the Black Power movement, I had a friend who had dead-straight hair, as we used to say, and was very light. So there she was in New Orleans, which was very hot, in a huge Afro wig in a restaurant one evening. She got up to go to the bathroom, basically to take a wig break. [laughter] She walked into the bathroom, and there, facing her, was a woman, a browner-skinned woman, who was also taking a wig break, but she had taken off her straightened wig and, yes, and underneath was a small version of the Afro that my friend craved. According to my friend, first they saw each other in the mirror and then they exchanged a look that meant, "Something will be learned from this," but they then each had to put the wig back on and return to their place, [laughter] but I think my friend ceased to wear her wig shortly after that. But it happened and that's comic, though not entirely, but terrible things were done in the name of all of that.

A.W.: Exactly. And I hope we learned; I think we did. I think now it's more a matter of choice.

M.J.: And I think the whole view of mixed-race children and all that, there's more flexibility, there's more room, absolutely. Which characters did come—because I'm still thinking of your moving from the U.S. to Africa and in *The Color Purple* Nettie making her way to Africa—who did come to you first? Because you describe yourself as writer and *medium* in thanking people in *The Color Purple*. Who came to you first and how?

A.W.: Okay, well, I had a stepgrandmother whose name was Rachel, and she loved me very much. My own grandmother had been murdered by a man who wanted to date her, and she said no, and he just shot her dead in front of the church, and she died in my father's arms, but in any case I had this stepgrandmother Rachel, and all I knew about her is that she had two children, nobody ever knew what happened to them; she had married my grandfather, who was not the sweetest husband you could imagine; and she was this loving though servile kind of person, and I wanted so much to honor the love that she managed to give to us that I decided to try to write in her voice, but I could never remember much more of her voice, her actual voice, than an expression that she used to use, which was "sho do." "Sho do." And I was then able to construct an entire book [laughter] out of her "sho do," and so that was a kind of start, and it was a way of honoring, also, the people, my grandfather, her, my grandfather's lover, you know, all of these people, it was a way to spend *time* with them, because I was so little that, you know, most of my siblings, all of my siblings left pretty much before I got, you know, big, and then the grandparents were getting really old, and so all you could hear was like these little fragments of "Well, then they did so and so," and "She was wearing this," and "Oh, that hat."

But I think there was something in me that so loved them, that so loved the remnants that were left of them, that I resolved to spend a year trying to be with them, and so when you read *The Color Purple*, you actually are reading someone who is actually feeling like she is with these people, and the only way that—since they're all dead, the only way that I could possibly do that, and it was a wonderful time, it was truly wonderful. They were so funny. And that was the other thing that was so annoying, people that were complaining about *The Color Purple*, they're all like, it's so, you know, depressing and tragic and this and that, but that's life, life has all that in it, but what you need to counter that is your own sense of honor, and these people I thought were just hilarious.

M.J.: How did Nettie find her way to Africa? I keep asking that because Nettie's—the children who lived with her, Celie's children who live with Nettie in Africa, show up in two more books, *The Temple of My Familiar* and *Possessing the Secret*.

A.W.: Okay, well, Nettie is named after my mother's mother, Nettie, who died when I was two. Now, this woman was battered terribly by my grandfather, the other grandfather; he was also a batterer.

M.J.: Did you ever see them battering each other?

A.W.: Never, never, I never saw any of that. This was all legendary; well, some of them had unfortunately the scars to prove it. No, I never saw that. This woman, my grandmother Nettie, who died when I was two, never went anywhere. Here's where the slave thing just goes right into what followed slavery. During slavery, you could not leave the plantation. The women *never* left. The men might get a pass to do something, but the women were *there*. So this Nettie, after slavery, not very long after slavery, also never went anywhere. This is what my mother used to say. "My mother never went anywhere." So I said, you know what, this woman is going to be named Nettie, and she's going to go everywhere. [laughter] And not only that, then two children that nobody ever knew. My stepgrandmother was the least quote "sexy" person you can imagine, so how she even got those children, you know, was just such a mystery, and you know it was a terrible way, I'm sure, but because she had had them, and because they had disappeared, I said, "Well, I'm going to give her some children, they're going to travel with Nettie, and they're going to one day come back to her because she deserves to have her children." So *there*.

M.J.: But did they—the way you describe in later books you really do have visions, and this is a little different, so it began to change in later books.

A.W.: Yes, because I did. I did. In fact, the reason I love *The Temple of My Familiar* is because when I was writing *The Color Purple* I was just in service; I don't know if you've ever had the experience of just knowingly putting yourself at the service of whatever it is. So I was like a priest, not the kind of priest you hear about in the news these days, but, you know, a priest priest, where you really know what you're supposed to be doing, and you're there, you're on the job, you give up everything else to do that, so I was serving these ancestors, basically, and I did it as well as I could possibly do it, I was just—it was like prayer, the whole year, and then I finished it and I just cried, you know, because I missed them so much when they left. But then, after I finished that novel, *they* turned around and gave me, it seemed to me, *The Temple of My Familiar*, which started with a dream.

I had bought a little house in Park Slope and I had gotten a divorce and I—long story—but I bought a little house, and it was only twelve feet wide, so we used to call it a sliver of a house. And one night in that little house I had a dream that I went down the stairs and I went to the basement and in the middle of the floor there was a trapdoor, a round trapdoor with a metal thing, and I lifted that up and there were more stairs and I went down there, too, and in this subbasement there were all these people from South America, and they were all making incredibly beautiful things. Beautiful things, I mean, weavings and things with feathers and, you know, just incredible—and they were all speaking Spanish and some of them were even speaking I think Quechua, or Mayan. Who were these people? I had no idea. Years went by. I wrote whatever, this and that, and then one day I realized that I had to start this new novel, and I started dreaming in Spanish, and I hired a tutor, because I didn't speak Spanish, so I hired my daughter's teacher to tutor me in Spanish, and I started writing *The Temple of My Familiar,* and that's who they were, they were the people in this new book, and I felt it was just the most generous gift.

M.J.: And then what about *Possessing the Secret of Joy*; what drove you to that, which is the female genital mutilation or, as you refer to it, FGM?

A.W.: Well, the son of Celie marries a woman who is genitally mutilated because in her culture they think that unless you're that way, you can't marry and you're no good. So when we were making the film in Burbank, or wherever that is down there, one day she arrived. She came from Kenya, this wife came from Kenya, the wife-to-be, the fictional wife, and I was looking for her to see how she was walking, whether she had been mutilated, and I don't think she had been, but in any case, it made me realize that I had to—for me, if I create a character who has a whole hidden story, especially of suffering, I cannot just leave her or him there, I have to pay attention to this person because I understand *fully* that this is not just about fiction, that every character, quote "character," is living somewhere in the hills of Kenya, somewhere in Benin, somewhere in Ghana, somewhere in Alabama, so I decided to take the time, which was I think a little over a year, maybe two years, to write a story about this woman and how she decided to be genitally mutilated, and that's how that happened.

M.J.: It's not just about fiction.

A.W.: No.

M.J.: No, I mean, I feel that in your books. Have you always known that?

A.W.: Yes.

M.J.: But it seems to me to become more and more intense.

A.W.: Yes. It's not; how could it be? You know, look at Charles Dickens. There was someone who fully understood that it's not about fiction, it's not just about fiction. We are capable, as writers, of changing some horrendous situations. I have been back to Africa many times and talked with people who five years or ten years before would have sworn that this didn't even happen, but now they know a hundred million women, horrible transmission of AIDS, great devastation of the communities, not to mention self-esteem and self-respect, you know, so we're actually, it's within our power to do some really good things just for the health of people. Even if you don't want to go into the spiritual whatever, just on this basic level of health, we can do some incredible things as writers.

M.J.: Two things are actually warring in my head. One thing—well, I'll say this first. I am always struck at your—and very appreciative—at how willing you are, amidst quite a panoply of spiritual practices and healings, to put black people in therapy and in psychoanalysis, because it seems to me that this is another taboo. [laughter] For many centuries— no, generations, let's say, psychoanalysis seems centuries old, but it's not—you know, the myth was that we were too strong for that. Whatever we had endured, and also, then the myth, based on some truth, arose that it couldn't encompass our experience and therefore couldn't be encountered and expanded but simply had to be denied, but you're one of the only black writers I know who consistently has black characters encountering psychoanalysts and therapists, and I thank you.

[laughter]

A.W.: You're welcome.

M.J.: No, it matters, and now I realize I had to say it because it's one of those life and fiction connections. It removes—it's like writing about depression, it takes away a stigma, it really does.

A.W.: Yeah, I just really want us to be healthy. I want us to be healthy and wealthy and wise, you know. It's wonderful to be able to—for instance, in *Possessing the Secret of Joy*. Usually what happens with me is I will study something for a long time to understand it as fully as possible, so I spent like years studying Jung, and I love Jung, and I was actually able then to understand his theories and his way and I went to visit Bollingen, where he had his little tower by the lake, and I was able then to actually put Jung himself in the novel, and that was such a delight because I feel that the people like Jung give us new ways of understanding our behavior when they help us to see the shadow that we just don't want to face, that they are actually helping us to see the light, to see the light of health, of who we really are. People like that should be honored, and so I was delighted to have him show up in the novel as Imsi, the old man who goes to Africa. And he actually did go to Africa, you know. I don't think he—here's an interesting little place where I think Jung and I, because I'm, you know, *me*, and he was *him*, where we saw things very differently. He had one of these old-fashioned video things. What do you call these things?

M.J.: They used to take those home-movie-type things.

A.W.: Well, he had one of those. You know what I mean, this thing. So he went to this village, and he saw all of these young girls who were lying in a row and they were obviously suffering, but they weren't permitted to show it, so they were just like, you know, immobilized. So he took this picture of them, and he came back and first of all he said they were boys, because they had had their hair shaved off, but that's what happens, you know, and then he went on about, you know, some kind of initiation, blah blah blah blah, but what he had actually seen, I think, was what I saw when I went, was that these were girls, little girls, who had been mutilated and they were lying in the row.

So I believe that psychoanalysis is really helpful, and I have spent some really wonderful—and it's fun, really, once you, you know. You shouldn't have somebody who's just going to sit there and not say anything much and just tell you to pay the money and come back Thursday. [laughter] You don't need that. You need somebody who's alive, who's alive to life, and who loves life and lives life.

In fact, by now, we must never, never put ourselves under the dominion of anybody who's half-dead [laughter]. I mean, check people *out*! [laughter] They will try to fool you by looking all, like, well-dressed and calm and collected and everything, but if they don't have the spark of life they are no good to you, and don't waste your time. See, the finger thing comes when you get to be sixty. [laughter]

M.J.: Put down the rose and lift the finger.

A.W.: Exactly.

M.J.: I think that you all should be able to talk to Alice Walker. . . . It's kind of shadowy back there, but if people, ah, they can approach microphones? Yes. Okay!

Q.: Good evening. I just wanted to say it is an absolute pleasure to be here tonight. I have two questions, fifty-two seconds, I'll promise. First, I just moved here from Nashville to New York City. I'd like to know what was your biggest cultural shock when you moved from the South to the North. Which you can answer hopefully quickly. The second one a little bit more provocative. My mother, who was a fair-skinned, dead-straight-hair kind of person, she is not a fan of *The Color Purple*, because she feels like it totally misportrayed black men and it aired our dirty laundry, so I wanted to know how do you deal with black people who are critics of that particular book.

A.W.: Let's see, the cultural shock. Not enough flowers. Not nearly enough flowers, and also that black people seem very ashy. [laughter] And you can also tell that they thought that not being ashy was really wonderful. Or not being shiny. They thought shininess was like—like country bumpkins were shiny. You know, I wrote a book called *The Same River Twice: Honoring the Difficult,* and it answers every question you can imagine about how I responded to all the people criticizing, you know, this and that. You know, maybe your mother just doesn't like the book, maybe she has her own issues, I would imagine, because it's a book that is just full of love, it really is, there's nothing in that book but love, even the people who are hating each other are coming out of love. It takes love to create people, clearly, who are doing self-hating things. It takes a lot of love to do that. I like to—I sort of think about Che Guevara, who said the revolution comes out of love. It's the same with creativity. It's the same with writing novels, singing. You know, like when Stevie Wonder sings to us, you know that man is singing out of love. He's often telling us some very sad things, but we know that he just loves us. So if your mother with the lightness, the hair, there's a lot of pain there, so just be patient with her, and tell her to come see the musical.

[laughter/applause]

Q.: Hi. I have a question about you being able to embrace your creative-writing niche at a time when that may not have been easy. Like, basically nowadays, they say, forget creativity, get a job, make money. And when you have that creative niche and you want to kind of get into it, how do you—how did you do it, basically?

A.W.: You know, life will give you some sort of spur. I think—I had had an abortion, actually. This is where my first book came out of, and I was very, very happy that I was not going to be trying to raise a child that I knew I couldn't raise, and I had also been facing suicide around this issue, and so when I realized that I could have my life, the response was just this outpouring of poems. And I gave these poems to my teacher— I was at Sarah Lawrence by then—and she gave them to a publisher, and you know, then I just kept writing, but luckily for me, my feeling of self-worth and self-respect meant that money just didn't matter as much to me as feeling good about myself did, and I knew that writing was a way that I could really utilize my whole being. It's such a wonderful discipline, writing, in that way. So I would say to you that, just forget about the siren song of the big bucks. Try to make enough, or get a grant or something, grants are good, something that will give you six months to a year to work on something that you really feel you must do, and do that.

Q.: First of all, I just wanted to say thank you for everything, and especially on the eve of *The Color Purple* opening on Broadway— congratulations. I wanted to hear you speak a little bit about the transition from the written word to the spoken and acted word, and what you find particularly fulfilling or thrilling and what you find challenging about that transition.

A.W.: The written to the spoken?

Q.: Yeah, from the text of *The Color Purple* to it becoming a movie and it becoming a play and it being embodied not just in your mind and in the reader's imagination, but in actual bodies.

A.W.: Oh, right, yeah. Oh, it's been magical, really, you know, it's like when we were making the film, it was just—there were all these synchronicities. And synchronicity is a sign of life, so whenever your life is full of synchronicity, you know you're right on it, you cannot do a wrong thing, it's all just good, you know. So there we all were down in Burbank making this film and we had these incredible synchronicities. I mean, one of the big ones, of course, you may know, is that Oprah is Harpo spelled backward. The other one was that when Celie was giving birth in the film, Steven Spielberg's wife was also giving birth. It was like an endless kind of thing, and it's been so long that I don't remember all of them. I have learned to really trust that generally speaking good people turn up in my life and when they are not good people, I try to help them move along, [laughter] but for the film I felt that Quincy Jones and Steven Spielberg were really good and I felt the same way with the producer who came to ask me if he could make a musical of the novel. And then what happens, this is part of the real magic. You know how I was saying how I missed my parents, my grandparents, my siblings, because they all went away, or they were all very old, and I felt like as a little child I just had all this *love* for them, and I couldn't really be with them because they were gone. So now what happens? Well, I walked onto the set for the movie. There they all were! And then I walked to look at the people doing the musical. There they are again! I have this feeling that they're not going away until I am really fulfilled in this desire to be with them. When I have had enough of them, you won't see any more movies or musicals. But I'm not done yet. I still miss them.

Q.: Hi. I just wanted to ask just an overarching larger question. You mentioned briefly that we are ahistorical, in the context of the social structures that currently exist in the U.S., like the disparities in education and the minority and black students, the incarceration rates and politics, and I just wanted to ask, how do you think our lives would be different if we as a people were exposed to the true histories of, like, race and class and gender and how they have played a part in forming our country, or do you think our lives would be different at all?

A.W.: Oh, I think our lives would be so much different if we knew our own history and we knew how things got to be this way, and also that we could see how they make a circle. We are going back in some ways to places we have already been and we really don't, we really shouldn't be able to, we shouldn't *have* to do that, and if we had a firmer grasp on the history, and on who we actually are, and what people have already created these wheels, we wouldn't be doing them over, and sometimes I feel a sadness about that, because I can see how young people especially, from the cradle really and before, even in utero, they are so attuned to television and other media, and I really appreciate these media, I mean, they are magical in themselves, but you know you cannot actually understand who you are if you are constantly being bombarded by things to buy, you know, how to look, you know, how thin you can be, how this, how that, so we've become extremely distracted in a way that actually did not exist when I was a child; we were not distracted in that way, and so I would say that we really, all of us, not just African Americans, but people in the world, have to learn how to turn off the distraction in order to connect again to what is vital. We will never get our people out of prison if we are all watching—I don't know what you're all watching, but you know, you have to really have a certain amount of a sacred solitude in which you develop what is a priority for you in this lifetime. You cannot do that if you are distracted and just pulled this way and that way all the time, so I don't know if that answers you, but those are some thoughts.

Q.: I identify something with you during the question-and-answer. I was an immigrant from Hong Kong and you mentioned the children being alone and the parents working, and people are saying this was changing. Can you name some things that the immigrants can help their children feeling that way—how to deal with that feeling?

A.W.: Well, I don't know, but what comes to mind is to say to this group what I say almost everywhere I go, which is that the time that we live in is so dangerous, is so precarious, for all of us, for our children, I cannot imagine what it looks like to our children, but it is very important that we form circles, that we form circles in which then the children who come into our circles feel that support, they feel that they have a community. Many of us have left communities. And some of us will never actually have the community of origin that we were born into—that's gone. But if we creatively make circles . . . You know, I have, I belong to two circles: one is a women's council, we meet four times a year, and then I belong to a sangha, which meets every month, and these are both circles that if there were children, little children around, they would be coming in, you know, grabbing a cookie off the table, where there are these *grand* women, sitting and talking about the fate of the earth and the fate of the community and the fate of *them*. This is what our children need. They need to know that there are adults *somewhere* sitting together and discussing, at least, what it's going to take for us to survive this brave new world.

Q.: I have a question, pretty simple—you basically answered my question already about young adults realizing how much we need to connect with our history and how much we need to learn from that and move on with our future—but my question now is going back to the movie *The Color Purple* and the night of the Oscars. Now, I understand that the movie wasn't recognized at all, and I just wanted to know what was your reaction to that night. I understand that God has a purpose for everybody and everything happens for a reason, and if anything God will bless you with that opportunity in the future, but at that moment in time, what was your reaction?

A.W.: Well, one thing you understand really early on in this kind of thing is that you don't need awards. You don't. [applause] You know, you don't. So, or another way of putting it, is that the award is *life*, and we won, we got it. What more do we need? So I was thinking, you know, they told me, well, Steven really wanted an Oscar, well, I thought, "I'm going to call up my friend in the country and have him just make him one." [laughter] It is true that if you have Oscars, you get more money, and you do this and that, but in fact one of the things I hope I've conveyed is that the creativity is the joy, when you're actually doing it, that's the award, not the other thing. So, personally, I felt very glad that we didn't get an award, and the reason I felt that was I didn't know any of the people who were giving the award. Now if my first-grade teacher had been one of those people, if even my high school teachers had been some of those people, if some of my uncles and aunts had been some of those people . . . but what are we talking about? We are talking about a few, you know, very well-to-do, basically white men in Hollywood. Do they know what they're doing? [laughter]

So it was not really that difficult. Actually it was not difficult for me at all. But I did feel. I felt for Oprah. I felt for Whoopi. I felt for Danny. I mean, all the people who were nominated. You know, there were eleven nominations. So there we all were in this huge hall, which I don't know if you know this, but you know, it looks very sophisticated on the TV, but outside, it's not, because you come in and there are these people on bleachers, like in high school, and they're yelling and they're screaming, and it was really not that wonderful. So I wanted *them* to have that affirmation, but we must deeply understand, especially in this culture, *especially* in this culture, that you do not need an award from people you don't know. You do not. It is meaningless on a deep level. It is absolutely of no use whatsoever if they don't really know you. Do you understand what I'm saying?

Q.: Hi. Thank you, Miss Walker and Miss Jefferson, for tonight. My question is just, as having loved your novels, but as an adult having come to understand and really identify with your essays, my question is how do you deal with—well, what I identify with is that you kind of, I felt like, were the first person to kind of call out and tell things like they were that I had noticed about the world. And I just wonder how you deal with the frustrations of ignorance. Like for me, it sometimes often turns to rage just dealing with racism and sexism. And I'm always the person who's the naysayer and oh here she goes again, bringing some realism into it and stats and everything else, so how do you deal with that within yourself, and also I feel like I want to *help* people, and often it comes out where I'm pushing then away because I get so wired up about it.

A.W.: I don't know. Actually, what comes to mind is how in my last novel—I have spent, again, two years studying Buddhism and

shamanism, and those are the twin pillars of that novel, and I was showing how, even though we think that they are very far apart, Buddhism
and shamanism, because one is like it's not really a religion, but it's a
philosophy, and it's all written and everything, and then shamanism
tends to be somebody with a drum and herbs and dances and ritual,
you know, and so we think that they are just like yay apart, but in fact
they are so similar, because the aim of each one is to open the heart, because they understand that with a closed heart, you really can't do anything; you have to open your heart. So then imagine my surprise when
I—I don't read reviews but people always tell you. [laughter] You know,
they'll say, "Did you know?" and I'll say, "No, I didn't know that." But
imagine my surprise when this whole aspect is just completely—it's as if
it didn't exist.

And not only that, I was also very interested in indigenous medicine.
You know, this is medicine that is older than anything you're taking,
and more people have been taking it, and more people have been getting
well with it. So I wanted to know about it, so I studied it, I took it myself.
I can't tell you how many times I threw up trying to *learn* about medicine that people have used for so long. And then to understand that
when it reaches the desk of someone who lives in New York, or wherever, and they have no notion that there is this whole history, this lin-
eage, this world of medicine and shamans, and so they write really
disrespectful—just madness, really, because it's so provincial and insu-
lar, you know? So what do I do? There's nothing I can do. All I can do is
write my books. What I do when I love a writer, say, for instance, Charles
Dickens or that man that I love so much whose name is just completely
gone, but anyway, but what I do when I really love someone's work is
I trust them not to give me, then, five books down the line, absolute
garbage. Usually it's just not in the artist to do that, unless they've just
completely sort of sold out and gone over, you know. Generally speaking, if someone you know cares deeply—and you can tell, you can really
tell. Read *Oliver Twist*. Charles Dickens really, really cared. So then you
just really trust that they are going to continue to probe deeply, to try
to see clearly, and to share this with *everyone*, because our existence is
in the balance right now. It's not even, you know, like, tomorrow; it's
now, it's yesterday. So there is just on my part the feeling that eventually
I can wait. And I don't even have to be here for the people to discover
my work that has been misrepresented. Eventually somebody will find

it. I mean, look at Zora Neale Hurston; we found her. This is what we can do.

M.J.: I think that that is a fine place to end but really to begin again. Thank you.

A.W.: Thank you.

15

"Outlaw, Renegade, Rebel, Pagan": Interview with Amy Goodman from *Democracy Now!* (2006)

AMY GOODMAN: I was just saying to Alice that I think one of the last times that I saw her was right before the invasion. It was International Women's Day, March 8, 2003.

She was standing in front of the White House with Maxine Hong Kingston, Terry Tempest Williams, and a number of other women. It wasn't a large group, about fifteen or so women, and they stood there, arms locked, and the police told them to move, and they said no. And they all got arrested.

We were trying to get their message out on community radio. I was interviewing them on cell phone. The police didn't appreciate that. So, really, the last time that I saw her was in the prison cell with her. But, Alice, you said that day, as we were in the paddy wagon or in the police wagon, that it was the happiest day of your life. Why?

ALICE WALKER: Well, you were there. I have so much admiration for this woman, so much love for Amy. . . . So I was very happy that she had appeared to talk to us about why we were there. Nobody else was asking.

And so, there we were, arrested in this patrol thing, and actually I did feel incredibly happy, because what happens when you want to express your outrage, your sorrow, your grief—grief is basically where we are now, just bone-chilling grief—when you're able to gather your own forces and deal with your own fears the night before, and you arrive, you show up, and you put yourself there, and you know that you're just a little person—you know, you're just a little person—and there's this huge machine that's going relentlessly pretty much all over the world, and then you gather with all of the other people who are just as small as you are, but you're together, and you actually do what you have set out to do, which is to express total disgust, disagreement, disappointment about the war in Iraq.

About the possibility of it starting up again, all of these children, many of them under the age of fifteen, about to be terrorized, brutalized, and killed—so many of them—so, to be able to make any kind of gesture that means that the people who are about to be harmed will know that we are saying we don't agree—just the ability to do that made me so joyful.

I was completely happy. And I think that we could learn to live in that place of full self-expression against disaster and self-possession and happiness.

A.G.: You have had a continued relationship with the police officer who put handcuffs on you.

A.W.: Yes, because he really didn't want to do it. And I could see that they really did not want to arrest us. And he, this African American man, truly did not want to arrest me. And I totally understand that. Would you want to arrest me? No. No, no. You would not. So even as they were handcuffing me, they were sort of apologizing. . . . I thought that you put the handcuffs [with] your hands in front, but they put them behind you. . . .

Then later, after we were released. . . . They take your shoes, I was there trying to put my shoes back on, and he came over, and he got down on his knees, and he said, "Let me help you." And I said, "Sure."

And I put my foot out, and he helped me with my shoes, and we started talking about his children. Well, first of all, he told me about his wife. He said, "You know, when I told my wife that I had arrested you, she was not thrilled." And so, then I asked him about his family, and he told me about his children, and I told him I write children's books. And so he said, "Oh, you do? Because, you know, there's nothing to read. The children are all watching television." I said, "That's true." So it ended up with me sending books to them and feeling that this is a very good way to be with the police. . . .

I realized fairly recently—I went to Houston to the Astrodome to take books and other things to the [Katrina evacuees], and the police, a lot of them [were] also African Americans. . . . It was very clear that they, like the people who had lost their homes, really wanted some books. But, as one of them said to me, "I really would like a book, but I'm not the people. I'm the police." And I said to him, and then some of the people said that, too, they said, "You know, these people are the police, they're not the people."

However, I said to the people and to the police that the police are the people, and we have to remember that the police are the people. . . . And so, there they were, these big guys who probably had not had anybody offer them a book to read in years, if ever. They had gone into the army and into the police force because they did not have an education. That's part of why they're police. . . .

A.G.: I was reading Evelyn White's biography of you, called *Alice Walker: A Life*, and she goes back to 1967, and you had just come to New York, and you were submitting an essay to *American Scholar*. It was 1967, so you were about twenty-three years old. And it was entitled "The Civil Rights Movement: What Good Was It?" You won first prize. It was published. "The Civil Rights Movement: What Good Was It?"

Can you talk about the civil rights movement to the antiwar movement? The antiwar movement, what good is it?

A.W.: Well, as I was saying about the civil rights movement . . . sometimes you can't see tangible results. You cannot see the changes that you're dreaming about, because they're internal. And a lot of it has to do with the ability to express yourself, your own individual dream and your own individual road in life. And so, we may never stop war.

We may never stop war, and it isn't likely that we will, actually. But what we're doing as we try to stop war externally, what we're trying to do is stop it in ourselves. That's where war has to end. And until we can control our own violence, our own anger, our own hostility, our own meanness, our own greed, it's going to be so, so, so hard to do anything out there.

So I think of any movement for peace and justice as something that is about stabilizing our inner spirit so that we can go on and bring into the world a vision that is much more humane than the one that we have dominant today.

A.G.: Speaking about movements, Rosa Parks died recently. It was the fiftieth anniversary, on December first, of the Montgomery Bus Boycott.

The corporate media, in describing Rosa Parks, talked about her as a tired seamstress who sat down on that bus, and when the white bus driver said, "Get up," she simply refused. She was tired. She was no troublemaker.

But Rosa Parks, of course, was a troublemaker. Can you talk about the importance of movements and what it means to be an activist, why it doesn't diminish what you do but actually adds to Rosa's . . . reputation and her legacy.

A.W.: I was thinking about Rosa Parks, because I was in Africa when she died, and I missed everything.

A.G.: Where?

A.W.: I was in Senegal, in a little village south of Dakar. I was visiting this great African writer, Ayi Kwei Armah, who wrote a famous and wonderful book called *Two Thousand Seasons*, which I recommend to everyone. He's a great, great writer, but when I got back and I realized that she had died, I didn't actually feel like doing anything. I waved. I waved to her.

What I remembered about her was the last time that I had seen her . . . one day in Mississippi, we happened to be at the same event. I think she was being honored for, you know, everything that she had given us, and we were at the same table, and I think that I may have offered to escort her to the restroom, and I was in there with her. And she—while she was getting herself together to go back out into the reception, she suddenly took down her hair, and Rosa Parks had hair that came all the way down to her, you know, the lower back, and she quickly ran her fingers through it.

I was just stunned. I had no idea. She then twisted it up again, and she put it the way you've seen her, you know, always with the little bun, very neat, and I said to her, "My goodness, what's all this, Miss Rosa?" And she looked at me, and she said, "Well, you know, I'm part Choctaw, and my hair was something that my husband dearly, dearly loved about me. He loved my hair." And she said, "And so, when he died, I put it up, and I never wear it down in public." Now there's a Rosa.

So, you know, writers are just—we live by stealth, and so I immediately had this completely different image of this woman: the little, quiet seamstress sitting on the bus, even the activist who was so demure and so correct. And I thought, this woman, hallelujah, was with a man who loved her and loved her with her hair hanging down, and she loved him so much that when he died, she took that hair that he loved, and she put it up on her head, and she never let anyone else see it. Isn't that amazing?

So to answer your question, for me, to be active in the cause of the people and of the earth is to be alive. There is no compartmentalization. It's all one thing. It's not like I just exist to go into a little room and write. People have that image of writers, that that's how we live, but it's not really accurate, not the kind of writing that I do. I know that what I write has a purpose, even if it's just for me, if I'm just trying to lead myself out of a kind of darkness.

So it broadens everything, being active in the world. You see the world. It's like, you know, I'm learning to paint now, and what I realize, learning to paint, is that I'm learning to see. And activism is like that. When you are active, and you must know this so well, that the more you are active, the more you see, the more you go to see. You know, you are curious. One thing leads to another thing, and it gets deeper and deeper, too. And there's no end to it.

A.G.: How do you write?

A.W.: What do you mean?

A.G.: Well, Isabel Allende said that she starts each new book on the same day of the year. I can't remember the date. Maybe it was January 9, something like that. . . . What about you? What is your process?

A.W.: I start each book when it's ready and never before. And what I do is I try to find—if it's forming, you know, and if I'm attentive to my dreams, I know that it's coming, and I know that it's time to take a year or two. In the early days the big challenge was finding the financing to do that, because for many years I was a single mother. I was lecturing and making a living that way, or teaching, and so I had to think hard and plan, and some of my early journals are just pages of additions of how much this costs and how much that costs, and how much is left at the end of the month, and whether I can afford this and that. So that was the challenge, to find the time, because what I understand completely is that you—in order to invite any kind of guest, including creativity, you have to make room for it. . . .

I learned, partly through meditation, which I have done for many years, that you can really clear yourself of so much that's extraneous to your purpose in life, so that there is room for what is important to your spirit, something that has to be given space and something that has to be given voice.

A.G.: How did you start *The Color Purple*?

A.W.: I got a divorce. I got a divorce, because I really knew that I could not stay in my marriage and write about these wild women. And also, I left New York. And I—and it started really just because one of the characters, while I was walking through Manhattan, said through my consciousness, "You know, it's not going to work here. We are just not the kind of people who would come forth in Manhattan."

So, they basically carried me through all this incredible anguish of divorce, because I, unlike many people who divorce out of hatred or anything, I actually loved my husband very much. He's a very, very good person, but I needed to write this book, and he claimed that the hills in San Francisco made him nauseous.

So I came here, and I ended up in Boonville, because I needed to be in the country, and so I had enough money to work on it for maybe a year, because I got a Guggenheim grant, $13,000, and I just headed for the hills. We rented a little cottage in an apple orchard, and I didn't know how long it would take, but it took just about a year.

A.G.: Did you ever envision then the kind of impact it would have on the world? Did you think about the people you were writing it for?

A.W.: Oh, I thought about the people I was writing it for. The people I was writing it for are the people who are in the book. That's who I was writing it for. It never crossed my mind to really be that concerned about the people who would be reading it now, and that's still true. I mean, I'm happy that people relate to it and love it. I think it's worthy of love. But my contract was always really with the people in it and whether I could make them live in the way that they deserve to live, and it was a very high, very high experience to be able to do that, and when I wrote the last page, I burst into tears just from gratitude and love of them and of being . . .

I don't know how many of you know the work of Jean Toomer. He's just a wonderful writer. But he talks about how in every generation, there is one person—or, as he puts it, there is one plum left on the tree, and all of the other plums are gone with the wind and so forth. There is this one plum, and that plum with one seed, that's all you need, really, to start it all over again, and that's another reason for us to be more hopeful about life.

So I really had that feeling of being this one plum with this one seed, because from what I could see, there wasn't anybody else who had the same kind of love for these particular people that I had, or the capacity to be faithful to the vision of them that I held. So I felt very blessed and very chosen, in a way, like my ancestors were really present with me the entire time I was writing. They never went away. They were just really there, and I have felt their caring, and I still feel it. And it means that I never feel alone. It's impossible.

A.G.: For someone who hasn't read the book, for a young person who is wondering why they should bother picking up *The Color Purple*, what would you say it's about?

A.W.: Well, I was just in Molokai last week. I just got back a few days ago, and Molokai is the island that is least known among the islands, and it's because it used to be a leper colony, and there are actually lepers who still live there. And I was looking through a book about Molokai and about Kalaupapa, which is where the lepers are, and there was a photograph of this man who had leprosy, and it had eaten away his nose and most of his mouth and his ears and a lot of his face, and he just had this incredibly beautiful beaming face. What was left of his face was just completely aglow. And what he said he had learned from living in this place of lepers all of his life was that the most horrible things can happen to people, and they can still be happy. So I feel that when you read *The Color Purple*, no matter what is happening in your life, or how difficult the whole huge miasma of sorrow that seems to be growing, there's a way that you can see through the life of Celie, that if you can continue and if you can stay connected to nature and also to your highest sense of behavior toward yourself and toward other people, if you can really keep that struggle going—you may not always win it.

You remember how Celie said to Harpo at some point that he should beat Sofia, that he should beat his wife, well, that was a low point, but she was still struggling to be someone who would outgrow that kind of thinking. And so, what you learn is that life can be really hard. People can abuse you, people can take advantage of you in terrible ways, but there is something in the human spirit that's actually equal to that and can overcome that, and that is the teaching of *The Color Purple*.

A.G.: You write in *The Same River Twice: Honoring the Difficult*, "What I have kept, which the film avoided entirely, is Shug's completely unapologetic self-acceptance as outlaw, renegade, rebel and pagan." Do you see yourself that way?

A.W.: Oh, absolutely. Yes. Why wouldn't I be? I know I'm very soft-spoken, but I have endeavored to live my life by my terms, and that means that I am a renegade, an outlaw, a pagan. What was the other thing?

A.G.: A rebel.

A.W.: A rebel, oh yes. Oh yes, and there is no reason not to rebel. I learned that really early. There is no reason whatsoever. You know, I don't look at television hardly at all, although I'm saving it for my old age. But when I do see it, and I see how relentlessly we are being programmed, and I see how defenseless our young are, I realize all over again that rebellion, any way you can manage it, is very healthy, because unless you want to be a clone of somebody that you don't even like, you have to really wake up. I mean, we all do. We have to wake up. We have to refuse to be a clone.

A.G.: [Will you speak about] making *The Color Purple* into a movie?

A.W.: It was a great risk, but I grew up in Eatonton, Georgia, actually not even in the town, way out in the luckily beautiful countryside. But our entertainment was on Saturday night to, you know, bathe and get dressed and go to see a film. Now, these were all, in retrospect, really pretty awful films. They were all shooting and killing each other, you know. But that was all that we had really in the way of entertainment that wasn't the church and our own entertainments. So that's what I grew up with. And my mother who worked so hard and never left the house or left the fields, she would sometimes be able to go, but after eight children, it was sometimes difficult to even move, but she enjoyed these movies.

And so, the risk that I took was in a way to offer to my mother and people like my mother something that they could identify with, something that they could, you know, have some real connection to. I mean, my mother never met Tom Mix and Lash La Rue. These were all these characters that were shooting and killing.

So I thought about, you know, the segregated theater. When I was growing up, we had to be up there in the balcony, and the white people were down here [on the floor], and, of course, the seats were better down here. So I wanted to change that to the degree that I could do so. And so that's part of the reason I wanted to make a film.

And I think—you know, I had never heard of Steven Spielberg when he appeared. I think that, for many people, that's amazing, given how famous he was, but I had no idea who he was. And that's the other thing, when you are working on your work—and I think it's really important that I talk to you about this a little bit as an elder—when you are working on your work, you really don't have to be concerned about what other people are doing.

You know, there's an expression: "Everything that rises must converge." At some point, if your work is as true as you can make it, it has its own luminosity, and it inevitably brings to you and your work all the people that you need. So enter Steven Spielberg to make the film, which turned out to be a very good thing. People thought it was a terrible choice, but what I looked for in him and in other people is the willingness to listen and the willingness to grow, to learn, and he had all of that.

A.G.: The questions that were raised—here you had written it, deeply out of your own experience, then having a white producer produce it and going on to Broadway, well, that's just repeated over and over. What were your thoughts of having your experience, your writing, your art, channeled through them?

A.W.: Well, I have fallen in love with the imagination. And if you fall in love with the imagination, you understand that it is a free spirit. It will go anywhere, do anything. So your job is to find trustworthy companions and cocreators. That's really it. And if you find them—and I don't know how you do, I can only go by how I feel about people.

And so with the play, this young man, Scott Sanders, who is the primary producer, went to great lengths to woo me, because I was not interested in doing a musical, partly because of the suffering that had occurred after making the film. There was so much incredible controversy after the film, and a lot of it excruciatingly hurtful. And even though I had ways to buffer myself, and even though by nature I can continue to function and do things that I need to do, it was still very painful. So I didn't really want to go back to that. . . .

That anybody reading *The Color Purple* or seeing the film, actually, that they could read it and see the film and still think that I hated . . . my father, my grandfather, my brothers, my uncles, just because they were black men—and, you know, this would mean that I hated Langston Hughes or Jean Toomer or Richard Wright or Ralph Ellison or—it felt so incredibly mean. It felt very mean, it felt very small, and it was very painful.

A.G.: And so how did you get through it?

A.W.: Well, I came down with Lyme disease in the middle of all of this, and I experienced it actually as a spiritual transformation, even though I didn't know that was going to be the result. It was very frightening. But I came out the other end of the bashing that I had received, the physical debilitation from Lyme disease, the breakup of my relationship with a partner at the time. I came out of all of that with a renewed sense that life itself, no matter what people are slinging at you, no matter what is happening, life itself is incredibly precious and wonderful, and that we are so lucky that we wake up in the morning, that we hear a bird, that we . . .

You know, just if you think about little things, they seem little, but they are so magical, you know, like eating a peach. I came through that period understanding that I am an expression of the divine, just like a peach is, just like a fish is. I have a right to be this way. And being this way, *The Color Purple* is the kind of work that comes to me. I can't apologize for that, nor can I change it, nor do I want to.

So there was this marvelous feeling, you know, that I had already been through a kind of crucifixion by critics. . . . And not to compare myself with Jesus, but I really got it, that there is a point at which a certain kind of crucifixion leads to a certain kind of freedom, because you cannot be contained by other people's opinions of you. You will always, I think, after you go through this kind of thing, feel somewhat removed, as I do. You know, I basically stopped reading reviews. And it's fine. I have realized I don't need them. I really feel that if more people could pay less attention to other people's opinions of them, they would be so much happier.

A.G.: Alice, I wanted to ask you about the Sisterhood. Who was this group of women writers in the 1970s that you gathered with?

A.W.: Well, the Sisterhood was the brainchild of myself and June Jordan, because we looked around one day—we were friends—and we felt that it was very important that black women writers know each other, that we understood that we were never in competition for anything, that we did not believe in ranking. We would not let the establishment put one of us ahead of the other. And so, some of us were Vertamae Grosvenor, Ntozake Shange, Toni Morrison, June Jordan, myself, and I think Audrey Edwards, who was at *Essence*, and several other women that I don't tonight remember.

The very first meeting was at June's apartment because it was the larger of—I had moved out of my marriage house into basically two small rooms. And so June had this beautiful apartment with lots of space, and the women gathered there, and I remember at the very first gathering—I had bought this huge red pot that became the gumbo pot—I made my first gumbo and took it to this gathering of women, all so different and all so spicy and flavorful like gumbo. And we have this photo. There is a wonderful photograph that someone took of us gathered around a large photograph of Bessie Smith, because Bessie Smith best expressed our feeling of being women who were free and women who intended to stay that way.

A.G.: You talked about criticism earlier and how you decided never to read reviews. Can you talk about it in terms of Toni Morrison's early work and the response of the critics?

A.W.: Well, I thought that her writing was beautiful. I had read *The Blu-est Eye* and, in fact, was passing it out to people. And I was very upset that it didn't get much of a long life. I think—I don't know if it went out of print, but it certainly was sort of below the surface. And then I read *Sula*, which I just fell in love with. And I remember that there was a review of it in the *New York Times* by . . . someone who basically said that in order for Toni Morrison ever to be anything in the literary world, she had to get out of writing about black women, and she had to broaden her horizons and that way, she would maybe connect. And I was just completely annoyed. And I wrote a letter to the *Times*, re-minding [the writer] that we will never have to be other than who we are in order to be successful.

A.G.: Here is the letter. Alice, here is the letter.

A.W.: Oh, okay; it says: "Dear sir: I am amazed on many levels by Sarah Blackburn's review of *Sula*. Is Miss Morrison to 'transcend herself'? And why should she, and for what? The time has gone forever when black people felt limited by themselves. We realize that we are, as our-selves, unlimited and our experiences valid. It is for the rest of the world to recognize this, if they choose."

16

Alice Walker on Fidel Castro with George Galloway from *Fidel Castro Handbook* (2006)

GEORGE GALLOWAY: Fifty years ago Cuba was an apartheid state. Even President Batista, a mulatto, was barred from the exclusive whites-only clubs. You went to Cuba for the first time in 1978. What were your impressions of the relations between Cubans of different ethnic ancestries?

ALICE WALKER: I went to Cuba in 1978 and there was of course lingering racist behavior and attitudes, which my group of cultural workers—artists, musicians, dancers—pointed out. The Cubans had a good understanding of how hard it is to change ingrained notions of superiority but assured us they were dedicated to doing so. They pointed out that racism itself had been made illegal in Cuba. This was a profound and novel idea that I wished to import to my home state of Georgia, USA. And the rest of North America as well. I had by then toiled long years in Mississippi beside my civil rights lawyer husband and watched the slow, sometimes life-threatening process of dismantling racist institutions case by case. There was no comparison between the racism of Mississippi and that of Cuba. Or the response to it. Mississippi was by far the more dangerous place to be.

G.G.: Fidel has always reached out to the "wretched of the earth," whether poor whites or blacks, the peoples of Southeast Asia at the time of the Vietnam War, the peoples of Africa, the indigenous peoples of the Americas. What is your impression of Fidel and what he has done for Cuban society?

A.W.: It is always apparent to me that Fidel is a deeply religious man. In the Gandhian sense: "I call that man religious who understands the suffering of others." More than any other leader of our time, or of the last century, Fidel has made it his business to understand exactly why people are poor, in whatever country they are in; why they are at war or at peace; why they are suffering. He has a fine, large intellect, which he uses to comprehend and defend the wretched of the earth. And what is most admirable about him, in my opinion, is that he has never once abandoned his scrutiny of the material conditions of the world in an effort to find solutions to the horrible inequities that exist. He thinks about the same things I do: infant mortality rates; how many calories it takes for a child to do well in school; what is the best way to develop a society in which people feel connected and not alienated. When I am in Cuba I feel safe. Once I was vacationing in Jamaica with my daughter and she was in a motorcycle accident that broke her foot. On the whole side of the island we could not find one doctor, only a couple of nurse practitioners who had only kindness and a bandage to offer us. In Cuba, even during the periods of almost no food or medical supplies I know my daughter's foot would have been looked after by a doctor, and moreover, a doctor who lived nearby. The Cuban people take such things for granted. They take a lot of things for granted. Free education, health care, low housing costs, their leader's obvious love of them. His pride in their endurance, stamina, compassion for the beleaguered of the world, their innumerable accomplishments. I have never felt affection, as an American, from a national leader in the United States. When there has been a semblance of genuine, as opposed to photo-op, caring, it has been partisan. And therefore painful. There has been no substantive and sustained attempt to deal with the underlying foundation of genocide and enslavement that created North America's wealth, still in the hands mostly of white families. Yes, I know Oprah has a billion dollars, which she uses very well, but this does not mean capitalism, rooted in Indian killing and African enslavement and torture and murder, works.

Cubans, generally, I have found, are intelligent, compassionate people who are curious about life. Partly because their leaders are. They hold a vision of what is possible different from that most North Americans possess. That is because they are taught more of what is happening on the planet and why. Global warming, for instance, which is only now becoming a hot (so to speak) topic in the U.S., has been in the consciousness of Cubans for years. That is why when a hurricane struck Havana some years ago the entire city was evacuated before it arrived. Think of the confusion of the U.S. government during Hurricane Katrina in New

Orleans. It is enough to make us weep. And we will weep, because more of that—confusion, denial, incompetence—is surely in our future.

I was not surprised when Fidel and the Cuban government offered to send supplies and doctors to New Orleans—this is behavior I expect of Cubans after all these years watching them respond to the disasters of the world. And I was ashamed when their generosity was refused, by my childish government, as so many of my people suffered miserably in alligator- and snake-infested water, and many of them died. This disregard for the black poor, like the disenfranchisement of black people during the last two elections, we can never forget. It is a permanent bruise to the heart.

G.G.: In the early years of the Cuban Revolution Fidel made contact with many prominent black Americans, such as Angela Davis, Malcolm X, Harry Belafonte, and later with people such as Jesse Jackson and Muhammad Ali. How is Fidel viewed by black Americans today?

A.W.: I only know a couple of hundred black Americans well enough to guess what they might think about anything. In the world, however, one senses there is a deep respect for Fidel. It is based on the fact that he has stood his ground. That my country's attempts to shut him up and to assassinate him have failed. I have written elsewhere that he is like a lone redwood tree in a forest that's been clear-cut. It is painful to imagine what might have been our current situation if Patrice Lumumba had survived, and Che, and Martin Luther King Jr., and the long list of names most of us will never be able to connect to each other, but which are connected by their resistance to the terrorism and tyranny of the United States.

G.G.: In an interview you once remarked that you had heard that Fidel could not sing and he could not dance, so it was just as well he had all those other good qualities. What do you consider his finest qualities?

A.W.: I have had the pleasure of meeting (with a group of people) with Fidel twice. It's true he talks a lot, and it is incredibly interesting because he enjoys explaining his information. He is a natural teacher. And he has a robust sense of humor. I realize many people, encountering such a force, would immediately think of him as a dictator. But it's different when someone talks a lot and it's about sending doctors around the globe to serve the poor, or it's about why so many young men are suffering from a mysterious eye disease (this was the topic at one of the meetings) or about the exploitation of the South American countries by the United States and Europe over centuries. His grasp of world realities is so profound that he has not one iota of the nervousness that most so-called white leaders display in the presence of alert people of color. This is delightful.

But let's linger a moment on the singing and dancing. These are profoundly important to the human spirit, and because Fidel's is a singing and dancing intellect, I wanted him to embody dance and song in himself. For his own enjoyment. Che was likewise without this embodied solace. Because I love these men, honor what they have accomplished, realize they have dedicated their lives to the alleviation of misery, I want them to have this medicine which I so frequently use. And there is also a part of me that says: you're Cuban, damn it! And before that, Spanish. What about that soulful music you had in Spain, and flamenco! And then of course I remember Catholicism and its heavy suppressions of the life force.

In Fidel this passion is expressed in his priestly dedication to revolution.

Fidel is eighty. It is perhaps selfish of me, but I wish he would retire to the countryside or seashore and enjoy a lengthy period of silence. It would be wonderful for him. And that there might be small children brought by to play with him for a couple of hours each week. I would want him to have a cat that falls asleep on his chest. And if there's a wife, as there must be since there are children, that they hold hands day in, day out. And fall asleep together in the hammock. Enough of leaders being used up, becoming, as Fidel was quoted as saying, "the slave of the revolution." The world is indescribably beautiful. One day of truly witnessing it is enough to revitalize the heart, stilling many worries about the outcomes of the future. I would wish many such days for Fidel.

> Happy birthday, Fidel.
> May you be happy.
> May you be peaceful.
> May you be joyful.
> May you have health and ease

Of Being
May you smile again
from inside your
fierce spirit.
May you discover naps and cats and
Small children
Who will be charmed
and mystified
By
Your beard.

May you hear us
In our millions
Say to you

As we used to say
In the little country church
Where I am from
"Well done." Good and Faithful
Servant
Well done.
Fidel. Faithful.
You have had the success that
Eludes
So many:
You have lived up to your name.

17

A Conversation with Marianne Schnall from feminist.com (2006)

MARIANNE SCHNALL: Congratulations on this amazing book *We Are the Ones We Have Been Waiting For*—it contains so many important insights and observations the world needs to hear. In this "me" society we seem to have turned such a deaf ear to what is really important. It's said that the truth hurts. Do you feel it is your calling to scream the truth out loud?

ALICE WALKER: Not at all—I never scream, and I think that silence is the best way to get real attention. Especially from the deep self. So I think the people who are in solitude in the mountains, or who live in temples or are contemplatives, the people you never hear from, you never know are there, somewhere in some deep, dark cave, meditating—I think those people are basically responsible for a lot of the sanity that we do have. And in my own case, I know that what I can bring to the world comes from a world of deep silence and quiet. And that is where my compass—my moral compass and my internal guide—that's where they live, in that deep quiet. So by the time whatever I'm offering gets out into the world, it may sound quite loud, maybe, but that's only, I think, to people who are not used to being in quiet and silence. Sometimes it might seem loud because it is a voice they have been silencing.

M.S.: That reminds me of something you wrote in your book, about the need for a "pause"—a pause to reflect. And I think I probably chose my words wrong, because I definitely did not mean to imply that you "scream"—I guess I meant more that part of your calling seems to be to bring light to the truth; that is probably the better way to say what I was trying to say.

A.W.: Well, I think that I do feel that my nature is to express what this self, this particular self at this time, experiences in the world. And that is so organic—I use this metaphor a lot, but I'll use it again—it's like a pine tree producing pinecones, or a blackberry bush producing black-berries: it's just what happens with this being, now. Going through the world and seeing what I see, and feeling what I feel. And wanting very much to touch other people with that.

M.S.: The subtitle of your book is *Inner Light in a Time of Darkness*. Is this where the real change that is needed in the outer world begins, in our own individual inner worlds, first?

A.W.: It has to be there. And not only that, we do carry an inner light, an inner compass, and the reason we don't know we carry it is because we've been distracted. And we think that the light is actually being car-ried by a leader or somebody that we have elected or somebody that we very much admire, and that that's the only light. And so we forget that we have our own light—it may be small, it may be flickering, but it's actually there. And so what we need to do, I think, is to be still enough to let that light shine, and illuminate our inner landscape and our dreams—especially our dreams. And then our dreams will lead us to the right way.

M.S.: We work with Omega Institute—and I just finished watching your beautiful, inspiring talk that you gave at one of the Women and Power conferences a few years ago. There was so much in there. And you had talked about your concern about the fascism and imperialism that's in the world today. Has America as a country spiritually lost its soul? And do you see a hopeful, antifascism peace movement that's growing?

A.W.: Oh yes, I do. I mean, look at us—look at the millions of people who turn out, and who turned out against the war. The people who are refusing to fight in the war and the soldiers who are throwing down their weapons and going to jail. And the mothers and the fathers who are speaking up—there's a couple who's taking their son's coffin from town to town because their son died in the war. But there's a massive, worldwide movement, I think, that is completely antiwar. And I think of that as a kind of enlightenment that we could not have had in earlier ages because we couldn't see war and its causes quite so clearly. And people were so misled by the church and other institutions that they couldn't see that basically the powerful and the rich, and the people who wanted to stay that way, actually made these wars, most of them for their own benefit. And so they could rip off the resources of people living far away. Now we can see that. Now there are enough women in the world who are educated and smart, and can really run it on down to their parents, and to friends, and to the media. It's a wonderful time. It seems so bleak, but I maintain that it's one of the best times to be alive, and I'm very happy to be here now.

M.S.: I've been thinking that maybe things needed to get so blatantly off course so that we can actually see the state of humanity in order to realize the urgent change that's needed.

A.W.: Unfortunately, that seems to be the way it is with humans. They need to be really scared on some level, and they need to worry about self-preservation and survival. And then it's an instinct—they have an instinct for thriving and continuing. And so that's part of who we are. It's a shame, though, because if we could develop in ourselves a lot of compassion for other beings, we wouldn't have to watch their destruction and humiliation and terrorizing of them in order for us to be moved, to be fearful of what could happen to us.

M.S.: In the world today, there is a growing awareness and more and more people wanting to contribute to change in the world, but not even knowing where to start. As such a longtime activist, what words of encouragement would you offer to other activists in the world?

A.W.: There's always something to do—always. And the reason that's true is that you always can work with yourself. You don't have to go out and worry about what other people are doing or how to start this or that out there; you can start ever so much in yourself. And that will evolve outwardly. So if you just hold that thought—that it really is up to each of us, and we're all trying to get to a place where collectively we can effect change. But we can't really do it from being a collective before we are actually self-collected.

M.S.: Do you think the rising of women, and feminine principles in the world, is a natural, evolutionary shift we are experiencing now?

A.W.: I think it is because the feminine has to rise in order for there to be any hope of continuation of the species. And I think that most people actually feel that on some level. What is a little frightening though is how many women—you know, people who in this lifetime have female bodies—are really fleeing the feminine. And you see it most clearly in language. As I mention in *We Are the Ones We've Been Waiting For*, that women and girls are taught and programmed actually to think of themselves as "guys." And it's a way to basically evade being deeply feminine on a daily basis. And you'll notice too that there's a kind of repetitiveness—like it's being constantly reinforced that you are not feminine, you are something else.

And I think it bears scrutiny and it bears sitting with and really deciding one way or the other. You might decide, well, damn it, you'd like to be guy, you want to use that word and other things that are similar, but you really need to make it a conscious decision. I think women have to be so conscious about what they want to be called, what they actually are—it should be our choice, and it should not just be society's programming, or the media's programming, or masculine or patriarchal programming—which is actually what it is.

M.S.: Speaking of language and linguistics, with a site called feminist. com, I am always amazed at the misconceptions there are about feminism, and the many women who clearly are feminists but who would never call themselves that. You came up with the term "womanist." For people who may not be familiar with that term, can you describe how that term came to be and its relevance today?

A.W.: Well, first of all it's feminist, but it's feminist from a culture of color. So there's no attempt to evade the name "feminism," which is honorable. It actually means "womanism"—I mean, it's French in its essence, *la femme*, so "feminism" would be "womanism," actually. Womanism comes, though, from Southern African American culture because when you did something really bold and outrageous and audacious as a little girl, our parents would say, "You're acting womanish." It wasn't like in white culture where that was weak—it was just the opposite. And so, womanism affirms that whole spectrum of being which includes being outrageous and angry and standing up for yourself, and speaking your word and all of that.

M.S.: When I interviewed Jane Fonda, she talked about how later in her life she experienced an "aha" moment where her "feminist consciousness slipped out of [her] head and took up residence in [her] body, where it has lived ever since." Do you think women need to experience a type of aha moment, their own personal epiphany, when they finally get in touch with their own feminine power?

A.W.: Definitely. I don't know if that's the only way they can do it, but anything that encourages women to accept themselves as who they are and what they are and to honor the feminine in them would be very, very helpful for the world's healing. Because the world is becoming so patriarchal, even more patriarchal in some ways, but also, just more dismissive and discarding of the feminine. And you see that in the way that very young girls are sold—often because their parents are really poor, but generally speaking it's the father who does the selling. And then these children basically are sold into slavery. And they live and die in brothels in many parts of the world. And it's as if the feminine there—when the feminine is so degraded anywhere, it's a blow to the feminine everywhere. Now, that's when we should be screaming—jumping up and down everywhere—and saying that this is such an insult to the Mother and to the feminine that we cannot stand it, and we will not. And we should liberate all these children from these horrible prisons that they're in as these slaves to just whoever can come in and pay a few rupees or whatever the money is.

M.S.: I also recently interviewed Gloria Steinem, who I know is a friend of yours. When I asked Gloria how we can help women better stay in touch with ourselves and make empowered choices for our lives, she said, "I think that the most effective means we have is to talk to each other in groups. Human beings are communal creatures." How important is this notion of telling our truths to each other and being supported by friendship and the power of sisterhood?

A.W.: It's totally crucial. In fact, I advocate that every woman be a part of a circle and a circle that meets at least once a month, or if you can't do that, once every two months or every four months. But you have to have a circle, a group of people, women—smart, wise, can-do women—who are in the world doing their work, and you need to meet with them as often as you can, so that they can see what you're doing, and who you are, and you can see the same. And you can talk to each other about the world and about your lives. In a circle of trust and safety. It's crucial. It is crucial for our psychological health and our spiritual growth—it's essential.

M.S.: In talking to Gloria about women's media, she remarked that only Oprah has the power to put some non-product articles in her magazine. I know Oprah has been a longtime supporter, colleague, and dear friend of yours. How do you view and understand Oprah's importance and popularity as one of the most powerful women in the media, and certainly as one of the most powerful African American women, possibly in the world?

A.W.: We're not really close friends—we're mutually respectful people. I met her when she worked on—you know she was Sofia in the movie of *The Color Purple* and later, recently, she became a producer of the musical, very late in the process, and did a lot of the publicity for it. And I have admiration like so many people. I think we love Oprah because she speaks her mind, and she is honest about her life and about the processes. And I think the world really is hungering for women of power. We love her partly because she's powerful. And because to see someone with so much power, and she uses it, I think, so often for such good. To see that is just a tonic for the spirit. And we need so many more people like that.

Now, there have been women with a lot of power—for instance, Margaret Thatcher. But she didn't inspire people with the love and devotion that Oprah does, because her power was so patriarchal and because we rarely thought she was always saying what she thought. It was very clear that she was still surrounded by men and becoming more male every day. And you can't really say that about Oprah. I'm not a big TV watcher, so I don't watch her closely as, for instance, my sister does, who watches it every day. But my sense is that she is living a very large life, of her own design. You may not particularly care for the design, but it is what she wants to be doing with her life. And if more women could see that, and enjoy it, I think there would be much more loose and inclusive and free feeling, sense of possibility, and enchantment among women in the world.

M.S.: In your Omega talk you spoke about the concept of the Dark Mother. How do you see the significance of Africa for humanity and the world—Africa as our communal birthplace?

A.W.: Well, as I'm talking about in *We Are the Ones*, we have an African mother. That is the common mother. And we have been taught to be so different and separate. And that's an illusion. And it's an illusion that has made us really murder each other and just do horrible things, especially to people of color, because white people have more often been in the power to do that on a mass scale. You know, like the rape of Africa, the absolute subjugation of the people, the stealing of resources, the enslavement of people—all of those things. And when humanity understands, really with the heart, that they have been doing all of this to their mother, I believe there will be a great shift in the world. Because you can only do those terrible things that people do when you have that illusion of separation.

And when you lose it—it's like when you really think that you are so, so very different from, say, your cat. Because I have a cat and I adore her. And you hang out with the cat and you live with the cat, and finally it really dawns on you that basically you and the cat like the same things! You know, you like to be warm, you like cuddling, you like food, you like to lie in the sun—and then you kind of get it: "Well, you know, I don't want to harm this cat, I don't want to eat this cat, I don't want to steal this cat's anything." So I'm hopeful that now that geneticists have actually done the work of linking us by DNA to our African mother that at some point that is going to sink into human consciousness and lead to an understanding of who the Mother is. Hopefully, the human mother and then of course the Earth Mother.

And you see how that has changed. I don't know if you remember this, but not so long ago only Native Americans, and indigenous people elsewhere and aboriginal people elsewhere—only those people talked about the Earth Mother. The earth as mother. And then this man—Lovelock, I think it was—found the Greek word "Gaia" for the Earth Mother/Goddess Mother, and was just astonished that, you know, hey—it's alive. Now everybody knew it was alive. All of the people who have lived on this planet for thousands of years, praying to the earth and thanking the earth, they completely knew—of course it's alive! So that's a good example of how consciousness changes, and if people can get it that they come from the Earth Mother, then they one day will understand that they also come from a human mother, the same mother, and she is due immense respect and love and appreciation.

M.S.: I know that the environment is a cause you care deeply about. The other site I run is an environmental site, ecomall.com, and I do think there has been increasing environmental awareness. Do you think that with all the recent attention to the dangers facing our planet due to global warming, we are finally starting to wake up to the current environmental crisis?

A.W.: I do, I think so. I think Katrina did it. You know, the tsunami in Southeast Asia was amazing, but it was far away, and I think that when Katrina hit . . . You know, interestingly, before Katrina, there had been an enormous amount of devastation and a lot of terror and fear in the islands, like Cuba and Jamaica and all of those islands, because they are all in that area. And it had been so sad to see how little attention was paid by this country to that devastation. And then when Katrina ripped across the Gulf, I think that woke up a lot of people. And then politically, I think a lot of people were awakened because then, for instance, Cuba immediately offered to send aid to help the people who were stranded and to send medicine and doctors, and in our country we refused the offer. And it wasn't the first time they had refused an offer from Cuba. And so many African Americans especially, and Americans generally, now see not only that we are in a lot of danger from "natural disasters," and that's what they are, disasters, but we are also in danger because we are led by people who watch us struggle, and suffer, and die while other people outside the country are offering help to save us—and they won't let that happen. So there's a general enlightenment happening about global warming and the inefficiency and *meanness* of our government.

M.S.: I don't know if you know of this Native American medicine woman named Dhyani, but she said something to the effect of, "You can tell how evolved a society is by how much of its garbage is recycled." How is how we treat the earth—our environmental awareness, or lack thereof—indicative of the state of humanity's consciousness?

A.W.: Well, I'll tell you, some of it has to be—I have a *Rolling Stone* article that I'm trying to get up my nerve to read and it's about how many hogs are slaughtered each year. By one company—Smithfield Foods, I think, or something like that. It was 27 million last year. And that's basically the population of like—I don't know—thirty-two of the largest cities in the land; that's the number of hogs they kill each year. I mean, it's just almost unbelievable. And I'm going to go and check it as soon as I get off the phone, because I read it [laughs to keep from raging] and then I just had to sit down. Because they were talking about the amount of waste that this one company generates, and where it goes, and you multiply that by all of the other pollution staying in the animal kingdom—or what would have been the animal kingdom, but now it's like the animal dungeon. But, you know, you have your chicken farms and your hog farms and your geese farms, and your cattle places. And that alone, just the cycle of the kind of brutality that goes into killing all of those creatures, and then sort of mindlessly eating them, and almost nobody even thinks about where all of their waste is going. And it gets recycled through us one way or the other.

So I think consciousness is very poor, actually. And that person that we were talking about earlier, like "What do I do? Where do I start?" Well, you can just start right there with your consciousness about what you're recycling through yourself.

What is so striking about the photographs that accompany the article in *Rolling Stone* about the factory-farming of pigs—and this is a must-read for humanity—in which we see the human look of fear and suffering on the faces of the pigs about to be slaughtered, juxtaposed with the face of the man who is responsible (along with the blissfully ignorant public) for their mistreatment, and, physically, they resemble each other so much! Only the man is sitting behind a desk and wearing glasses and clothing, and the pigs are covered in filth from the degrading circumstances of their captivity; and his look is less honest, by far. We must begin seeing other creatures as equal. Existence makes us all equal.

M.S.: I know you have written a lot about female genital mutilation and other forms of violence against women in Africa—are conditions worsening or improving, and how can we address the problem?

A.W.: Well, someone just sent me an e-mail about the fact that some scholars very high in the hierarchy of the Muslim world met recently in Cairo, and they made a resolution that female genital mutilation is not to happen henceforth among Muslims. And my friend Pratibha Parmar is visiting, and she and I made a film called *Warrior Marks* that talks about female genital mutilation, and we just almost cried, because it's such a major acknowledgment from people who have traditionally ignored the problem. Basically people like these scholars have ignored the problem for six thousand years. So there is change, and a lot of it has to be about making sure that men, and maybe starting really young, really understand that they are endangering themselves. Because they really are very self-interested people, most men—and I say that because when I started talking about female genital mutilation and writing about it, many men in Africa and elsewhere just completely denied it and just didn't want to hear about it. Until I said, "Well, you know, you notice how AIDS is spreading, and one of the ways that it spreads is through these fissures and tears that happen when you have intercourse with someone who has been mutilated," and that really sat them up very straight.

And so, you know, we have to do a lot more educating of men, and I know that many feminists feel like they're tired of that and they can't do that, and da-da-da-da-da. . . . And nobody's more tired than some of us, but it seems to be really important. Especially if we're thinking of our sisters' and daughters' health. And not only that, so many of us by now have these wonderful feminist sons and grandsons, who really are allies, and we should give them the respect as allies, in changing a lot of the things that are wrong and done against women in the world.

M.S.: You write about how much you enjoy living in the country on a farm. Do you find it easier to be more creative in nature? And do you think part of humanity's problem is a growing disconnect with nature—that we need to be more in tune with nature for a healthy body, soul, and mind?

A.W.: I just think cities are unnatural, basically. I know there are people who live happily in them, and I have cities that I love too. But it's a disaster that we have moved so far from nature. That people no longer notice the seasons, really. Or they talk about all the beautiful colors in the fall; that's about all they know. They don't know how to plant—you know, they would starve if they had to try to grow their own food. They have no idea; some people think that apples grow underground and potatoes grow on trees—I mean, really! And they go to the market and they buy their food there and they often have no connection to who picked the food, the workers, and that's also really heartbreaking. As a daughter of a farmworker, to feel just how much they take for granted, the people who are buying their food without thinking about the people who produce it. And that leads to not caring that those people are being treated very much like slaves. Not permitted to go to the bathroom, for instance, for long periods. And then of course that endangers the people who eat the food, because like, you know, with that E. coli bacteria that was in the spinach? Part of that could very easily be if you don't let people go to the bathroom, you know, they have to go somewhere. So it's just one of those cases of insisting on human decency everywhere, with everyone. And therefore making it possible for your own health and well-being to prosper.

M.S.: There are so many unbelievably alarming statistics about world poverty these days. What do you see as the cause of world poverty and what can be done to help to alleviate the problem? Sometimes it just seems so overwhelming that it feels insurmountable; is it?

A.W.: No, of course it isn't. It's that some people have all the goods and money they can imagine having, and they've taken it from the poor people. In my book, I'm talking about a speech that Fidel Castro gave in which he talks about how the three richest people on the planet own more than forty-eight poor countries combined. Now, this is ridiculous—they don't need all that, and why don't people just insist that there is a limit to what people can have? This is where the world will have to go anyway; it's just inevitable. Because everything is just shrinking. Unless we want to go back to a time when, you know, feudalism or something, where the king had everything and the peasants had nothing. And I don't think we want to go back there. So it would make a lot more sense to say that, actually, you know what—you cannot have $50 billion. You just can't have it. Forget about having that, and just have enough for you and your grandchildren and your great-grandchildren, but you're not going to have that much while other people have nothing. Period.

M.S.: You are such a hard worker—as a tireless activist, as a prolific writer, speaker—how do you keep yourself motivated? What is the source of your energy?

A.W.: Love. I have a lot of love. And I think that I'm by nature a revolutionary. Some say all Aquarians are. Even Ronald Reagan thought he was one! And I feel very keenly that things could be so much better for so many more people and for so many more creatures, and for the earth; I just know that. I just know it can be better. And that people have it in them to rise to that. I know they do. And sometimes it's just a matter of touching that place that can be opened to the reality that, you know, we can do so much more than we think we can. My deepest desire is for people and the world to be happy. I will always believe this is possible and seek to learn how I can contribute. I have felt deeply blessed to have the vehicle of words, of voice.

M.S.: Women often struggle with getting older. How can we help women embrace the aging process and value their role as elders and a source of wisdom and power in our society?

A.W.: Well, I was just thinking about that this morning because I was thinking about how—I didn't follow this, but apparently Bill Cosby made some comment about something like, black people should take more responsibility for their predicament and the choices and ways of their children and everything, and he was roundly attacked. He was really attacked, and I think several people actually wrote books about how he dare not say such things. And I was thinking about how, actually elders—and this has been traditionally true in most cultures and still is in many cultures today—elders really need to be listened to respectfully. Even if you don't agree. They really don't need to be attacked. You know, you can giggle at them and kind of ridicule them—maybe not to their face; I mean, I wouldn't do that. You can let it be known that you don't agree with them. But I think that the disrespect of actually attacking an elder who is obviously trying to bring some kind of light—I think that's not a good thing. And then elders have to be willing to assume the role of the person who gets to speak about society and where it seems to be going and what it needs. And because everybody in our society up to now has been trying to stay thirty, there's a problem with people knowing how to be, and how to speak, and how to take on the role of the person who can actually speak to the young with some kind of integrity. So this is shifting, I think. And I think the war has called out many of the people into that role, who otherwise might not have gotten there.

M.S.: On the opposite spectrum, Amy Richards, who is one of the founders of feminist.com and does the "Ask Amy" column at our site, also co-founded Third Wave, an organization for young feminists, with your daughter. What do you think about the younger generations of women today?

A.W.: Well, they seem to be doing fine. I have to say that I'm not just noticing in that way, but the ones that come across my path, I think they seem really alert. In fact, let me just be specific—at a local college here, Mills College, there is a group of women who founded a journal called *The Womanist* and they came to tea last month. And we had a great time and they all seem so feminist, so alive, so alert, so into whatever they are doing. So I felt very happy that those of us who are older and who have blazed some of the trails, that we did that, because I could see that these younger women are determined to have their own lives, and they just take it for granted that "Yes, of course, I am going to do this, I am going to do that." So in that way, I think that they are doing really well.

M.S.: One of the big issues for women these days seems to be creating balance. How do you do that?

A.W.: I spend a lot of time, or as much as I can, in silence. And at home. And more and more as time goes by. I think all this zipping around the world is overrated. In fact, I did a year of studying medicinal plants. And one of them was ayahuasca, a medicine from the Amazon that people have used for thousands and thousands of years. And one of the things that I've learned was that I needed myself to be more rooted. And so I've been working on that. I feel that has been so helpful to me—to cut out movement wherever possible, instead of going here and there all the time. Talking a lot less—really talking a lot less. Being much slower, and much more grounded with my animals, the animals I live with, with my friends. Staying extremely simple. Dancing more too. Just learning to really, really love the ordinary—you know, that nice well-made bowl of oatmeal in the morning and walking with my dog—just what is ordinary. What is simple and true.

M.S.: I have also read a few interviews in which you talk about the spiritual practices that have most helped you, like tonglen and meditation. Can you tell us more about the practices that have served you in your life?

A.W.: Well, I learned Transcendental Meditation when I lived in New York and after a divorce. And it was so much like the way I had lived as a little child, which was just completely merged with nature. So much so that I didn't know I wasn't the tree I was looking at, you know? It was just a complete oneness—that sense of oneness and the ego goes somewhere else temporarily. And so that became the foundation of how I could move through the world, do my work, balance raising a child and being on the road a lot—out of necessity, really, making a living—teaching. And I have maintained some form of meditation, yoga, a lot of walking. Tonglen, which I learned some years ago, because it's a practice that, thanks to Pema Chödrön, we get from these amazing, ancient Tibetans who figured it all out. That you don't have to just drown in your sorrow and pain, that you can actually learn to live with it and to accept it and to take it in, make your heart really super, super big to hold it, and then to send out to yourself and to the world whatever it is that you would prefer. And lo and behold, I found that the practice worked.

And in general I find that the practices like Native American drumming, for instance, which I also do, chanting, sweats—all of these things really help us. I also am very fond of the *Motherpeace Tarot* deck and have used it for, I don't know, as long as it's been in existence I guess. And also the *I Ching*. The *I Ching* I consider one of the great, mysterious, magical gifts to humanity. It is such a divine oracle, it comes close to being a living being, like a tree or something.

M.S.: You write and talk a lot about the role of personal transformation. Obviously in your life you've been able to overcome a lot of the hardships that you've faced. Is part of this learning to find the blessings and lessons during times of adversity and crisis, to use them as a fuel for personal and spiritual growth?

A.W.: Well, what else would you do with it? I mean, sometimes these blows are so severe that you just think, "Well, it's not about whether I deserved it, it's just that that's what's happening." And since that's what's happening, what do you do with it? And so I have, you know, as the years have gone on, really gotten to that place where I do say to myself, "Well, wow—I bet I'm going to learn something pretty amazing right here, because this is so painful. Or this is so strange." And that has been true!

M.S.: I've read that you wouldn't necessarily call yourself a Buddhist per se, since it seems that you enjoy the wisdom from a lot of different traditions, but something about Buddhism has been very helpful and appealing for you. How do you see Buddhism's relevance in today's world? There seems to be a growing interest in the Buddhist teachings.

A.W.: I think it's because Buddhism makes so much sense. It is the most sensible thing. And because it works in its sort of prescriptions. I mean, like, for instance if you have the dharma—you know, you have the teachings, which are extraordinary. You have Buddha as a symbol and as a model for how to strike out to find your truth. And then you have the sangha, which is your circle of friends, who get together regularly to support each other. Well, you know, that right there is major. Because the teachings are just invaluable. You know, the things that we are learning through Buddhist teachings, just about how to work with the human heart, with human emotions. I mean, just the idea to finally get it that, yeah, everything is changing, everything is impermanent, it comes and it goes. You sit there in meditation and you just witness that. You see. And you lose a lot of your stress because you know that, okay, if I just am with this, it's going away. And so I think it's a wonderful thing. I love it. I just love it. It's a wonderful gift to us.

Think of what humanity would have lost if Tibetan Buddhism had been destroyed. And how many cultural and spiritual gifts we lose because they are destroyed. In both the human and then animal realms. Realizing the value of what other branches of humanity offer the human collective could motivate us to change how we relate to whatever is perceived as strange.

M.S.: As an artist, how is your spiritual energy connected to the experience of writing? When you're writing, do you feel like your ability is from a higher source, is that where your inspiration feels like it comes from?

A.W.: Well, if you take the position that all is the higher source, you know, all is God, all is light, all is love, all is what is—then you just feel like this little part of it, that's doing your part. You're doing your little jig.

M.S.: There's an old hippie saying about having the "juice" or being "juicy"—when you're in the flow, or flowing with the magic of the universe. . . .

A.W.: I always liked hippies. Sometimes they seemed a little shallow but I could really understand it [laughs]. I could almost always relate. They were certainly, partly because of their use of the plant medicine marijuana, very different, startlingly so, from their usually very white, unmedicated parents [laughs]. Racism needs a medicine, you know. Greed. Envy. Superiority of any kind. They all need a medicine, and plant medicines are sometimes very helpful. Hippies were very good for the white race in general and did a lot to make the world more trustful of it. But then they were crushed, as a movement, as so many of the rest of us were.

M.S.: There seems to be a growing awareness of how our inner reality is connected to our outer reality, even in the fact people are coming to Buddhism maybe because the suffering is so much. . . .

A.W.: Yeah, that will get them in. [laughs]

M.S.: Do you see humanity as evolving? What do you believe is the next step in our evolution in terms of humanity's consciousness?

A.W.: Well, I would like to believe it is that all creatures have the right to live without fear. And without fear of being eaten, for instance. And that's a real hard one because we have been addicted to meat, to animals as meat, you know. And I struggle with that myself, and I think most people do. But I do really believe that is where we're headed—that if we do survive as a species, we will get it. That we are no more precious than the rest of the species on Earth.

M.S.: I struggle sometimes with the notion of organized religion and how it relates to spirituality—and that so much of the wars and intolerance in the world are over religion. What is your view of the role of religion in the world today?

A.W.: Well, I think that some of it is self-destructing, because it's basically set up to be that way. I mean, when you have religions that don't like other religions and "my God is better than your God" and "your God is actually wrong." And then the foundation of so much of the patriarchal religion is the destruction of the goddess worship that was before it, and the destruction of the feminine. Which would have to mean not a good future for them, for the patriarchal religions in the long run, I mean the very long run, as it's turned out. Because you know, the feminine actually has to rise again, because, you know, we are here—the feminine exists. It is what is keeping them (and all of us) going. A world without the feminine is a dead world.

So I think that for many of us, what has happened is that we have perhaps taken some parts of the religions we were raised in, and we have incorporated them into our belief systems—with gratitude. You know, like the teachings of Jesus I really love, and I love *The Gnostic Gospels* and the Nag Hammadi scrolls, sermons, or whatever you call them, parables I guess. But we're making a new religion. Religion is going to be more self-styled. It's going to be less and less a group thing, because we're all taking from various traditions, and we're all also open to divinity just as who we are! It's a very one-on-one kind of thing. And once you realize that you are just part of the whole thing, then you just kind of worship that, and yourself, and everything—all is one.

M.S.: So many of us feel like we've been "wronged" in some way. What's the importance of forgiveness and the healing process for that?

A.W.: Well, it's one of the hardest things to do, but it's really necessary. Without forgiving, you don't really move—you can't. It's like this little prison that you're in. And it's so painful, because you feel like you don't deserve to be in prison, it wasn't your fault. And how dare you have to forgive these horrible people? But actually, you do. And that's a good place for tonglen practice.

M.S.: You have written a lot about humanity as one family. Are you optimistic that humanity will ever live as one family here on planet Earth?

A.W.: It could. I mean, that's about what I would say—that it very well could, and why not? Yes. I think people can do it. I think people have to believe more in themselves. For some reason, and you know we can find many reasons, people have lost faith in their ability to live the higher truth of interconnectedness and family.

M.S.: What's your prayer for the children of the future? What would you like to see?

A.W.: A certain fearlessness of being who they are and expressing themselves as freely as—I don't know, as freely as a pear tree or an apple tree expresses itself. Just be what it is that you are—and that is *just fine*. You don't have to be what you're not in any way. And live that and live that fully. And that is where you discover ecstasy. You can't really have ecstasy as something other than yourself. And life should be ecstatic. You know, not every minute, but you should definitely have enough ecstasy in your life from time to time to know that you are just completely wired into creation.

A Conversation with David Swick
from *Shambhala Sun* (2006)

DAVID SWICK: While your new book [*We Are the Ones We Have Been Waiting For*] has a lot of pain in it, you work through the pain and come to a place of hope and peace. Is pain an important teacher for you?

ALICE WALKER: Pain is a great teacher. You can work through pain and come to a place of peace when you accept that you will need to work as hard as you can. If you can be at rest with the fact that you will do your utmost under all circumstances, what else is there but peace?

D.S.: A lot of people, though, feel that no matter how hard they try, they are not going to be happier. They feel they cannot overcome their problems.

A.W.: That's because they believe in trying rather than in doing.

D.S.: How do you mean?

A.W.: If you just try to do something, you're not actually accomplishing anything. But if you resolve to do it, you accept that it is there for you to do and that you're perfectly capable of whatever it is. And of course there's no point in trying to do something you're incapable of. Then you use every conceivable atom, sinew, and instinct available to move whatever it is you're trying to move. There's a world of difference between that and simply trying to do something. That is basically how I work. I think if I had started out simply with the idea that I was going to just try to make the life that I have made for myself—and the work that I have made for myself, and for my community and the world—it's very possible that I would not have accomplished very much. Instead,

I simply set out to do it. And to do it incrementally, so that I could do just the amount that I was able to do each day.

It reminds me of what Ernest Hemingway used to tell people when they asked him how it is possible to write a novel. He would tell them that it's a matter of "across the river and into the trees." You resolve to get to the river, which is like the end of a chapter, and then, maybe in your dreams, you cross the river at night. Then, the next day, it's on into the trees. You do it in stages, rather than saying, "I'm going to just try to write the whole thing." You simply do what you can do today, and that's fine.

D.S.: Is perfection one of the things we have to let go of to live like that?

A.W.: But everything is already perfect. And if you can accept that everything is already perfect, the imperfection is a part of the perfection. What's to worry about? [Laughs]

D.S.: So often we think if we can't do it perfectly, it's not worth doing.

A.W.: That's a terrible mind-set! I look at my cat. My cat lived a very rough life before she arrived in my home. She has one tooth that's broken and another that's kind of long on the other side. She's snaggle-toothed. A stranger might look at her and say, "Oh, she has imperfect teeth." But I look at her and see the absolute perfection—the charming perfection—of her imperfection. It gives me so much information about the kind of life she has had, and the kind of soul she has probably fashioned.

D.S.: In your book you stress both yoga and meditation as essential practices for people living today. Do you think of yoga and meditation as complementary practices?

A.W.: Oh, yes, very much so. I've recently started doing a type of yoga that brings both of them together. Each pose is held for five minutes, which leaves you plenty of space and time to consider the pose, what it means to your peace of spirit, and to just breathe in, breathe out, in the way Thich Nhat Hanh talks about.

D.S.: What part does yoga play in your life?

A.W.: It is relaxation from stress. Yoga allows us to be calm and more present and not be physically overwhelmed by the calamities that surround us and the messages of disaster we're constantly exposed to. In one of the talks excerpted in the book, I was speaking to a yoga group and telling them about how I learned of all these horrible abuses on Native American reservations and boarding schools, and how that connected to my own Native American ancestry. I told them it was so overwhelming that all I could do, really, was yoga.

D.S.: What would you say meditation means for you?

A.W.: Many things. In the early days, I almost always disappeared in meditation and found it just delightful. Now, sometimes I can disappear, but I have reached a place, I think, where the meditation often happens spontaneously. At times that means a lot of attentiveness to something, and letting it fully develop, and then having real insight into it. On the other hand, meditation could arise as a calming, spacious feeling of connection with everything, dissolving into the all.

D.S.: Are there other Buddhist practices you do?

A.W.: I am so grateful to Pema Chödrön for the gift of the practice of tonglen: taking in the bad and sending out the good. She has managed to absorb and preserve and present these ancient teachings in a form that is so current. I find tonglen one of the most important practices we could receive in this time. It's always challenging and deeply rewarding.

D.S.: You meditate, you read Pema Chödrön and Thich Nhat Hanh, you have praised the work of Jack Kornfield, you go on retreats, and yet you say in the book that you're not a Buddhist.

A.W.: I'm not. The whole point of anything that is really, truly valuable to your soul, and to your own growth, is not to attach to a teacher, but rather to find out what the real deal is in the world itself. You become your own guide. The teachings can help you, but really, we're all here with the opportunity to experience the reality of hereness. We all have that. I trust that.

D.S.: Are you concerned that if you embrace the word "Buddhism," it would change the experience into something more formulaic and less alive?

A.W.: Yes. I'm just not interested in labels. I find all of them constrictive. They're hard to wear. And they're hard to wear because we're always—hopefully—growing. Not only that, there are so many teachers in the world today of many different stripes. The world is a marvelous place of learning, from every possible direction.

D.S.: Does that make this a fortunate time to be living in?

A.W.: We live in the best of all times.

D.S.: Why is that?

A.W.: There's so much to do! [laughs] We are so lucky. There's no shortage of work to do! [laughs] There's no excuse for anyone, in my opinion, to complain that they can't change anything. For instance, there are millions and millions and millions of hungry children, people who don't have clothing, people who don't have housing, trees that are begging us to let them live, rivers that are crying out to be clean, skies that are shouting at us to let the ozone layer live. There is no end to the ways we can have full self-realization. That's what has to happen, and that's what this time is pointing out. This is the time to have full self-realization as an earthling. It's time to be responsible and take charge of that. It's also a great time because if we fail, we lose the earth.

D.S.: Is self-realization the spiritual philosophy at the center of your life and work?

A.W.: Self-realization is certainly up there, and of course true self-realization comes with a realization of the connectedness to all, the inseparability of the self and the all. That leads one to understand oneself as an earthling, not an American, Canadian, African, or Indian. Beyond that I realize myself as the cosmos, the universe, the whole thing. How can we not be the whole thing? [Pause] As I sit and look out at the trees, I know clearly one day that's where I'll be. Hallelujah!

D.S.: You touch upon so many different influences in your book: the *I Ching*, the Tao, meditation, yoga, and so forth. In your life and practice, does Christianity have a place?

A.W.: I love Jesus; I think Jesus was wonderful. However, I think he has been distorted terribly. I want to see the wizardry of Jesus restored. I want to feel his dancing quality and his joyfulness. It's a terrible thing that they have left him in that tortured, naked condition, which is bound to frighten most children. Just imagine if he were depicted like the Buddha. I love the way the Buddha goes through all his changes and he's basically very happy. Suffering is not the end-all in life. It is a part of it, and then we rise above it, we work through it, we transform it. Jesus did that.

D.S.: You write that "heaven is a verb." Can you use it in a sentence?

A.W.: In looking for places to write novels, I've ended up with houses in Mexico and Hawaii. I rent them out to people on a sliding scale depending on need. I've created a little booklet about them, and in there I talk about being in Hawaii and "heavening on the beach in sight of a six-pack." Isn't that good? [Laughs] Are we there?

D.S.: You talk about grandmothers as a source of wisdom and power. Is this something you've recently come to understand, or have you long had a connection to the power of a grandmother?

A.W.: My maternal grandmother died when I was two, and the other one had been murdered when my father was a boy, but I had a strong connection with my stepgrandmother, who did give me unconditional love. As time went on, though, I saw the damage to the feminine that patriarchy imposes, and I understood that it's often the old woman—the grandmother, with all of that accumulated wisdom and compassion—who is depressed.

She is depressed because she sees things so clearly, and she's lost her fear of speaking. We need her. We are not going to get anywhere with-out her, so we might as well go and start liberating all those nursing homes, and calling home, and getting our grandmothers back with us, and asking them to leave the sitcoms, and get them to come out from in front of the TV and give us some guidance, some of the understand-ing that they have gained over all these decades. Sadly, many of them have been anesthetized, but many of them have not. They've just been silent.

D.S.: Do you see people being anesthetized as a big problem?

A.W.: It's huge! That's what television is for. That's what all these Game Boys and PalmPilots, and all of these whatever-you-call-them gadgets are for. I feel we became gadgetized as part of the corporate takeover of the world. Everyone was either looking into their hand or into their TV set or their computer and basically missed how our lives were being stolen by very greedy people who would rather have a lot of money than have community.

D.S.: Do you see our obsession with security as part of the anesthetizing?

A.W.: We need security, but it cannot come without community. How can you have security without community? You could have all the chain-link fences, and all of the gates, and all of the helicopters flying over your house you could possibly afford, but if you had trusting neighbors, people who really cared about you, you'd be much more safe.

D.S.: In the book, you say that it is time for the right hand to know what the left hand is doing. What do you mean by that?

A.W.: Many people live with two sides of themselves out of touch with each other. They complain about paying their taxes but don't complain about what their taxes actually buy, like cluster bombs. A million of these bombs, originally supplied by the U.S. government, were left in Lebanon. Children will come and pick them up, and they will blow up in their faces. Then you have all these maimed and dying children. But since your right hand, which wrote the check for the taxes, has learned not to care about the left hand, which has actually sent this off to the

IRS and the government and the military, you pretend you are innocent. Well, you're not. That's what I mean.

Of course, I know how difficult it can be to become fully aware and bear responsibility, and even though I figure there's very little I can do to actually stop the war, I feel like I can make every effort to be aware. Not to be aware is very soul shredding. People might say, "I didn't know they were making tanks big enough to level people's houses." Well, they should know that. You may not be able to dismantle the tank, or even stop paying for the tank, but you can know that's what is happening.

D.S.: Often, though, we feel that if we spend a lot of time finding out such disturbing information, we will just become more depressed.

A.W.: Have the courage to be more depressed. In a world like this, where we are—as Americans, anyway—paying for so much suffering, who wants to be Little Miss Sunshine? It's scary.

D.S.: You have said that when you write fiction, you write the book for the characters. Was there someone specifically you were writing this book for?

A.W.: Oh, yes, for our times. My regular publisher, Random House, didn't want to publish this book, because my editor said they didn't know what they could do with it. But I kept saying to them, "We live in a time when things are so dire, and politics especially. The political discussion is so discouraging that people need a book that is political but is at the same time infused with spirituality. They need a book that instructs them to step back and meditate, sit and contemplate, rather than dissolve into despair."

So I offered this book as a companion for this specific time, which I consider probably, along with millions of other people, the most dangerous, frightening, unstable time that the earth has known and that human beings have ever known.

D.S.: But your regular publisher didn't see it that way?

A.W.: No. I think they may not have understood how much nourishment we get from teachers who encourage this kind of awareness. Even when we feel we can't change things, it's important to have awareness of what has happened. If you are unaware of what has happened, it means you're not alive in many respects. And to be unalive in many places within yourself means you are missing a lot of the experience of being on this planet. And this planet is not to be missed.

19

On Raising Chickens:
A Conversation with
Rudolph P. Byrd (2009)

ON *THE WORLD HAS CHANGED*

RUDOLPH P. BYRD: For *The World Has Changed: Conversations with Alice Walker,* you have written a poem that marks the publication of your first collection of conversations and interviews. Tell us about the genesis of the poem and the questions you believe are central to it.

ALICE WALKER: With the election of a black man to the presidency of the United States, the world *has* changed. Such an event was unthinkable for many people until it actually occurred. For some, there is an unwillingness to believe this historic turn in North America's affairs is real. They need a poem that reminds them that disbelieving in a new reality can mean missing it altogether; this would be a waste and a tragedy for those who could benefit from shifting their understanding of what America is or can become. I was asked by a newspaper, I don't recall which or whether it was printed, to write a poem for the inauguration; my mind was very much on those who, from disbelief, could not rejoice. I was able to read the poem on *Democracy Now!* on the day of the inauguration. I co-hosted the program that day with its anchor, the most honorable Amy Goodman.

I also wanted to celebrate those of us who have withstood years of little hope and scant beauty coming to us from Washington. That we continued to believe in and then to work for change, in the person of Obama, was remarkable. We deserve a better world, and it will come, as we strengthen belief in our own power to create what we desire. Human beings must regain faith in ourselves and try to see more good in each other than bad.

ON WANDERING AND MEDITATION

R.B.: You have devoted the last year or so to travel, to seeing the earth, and to meditation. Why have you restructured your life in this way? What have you learned about yourself and the world during this period? And what effect has this period of wandering and meditation had upon your writing?

A.W.: I wasn't planning to travel beyond my writing and meditation retreat in Mexico. I settled in for the duration, thinking I would meditate on my cushion, which faces a fountain created by a local artist as an abstract sculpture of a mother holding her child/her heart, symbolized by a large reddish stone. I thought I would wander no farther than a local beach filled with Mexican families who strike me always as still knowing how to enjoy life. There are lots of moms and dads and children and the occasional dog, lots of thatched palapas for sitting out of the sun, lots of food. The day Obama won the election, I started a Web site and a blog. This would take care of the very occasional writing I thought I might do. However, true to a pattern I've noticed over the years, I am like a spring that goes dry from overuse but then, with rest, fills up again. I began writing almost daily on my blog, often about my attempts to get collard greens to flourish in my garden or a neighbor's field (where unfortunately ants ate them over-night), and to my surprise I soon found myself—within weeks of leaving Mexico—on my way to far-off destinations: Burma (Myanmar) and Gaza (Palestine).

But the old way of living and writing—tied to schedules, book tours, and publicity concerns—has no attraction for me. This period I'm in now, with its surprise writing and travel, also feels transitional. There is a sense of sinking back, with gratitude, into the vegetation. A call from the soul that wants a quiet so deep, a mental space so clear and empty, that I can inhabit it almost solely as spirit. And surely this is part of what aging is for: to prepare us for the slow absorption into the All, which I perceive to be a radiant and positive destination.

DHARAMSHALA AND GAZA

R.B.: You will be traveling soon to Dharamshala and returning to Gaza. What draws you to these very different places? Is there a history that the people in both places share?

A.W.: It isn't clear whether I will be able to have an audience with His Holiness the Dalai Lama in Dharamshala; I was forced to cancel an audience with him scheduled too close to the date I am to join a Freedom March in Gaza, December 31, 2009. We met many years ago, I think the first time he came to San Francisco. He came to speak to our youth, and I was also invited to speak. I admire him tremendously for his humble bearing of the huge responsibility life has given him as leader of the Tibetan people and, in a sense, leader of the rest of us who need a living example of how to maintain soul under nearly unbearable circumstances. When I travel to countries like Rwanda and the Congo and Palestine, I draw on his example of soul care and his dogged continuation of teaching that which he knows, having used it himself, to be effective: meditation and clear seeing. Also peace enhancement and anger management.

While in Kerala, India, I hope to spend time with the writer Arundhati Roy—and her mother! Roy's work is marked by an intense, even fierce compassion for common people; I want to visit the Kerala that produced this sense of commitment and belief in possibility. I've heard little about the senior Mrs. Roy, but I'm sure she will be revealed as formidable.

While in New Delhi, I will want to pay my respects to Mahatma Gandhi. I believe I'm to give a talk at the Gandhi Institute there. What always struck me about Martin Luther King when I was a student in high school and he was just beginning his charge against the Dictatorship of White Supremacy in our country was that he seemed to know us, people of color, so well. What we really, in our heart of hearts, were like. And he accepted us for what we were. I want to visit India to see what it was that Gandhi loved, understood, and accepted about Indians—so much so that he endangered his life to live among them and to teach and lead. That King thought us worthy of any sacrifice was clear to me as a student, and moved me to tears. How does he know? I wondered. How does he continue to believe in us? Who are we, after all? After four hundred years of slavery and post-enslavement degradation, we were, far too many of us, quite a wreck. But with those extraordinarily wise eyes of his, he saw us beyond our wreckage and with compassion held us dear. Knowing the divine within himself, he saw it in us. Namaste!

There are similarities between what has happened to the Tibetan and Palestinian people. Both peoples have been invaded, their lands confiscated, and their culture suppressed and largely destroyed. The Chinese and Israeli governments have behaved with similar cruelty toward the indigenous people. Both Palestinians and Tibetans have a strong history of resistance, and their cultures are deeply rooted in nature, in music, in religion/spirituality, and in art. They are also, very often, farming people, with a deep love of the land. This is one of the reasons I resonate with both of them. Whenever I encounter people who love their olive and fruit trees, their tomatoes, vegetables, and land, the farmer in me joins hands with them. I need no other, more political connection. But this is because of my paganism, no doubt. My belief that nature and we and "God/Goddess" are one and the same. My devotion to this intuitively arrived-at understanding.

ON INFLUENTIAL BOOKS

R.B.: At an earlier period in your career as a writer, you spoke of the importance of Jean Toomer's *Cane*, Zora Neale Hurston's *Their Eyes Were Watching God*, Flannery O'Connor's *Everything That Rises Must Converge*, Ernest J. Gaines's *The Autobiography of Miss Jane Pittman*, Charles Dickens's *A Tale of Two Cities*, Bessie Head's *When Rain Clouds Gather*, and Ayi Kwei Armah's *The Beautyful Ones Are Not Yet Born*. This is only a very slim sampling of the writers and their books you regard as important in your artistic development. What are those books in either fiction or nonfiction with which you are now in dialogue as writer and as earthling?

A.W.: Reading comes in layers: there's the reading one does to understand the current crisis, whatever it is; the reading for pleasure; the reading for soul.

Because I'm engaged in bringing more U.S. awareness to the situation in Gaza, where the Israeli government uses American taxpayer money (including, to my shame, some of mine) to destroy Palestinians—a lot of them children, women, and old people—I have been reading books by Palestinian and Israeli writers: Ali Abunimah, Saree Makdisi, David Grossman, and Marcia Freedman, among others. I like what some Indian writers are writing. I loved *The Mistress of Spices* and will read anything by Arundhati Roy. I recently read a wonderful book called *Leaving India*—not a novel but one woman's travel all over the earth to trace relatives and ancestors who'd left India to settle in odd places: Fiji, for instance. I wish I had a better memory and could recall all the novels I've loved and all the names of the writers. One novel, about Gertrude Stein and Alice B. Toklas and their Vietnamese cook, that I never forget is *The Book of Salt*, by Vietnamese American writer Monique Truong. I am also a big fan of the Hawaiian writer Kiana Davenport, who wrote *Shark Dialogues*. No one should go to Hawaii without reading her novels about it.

On a day-to-day basis, I am happiest reading the *Dhammapada*, the Upanishads, *365 Tao* by Deng Ming-Dao, and other books that teach spiritual lessons. I love the work of Jack Kornfield, especially his books on CD: *The Roots of Buddhist Psychology* and *Buddhism for Beginners*. Also *A Path with Heart*. I also love the work of Michael Meade, war resister, mythologist, and storyteller, also on CD. For decades I have been supported by the old stories collected and told by Clarissa Pinkola Estés. I think her two-volume set *Theatre of the Imagination* should be in the audio library of everyone. I have also benefited from reading Carl Jung and Laurens van der Post—van der Post because he lived in a time when Bushmen (Bushpeople) were still living their traditional lives close to the earth in Africa. We can learn a lot from their gentleness, compassion, and disinterest in gobbling up the world around them. I've studied Jane Goodall's work admiringly, as well as Malidoma Somé's. *The Healing Wisdom of Africa* and *Of Water and the Spirit* are strengthening gifts to human imagination and growth. The work of Pema Chödrön has meant a lot to me. I love books (books and houses—a decent house!—were what I most longed for as a child), but I've become very selective about what I read. I find I simply cannot read anything that lacks integrity or spiritual energy. Beside my bed are these: the *I Ching* (which I sometimes feel is my favorite book simply because I've used it for so long); the *Motherpeace Tarot: Deck and Book*, which I also use periodically; *The New Astrology* (Chinese and Western) by Suzanne White (a wonderful book and not only because she gets monkeys right); and *The Essential Rumi*, translated by Coleman Barks. Rumi and I belong, with millions of other enchanted readers it is heartening to realize, to the same star.

What many people don't realize is that the soul can benefit from instruction just as the mind can, and that this instruction is readily available. We just have to look, sometimes vigorously. It is a good thing to have a nourishing church experience every Sunday, for instance, but that is like going to a dinner where only a certain kind of food is likely to appear on the table. The soul may take a nibble, but it's quite likely that what it really wants isn't there. Unfettering the soul and letting it roam after its own peculiar nourishment is part of what assures spiritual development. We live in a time rich in all kinds of soul food, not just chops and overcooked greens, but organic produce and pure water, one might say.

I am fundamentally animist (everything has spirit) and pagan (I worship nature and the spirit of nature), but I am enchanted with wisdom wherever it is found. Buddha and Jesus, the poet Rumi, Somé, Meade and Kornfield, Chödrön, Amma, and Fidel are all dear to me.

ON THE QUESTION OF GENRE

R.B.: You have created beautiful and enduring works in the genres of the essay, poetry, the short story, and the novel. Could you elaborate upon the appeal and challenge of each genre? Given your obvious strengths as a writer of dialogue, will you ever write plays?

A.W.: I enjoyed writing the screenplay for *The Color Purple* once I actually started it. (Not used for the movie.) I can imagine writing plays. What gets in the way is the realization that I'd need actors. It is extremely satisfying to write in genres that don't require more than I myself can give. I can imagine being distracted trying to find the right actors for the roles, or even having to think about this. Also, at this point in my life, I seem to be returning to poetry, my first love. Over the past year, I've written a book of poems, *Hard Times Require Furious Dancing: A Year of Poems*. These came at a rate of several a week. Sometimes several came on the same day, like surprise guests.

ON CREATING CHARACTERS

R.B.: Along with the stories themselves and the majesties of language, what is most memorable about your fiction are the characters. What are the several elements that for you lead to the creation of characters? Could you describe your process of creating characters and also for naming them?

A.W.: I love creating characters! Because, like our children, they really create themselves. We get to sit back and watch something astonishing come into being that we had something to do with, but not everything. It's magical. Naming characters is also. For some books, I try to keep alive names I heard as a child, the names of friends, relatives, family. People I loved or whose names struck me as poetic in some way. I did this in *The Color Purple* as a way to honor family who would have no way of being remembered or honored otherwise. It amused me too to mix up the names so that sometimes a character (based on a real person) is mistreating his wife, who has the name of the real person's mother or daughter. I suppose this is a way I, posthumously for these people, attempt to teach them about each other. And to urge kindness. Similarly, Grange Copeland is not only named for the land itself—the grange—but also for the landowner, "Copeland," who owned land my family lived on when I was a child. The connection between land, farmer, and landowner, is very strong, but to my knowledge it is rarely deliberately intertwined in literature. Mem Copeland's name comes from the French *la meme*, which means "the same." This was a signal to readers about the prevalence of domestic violence before it had a name. As a student in college, I adored French and lived in the French House on campus.

Writing *The Temple of My Familiar* was an absorbing joy; creating the many carefully considered names in it made it more so. Dickens loved naming his characters. A companion and I enjoy watching Dickens on DVD and just finished watching *Bleak House*. Fantastic names! Lady Dedlock, Mr. Guppy, Mr. Smallweed. Each of them funny and perfect. I think naming characters is a way we writers play with our work, amuse ourselves as we go over a paragraph or chapter the umpteenth time.

YOUR PREOCCUPATIONS AS AN ARTIST

R.B.: In an earlier period in your career, you stated that your preoccupations as a writer centered on two overlapping areas: "I am preoccupied with the spiritual survival, the survival *whole* of my people. But beyond that, I am committed to exploring the oppressions, the insanities, the loyalties, and the triumphs of black women." What are your preoccupations at this stage in your life as a writer?

A.W.: What could it be but to be of assistance to the world in its dire hour of need? We've turned a scary corner, as humans. We may have ruined our nest. If I write about Palestinians being deprived of water and land, of Aung San Suu Kyi and the precious instruction she is capable of giving us—not only about democracy but also about morality—if I write about violence and war, collards and chickens, I can connect with others who care about these things. Hopefully, together we can move the discussion of survival, with grace and justice and dignity, forward. We will need to know many different kinds of things to survive as a species worth surviving.

ON BLACK WOMEN WRITERS: THE SISTERHOOD
R.B.: In 1976, you and your friend and fellow writer the late June Jordan established the Sisterhood. Could you recall the origins of this group? How often did you meet? Were the meetings structured in a particular way? Did you imagine at the time that the writers of the Sisterhood—June Jordan, Toni Morrison, Ntozake Shange—would have such a deep and wide impact upon American and world literature?

A.W.: June and I were rebels of the first order against ranking of any kind imposed from beyond ourselves. We thought we must create a space for black women writers to honor each other, to know each other, so that nothing from outside could make us fight over anything. Or even feel competitive. This was the Sisterhood's purpose. We met only a few times while I was still in New York. I moved to California, and later so did June. My connection with women's circles continued. I have been a member of an African American women's sangha for ten years and was part of a racially diverse Women's Council (now on break) for about seven years. Circles are crucial for human advancement in the time we are now in. In a safe place, where people can express their sorrows and fears without worry, we can shift the world's thinking, as these circles, millions of them, join together to usher in solid and useful thought that has emerged in the patience and safety of our homes.

ON THE RELATIONSHIP BETWEEN WOMANISM AND FEMINISM
R.B.: In *In Search of Our Mothers' Gardens*, you provide us with your widely cited definition of womanism, which has led to the creation of new fields of study in literature, religion, and black feminism. The final definition reads: "Womanist is to feminist as purple to lavender." In this formulation, you suggest that womanism is more radical than feminism. What is your current thinking on womanism and its relationship to feminism?

A.W.: As long as the world is dominated by racial ideology that places whites above people of color, the angle of vision of the womanist, coming from a culture of color, will be of a deeper, more radical penetration. This is only logical. Generally speaking, for instance, white feminists are dealing with the oppression they receive from white men, while women of color are oppressed by men of color as well as white men, as well as by many white women. But on the joyful side, which we must insist on honoring, the womanist is, like the creator of the word, intent on connecting with the earth and cosmos, with dance and song. With roundness. With thankfulness and joy. Given a fighting chance at living her own life, under oppression that she resists, the womanist has no or few complaints. Her history has been so rough—captured from her home, centuries of enslavement, apartheid, etc.—she honors Harriet Tubman by daily choosing freedom over the fetters of any internalized slavery she might find still lurking within herself. Whatever women's liberation is called, it is about freedom. This she knows. Having said this, I have no problem being called "feminist" or "womanist." In coining the term, I was simply trying myself to see more clearly what sets women of color apart in the rainbow that is a world movement of women who've had enough of being second- and third-class citizens of the earth. One day, if earth and our species survive, we will again be called sacred and free. Our proper names.

ON DEVELOPING A PRACTICE

R.B.: As you argue in *We Are the Ones We Have Been Waiting For*, we live in a world that is increasingly interdependent, and also a world in which fragmentation and isolation remain predominant. What are the practices that have been most helpful to you in maintaining a sense of purpose and balance in this changing world?

A.W.: Meditation has been a mainstay in my life. It has helped me more than I could have imagined prior to learning how to meditate. I don't meditate the same way I did earlier in my life, when the pressure to write, to mother, to travel, to be an activist, and to pay the bills was intense. Now I just live more meditatively, and it is very helpful that, understanding my nature and its needs for flourishing, I've created retreat spaces that help me keep my sanity and, quite often, my serenity. I discovered Mexico while I was pregnant with my daughter; we went there during my second trimester. I loved it and have gone there to rest in the sweetness of the Mexican people, in the kindness and courtesy of friends, every year for over twenty-five years. I also fell in love years ago with a Hawaiian musician who had the most delightful house on a beach in Molokai. The relationship ended, but we share the house still. I can go there when I'm dragging in spirit and sit and look at the moonlight on the water until I know all is well. That whether this small being is at peace or not, the tides will still do their thing: rise and fall and bring some boats to shore and refuse to let others land. With a complete and splendid indifference.

ON WWW.ALICEWALKERSGARDEN.COM
R.B.: In 2008, you launched your official Web site. What motivated you to establish a Web site? As an electronic medium, how does it serve your interests as a writer?

A.W.: I never thought I'd have a Web site. But once I realized I was finished with writing as I had always done it before—write a book, wait a year, publish the book, go on tour; by then you've almost forgotten why you wrote the book, etc.—I considered the Web site idea that one of my young friends in Mendocino, the painter Shiloh McCloud, had suggested. She would help me set it up, and then I could write from anywhere, since Anywhere seemed where I was headed. It has worked out well, I think. And blogging (I used to think the very word repulsive, I think I thought it sounded like snot or something) turns out to suit me. I'm Aquarian, and this is our age, and our element is air. We like electricity; our favorite color, next to the amethyst of our birthstone, is electric blue. The sky. I also like writing and charging nothing for it. I will do this as long as I can afford it. I'm very into my sense of being like anything else in nature that has not yet been captured by Monsanto: just dropping my seeds, my fruit, my nuts, and my leaves, because that's what this being does. I love the immediacy of it also. It is instantaneous. A marvel.

For a year, I didn't permit my administrator to show me one comment. Do trees want comments? But now I will sometimes view and share a comment. The ones that are rude or crude I never see; it wouldn't help me. It would be like telling a walnut to be an apple.

"MY ARCHIVE CAN REST WITH JOY IN THE COMPANY IT KEEPS"
R.B.: After almost four years of dialogue that began in January 2004, you appointed Emory University as the custodian of your archive in December 2007. Your archive opened to the public and to researchers in April 2009. What were some of the reasons that led to your decision to appoint Emory University as the custodian of your archive? How has your life changed since you made this very important decision?

A.W.: Emory is in the South, in Georgia, where I am from. You are there, a friend. There are others close to Emory who make me feel welcome. The Dalai Lama sometimes teaches there, and others who care deeply about us humans. My life has changed because of this decision. I feel free of the forty-odd years of history—in the form of papers and memorabilia—I had been keeping in my house! Ironically, I left boxes of personal journals at Emory thinking I would come there to work on them, but instead I seem to be writing forward rather than backward. This is a surprise to me, but I'm enjoying it. Perhaps I will one day come back to Emory and go through the journals and write a memoir or two, but maybe not.

ON CARL JUNG'S *THE RED BOOK*

R.B.: You are an admirer of Carl Jung. We can see the imprint of Jung's psychological system in your novel *Possessing the Secret of Joy*. You joined Jungians and other writers in New York City to offer commentary on *The Red Book*, Jung's recently published record of his dream life spanning more than four decades. What were some of the revelations of *The Red Book* for you?

A.W.: That it is exquisite! This is what the soul needs from us; that we investigate it using all of our tools created out of beauty. And out of dreams. Jung was not stingy about giving his spirit and soul what it needed to fully expand. He was not afraid of himself, a lucky reality. So many people are afraid of themselves, as if they were, to themselves, completely unknown quantities, and of course some folks may be. But part of our work as humans, if we wish to live in peace on earth and not project our fears and errors onto others, is to get to know who we are. The drawings are lovely and patiently exacted; the paintings are vibrant and intense. I have always felt with Jung, since first reading his work, that he is a kindred spirit. That is why I incorporated him as a character in *Possessing the Secret of Joy*.

ON *THE COLOR PURPLE*

R.B.: You have just completed the audio recording of *The Color Purple*. It will be wonderful for readers to hear your voice as they read or listen to the most celebrated novel in your corpus, and unquestionably one of the most important novels written in the twentieth century. What was it like to engage the written word in this manner? You have stated that you felt supported by the ancestors in the writing of a novel that possesses elements of family history. Did you feel supported by the ancestors as you translated their stories into this new medium?

A.W.: I did this recording with one of the worst colds I've had in my life! Ever so much coughing and sneezing. But, having waited twenty-five years to record *The Color Purple*, I was not willing to wait until I was better. The people in the book: ancestors, characters, spirits, whatever I've called them at different times, came through wonderfully. They are people who show up! And hold up! It was truly magical. I worked for four hours a day for four days and they were as present as when they first appeared to me in the early 1980s.

ON RAISING CHICKENS

R.B.: How did you come to decide to raise chickens at your country home in California? Aside from fresh eggs, what are the benefits that have come to you from reconnecting with nature and your rural Georgia background in this way?

A.W.: With Proust, who lived in Paris, it was the madeleine cookie that carried him back to *Remembrance of Things Past*. With me, with my rural background in Georgia, it's chickens. As I write about my chickens frequently on my blog, I find myself being led into a part of my memory that was suppressed when, as a child, I was injured. Like most children with injuries, I was so intensely involved with the change I had experienced—and continued to experience in the way other people now responded to me—that my mind couldn't pay attention to anything else. Years of my memory were erased or, rather, submerged. On a visit to Bali, in my forties, I was strolling along a dirt road in Ubud, and a hen and her chicks appeared in front of me; for no reason that I then understood, I was transfixed by this sight. Years later, I realize they were grace-launched messengers with ties to the unconscious sent to awaken me to the possibility of regaining some of what I had lost: my memory of many, many years of my childhood that I had completely forgotten.

What is fascinating is that now I see that writing fiction has been a way for me to have a memory, though it is largely, well, fictional.

NOTES

1. Alice Walker, "Three Dollars Cash," in *Her Blue Body Everything We Know: Earthling Poems, 1965–1990* (New York: Harvest, 1996), 161.
2. Ibid., 161.
3. Evelyn C. White, *Alice Walker: A Life* (New York: W.W. Norton, 2004), 361.
4. Alice Walker, "Beauty: When the Other Dancer Is the Self," in *In Search of Our Mothers' Gardens* (New York: Harcourt, Brace & Jovanovich, 1983), 386–87.
5. Walker, "Three Dollars Cash," in *Her Blue Body Everything We Know*, 414.
6. White, *Alice Walker*, 40.
7. See Gloria Steinem's *Outrageous Acts and Everyday Rebellions* (New York: Holt Paperbacks, 1983), 294.
8. The Alice Walker Archive, Box OBV 1, in the Manuscript, Archives, and Rare Book Library, Emory University.
9. Alice Walker, "On Stripping Bark from Myself," in *Her Blue Body Everything We Know*, 270–71.
10. Ibid., 271.
11. Alice Walker, "A Talk: Convocation 1972," in *In Search of Our Mothers' Gardens*, 38.
12. Ibid.
13. Ibid., 39.
14. White *Alice Walker*, 112.
15. Ibid., 114.
16. Ibid., 112–18.
17. Ibid., 125–26.
18. Ibid., 127.
19. For "Suicide of an American Girl," see Alice Walker Archive, Box 73, Folder 1.
20. Alice Walker Archive, Box 88, Folder 19.
21. Ibid.
22. Underwritten by the brokerage firm of Merrill Lynch, the Merrill Fellowships were awarded annually to students of Spelman College and Morehouse College through the generosity of Charles Merrill, trustee emeritus and former chair of the board of Morehouse College. The Merrill Fellowship came with

a cash award of $2,000. See Evelyn White's *Alice Walker: A Life* (New York: W.W. Norton, 2004,) 89, 130.

23. White, *Alice Walker*, 138.

24. This statement appears as a headnote for Walker's prize-winning essay "The Civil Rights Movement: What Good Was It?" in *In Search of Our Mothers' Gardens*, 119.

25. White, *Alice Walker*, 136–37.

26. Ibid., 137.

27. Alice Walker Archive, Box 2, Folder 4.

28. Ibid., Box 2, Folder 6.

29. Ibid.

30. White, *Alice Walker*, 154.

31. Ibid., 156.

32. Alice Walker Archive, Box 2, Folder 6.

33. White, *Alice Walker*, 156.

34. Alice Walker Archive, Box 2, Folder 6.

35. Ibid.

36. Ibid.

37. Ibid.

38. Ibid.

39. Ibid.

40. Walker, "The Civil Rights Movement: What Good Was It?" in *In Search of Our Mothers' Gardens*, 119.

41. Michael S. Harper, "Alice," in *Images of Kin: New and Selected Poems* (Urbana: University of Illinois Press, 1977), 66.

42. White, *Alice Walker*, 280.

43. Ibid., 413.

44. Alice Walker established Wild Trees Press in 1984 and operated it with Robert Allen until 1988. The mission statement of the press was "We publish only what we love." White, *Alice Walker*, 388.

45. Ibid., 326–27.

46. Alice Walker, "Writing *The Color Purple*," in *In Search of Our Mothers' Gardens*, 358.

47. Ibid., 355.

48. Alice Walker Archive, Box 51, Folder 1.

49. Ibid.

50. The key to *The Color Purple* identifies Celie as her great-grandmother, but in correspondence dated September 18, 2009, Walker states that the victim of rape and the model for the character Celie was her great-grandmother Anne.

51. Alice Walker Archive, Box 51, Folder 1.

52. Ibid.

53. Alice Walker to Rudolph P. Byrd, correspondence, September 18, 2009.

54. Alice Walker Archive, Box 51, Folder 1.

55. Ibid.

56. Ibid.

57. Alice Walker, "Writing *The Color Purple*," in *In Search of Our Mothers' Gardens*, 358.

58. Roland Freeman, *A Communion of the Spirits: African-American Quilters, Preservers, and Their Stories* (Nashville: Rutledge Hill Press, 1996), 150.

59. Alice Walker, "Writing *The Color Purple*," in *In Search of Our Mothers' Gardens*, 360.

60. White, *Alice Walker*, 358–59.

61. Ibid., 360.

62. Ibid., 359.

63. Ibid., 298–99.

64. Ibid., 22–23.

65. Alice Walker, *Anything We Love Can Be Saved: A Writer's Activism* (New York: Random House, 1997), xiii.

66. Ibid., xiv.

67. White, *Alice Walker*, 53.

68. Ibid.

69. Ibid., 64–65.

70. Alice Walker to Rudolph P. Byrd, correspondence, August 28, 2009.

71. Ibid.

72. Ibid.

73. *Anything We Love Can Be Saved*, xxii.

74. Ibid., xxiii.

75. Ibid.

76. Alice Walker, *The Same River Twice: Honoring the Difficult* (New York: Scribner, 1996), 38.

77. This phrase is based upon a statement written by Peggy and Bill Lykes of Tucker, Georgia, who recorded their impressions of the exhibition "A Keeping of Records: The Art and Life of Alice Walker" in the comment book located in the Schatten Gallery of the Robert W. Woodruff Library of Emory University. There the Lykeses wrote: "Alice Walker continues to change the world, heart by heart." Commemorating the opening of the Alice Walker archive to the public, "A Keeping of Records" opened on April 23, 2009, and closed on September 28, 2009.

CONTRIBUTORS

Isabelle Allende is a journalist, playwright, and novelist born in Chile. She is the author of articles published in newspapers and magazines in the Americas and in Europe. Allende is the author of seventeen novels, including the much acclaimed *The House of the Spirits, Eva Luna*, and, most recently, *The Island Beneath the Sea*. In the United States, she has held faculty appointments at the University of Virginia, Montclair State University, and the University of California at Berkeley.

Jean Shinoda Bolen is a psychiatrist, Jungian analyst, author, and activist. She attended the University of California at Los Angeles, Pomona College, the University of California at Berkeley, and the C.G. Jung Institute in San Francisco. Shinoda Bolen's many professional honors include being named a Distinguished Life Fellow of the American Psychiatric Association and a Fellow of the American Academy of Psychoanalysis and Dynamic Psychiatry. She is the author of ten books, including *The Tao of Psychology, Crossing to Avalon*, and *Urgent Message from Mother*.

Rudolph P. Byrd is the Goodrich C. White Professor of American Studies and the founding director of the James Weldon Johnson Institute for Advanced Interdisciplinary Studies at Emory University. He is the author or editor of several books, including *Writing the American Palimpsest: The Novels of Charles Johnson* and *I Am Your Sister: Collected and Unpublished Writings of Audre Lorde* (co-edited with Johnnetta B. Cole and Beverly Guy Sheftall). He is the co-founder of the Alice Walker Literary Society.

Ellen Bring is a journalist, activist, and a frequent contributor to *Animal's Agenda* based in Oakland, California.

Ani Pema Chödrön is an ordained Buddhist nun in the Tibetan Vajrana tradition. Educated at Miss Porter's School in Connecticut and the

University of California at Berkeley, she was an elementary school teacher in New Mexico and California prior to her conversion to Buddhism. Chödrön became a novice nun in 1974 under the tutelage of Lama Chime Rinpoche, and was ordained by His Holiness the Sixteenth Karmapa. She is the former director of the Karma Dznong in Boulder, Colorado, and is currently the director of the Gampo Abbey in Cape Breton, Nova Scotia. She is the author of *The Wisdom of No Escape*, *Start Where You Are*, *Heart Advice for Difficult Times*, and *The Places That Scare You*, among other books.

Claudia Dreifus is a freelance writer in New York City. She is a regular contributor to *The Progressive*.

William R. Ferris is the Joel Williamson Eminent Professor of History and Senior Associate Director of the Center for the Study of the American South. He has held faculty appointments at Yale University and the University of Mississippi. Ferris is also the former chairman of the National Endowment for the Humanities and the founding director of the Center for the Study of Southern Culture at the University of Mississippi. He is the author or editor of ten books, including *Give My Poor Heart Ease: Voices of the Mississippi Blues* and the *Encyclopedia of Southern Culture* (co-edited with Charles Reagan Wilson), and the creator of fifteen documentary films.

George Galloway is the Respect Party's MP for Bethnal Green and Bow in London, a seat he won after having been expelled from the Labour Party, after thirty-six years of membership, for his opposition to the Iraq War. He is the author of *Mr. Galloway Goes to Washington* and *I'm Not the Only One* and the editor of *The Fidel Castro Handbook*.

Paula Giddings is the E.A. Woodson 1922 Professor of African American Studies at Smith College. She is the author of *When and Where I Enter: The Impact of Black Women on Race and Sex in America*, a landmark work of scholarship in African American women's history. She also is the author of *In Search of Sisterhood: Delta Sigma Theta and the Challenge of the Black Sorority Movement*, and, most recently, the critically acclaimed biography of Ida B. Wells *Ida: A Sword Among*

Lions. Giddings has written for the *Washington Post*, the *New York Times*, the *Philadelphia Inquirer*, and *The Nation*. She is the senior editor of *Meridians*, a peer-reviewed feminist, interdisciplinary journal.

Amy Goodman is the host and executive producer of *Democracy Now!*, a national, daily, independent, award-winning news program airing on over eight hundred TV and radio stations in North America. She is the author or co-author of several books, including *Breaking the Sound Barrier*.

Jody Hoy is a freelance journalist and the editor of *The Power of Dreams: Interviews with Women in the Creative Arts*.

Margo Jefferson is Critic-at-Large for the *New York Times*. She has held faculty appointments at New York University and Columbia University. Jefferson has been a contributing critic to *The Nation*, the *New York Times Book Review*, the *Village Voice, Ms.,* the *Soho Weekly News, Dance Ink, Lear's, Harper's Magazine, Alt, Denmark,* and *NRC Handelsblad* in the Netherlands. She is the author of *Roots of Time: A Portrait of African Life and Culture* and *On Michael Jackson.* In 1995, Jefferson was awarded the Pulitzer Prize for criticism.

John O'Brien is a literary critic and the editor of *Interviews with Black Writers*. His work has been published in *Studies in Black Literature, Fiction International,* the *American Scholar,* and *New Orleans Review.*

Marianne Schnall is a writer and interviewer who has worked for many publications. She is the founder of the women's site Feminist.com and the co-founder of the environmental site EcoMall.com. Through her diverse writing, interviews, and Web sites, Schnall seeks to raise awareness about important issues and causes.

Tami Simon is the founder and publisher of Sounds True Recordings.

David Swick is a freelance writer and a frequent contributor to *Shambhala Sun.*

Claudia Tate (1947–2002) was a pioneering scholar in the fields of English, African American studies, and American studies. Educated at the University of Michigan at Ann Arbor and Harvard University, she was a member of a generation of scholars who laid the foundation for the field of African American studies in the 1970s. Tate held faculty appointments at Howard University, George Mason University, and Princeton University. She was the author or editor of *Black Women Writers at Work, Domestic Allegories of Political Desire: The Black Heroine's Text at the Turn of the Century*, and *Psychoanalysis and Black Novels: Desire and the Protocols of Race*.

Justine Toms and **Michael Toms** are with the co-founders and co-presidents of New Dimensions.

Alice Walker is a native of Putnam County, Georgia, and was educated at Spelman College and Sarah Lawrence College. She is the author of more than twenty-six books spanning the genres of the novel, poetry, and the essay. Walker's books have sold more than fifteen million copies worldwide and have been translated into more than twelve languages. She is one of the leading figures in what scholars term the renaissance in black women's writing of the 1970s. Walker is the author of *The Color Purple*, which received the Pulitzer Prize and the National Book Award for fiction and has been adapted for film and the stage, among other novels. Through her anthology *I Love Myself When I Am Laughing and Then Again When I Am Looking Mean and Impressive: A Zora Neale Hurston Reader*, she is chiefly responsible for the revival of scholarly interest in the life and writings of Zora Neale Hurston. Walker is the author of several collections of essays, including the landmark collection *In Search of Our Mothers' Gardens: Womanist Prose*. This collection contains her definition of womanism, which has catalyzed new research and theoretical models in such fields as literary studies, women's studies, and theological studies. Through *Warrior Marks: Female Genital Mutilation and the Sexual Binding of Women*, a companion volume to the eponymous documentary produced and directed by Pratibha Parmar, Walker has raised international awareness of the practice of female genital mutilation. Her activism also includes support of several social justice movements, including the civil rights movement, the women's movement, and, most recently, opposition to the wars in

Afghanistan and freedom for the Palestinians. The author of several prize-winning collections of poetry, Walker is the author of the forthcoming *Hard Times Require Furious Dancing: A Year of Poems*. In 2008, she launched www.alicewalkersgardens.com, her official Web site where she posts regular contributions to her blog. Walker appointed Emory University as the custodian of her archive, which opened to researchers and to the public in April 2009.

Evelyn C. White attended Harvard University, the Columbia University School of Journalism, and Wellesley College. She is the author of *Alice Walker: A Life* and the editor of *The Black Woman's Health Book*. Her articles, essays, and reviews have appeared in *Smithsonian, Essence, Ms.,* the *Wall Street Journal,* the *San Francisco Chronicle,* and the *Washington Post.*

Howard Zinn (1922–2010) was a historian, political scientist, social critic, activist, and playwright. He is best known as the author of the bestselling *A People's History of the United States,* which has been adapted into a two-hour documentary that aired on the History Channel in December 2009. Zinn was the author of twenty books and a professor in the department of political science at Boston University.

INDEX OF PEOPLE AND WORKS*

* All works are by Alice Walker unless otherwise indicated.